Brushes
With
DEATH
The Blood of Jesus

By
Richard Taylor

To: Sharon Griffin
Thanks dearly for your
support. Peace & Blessings

Brushes with Death
Copyright © 2012
Richard Taylor

ISBN: 978-0-615-70466-1

FOR INFORMATION CONTACT:
Richard Taylor
702 Appomattox Street
Norfolk, VA 23523
1-888-680-2847
www.brusheswithdeath.org

Printed in the USA by
Morris Publishing®
3212 E. Hwy. 30 · Kearney, NE 68847
800-650-7888 · www.morrispublishing.com

Dedication:

This book is dedicated to my family and friends who have always stood by my side with encouragement and advice. I thank you all for the immeasurable support in times of comfort and distress. There is no way possible that I would have accomplished this feat without the prayers of you all.

This work is also devoted to those fallen victims of society. Whether they be those who have left this earth due to the vices addressed in this novel; or whether they be those still entrenched in the struggles that beset so many in the human race. Those affected by poverty, addiction, alcohol, gambling, drug dealing, guns, violence, prostitution, promiscuity, crime, prison, lack of knowledge and other tragedies are continuously in my thoughts and this book is a tribute to the plight of the "hopeless."

Finally, I dedicate this novel to my daughter Italy, love of my life. The Most High has blessed me with a treasure that no amount of gold could compare. I pray the best for you and that God's blessing will continue to be upon yours and my life. You are my inspiration, my motivation and my universe. I love you always and forever.

Acknowledgements:

First and foremost I would like to acknowledge the Most High, the Creator. If it were not for the grace and mercy of Yahweh (God), and His spiritual guidance, neither I nor this work would be in existence.

Next, I would like to thank my mother and father, Rodger and Aletta Taylor for the foundation that they provided me that continues to benefit me in the present day. Also, I thank my sisters, Karen and Kamia, along with other immediate friends and family members who have assisted in the growth, maturity, and overall well-being of the author.

Additionally, gratitude extends to Mike Williams, Terrence, AJ, and David, Terry, L, Val, AB, Pook, Twan B, Rock, Peg, Kel, grandma, Fran, Charmaine, Pee, Te', Billy, Keontae, Deshanna, Jacorey, Bless, Keith, Sheila Jaqueese, Ann, Mary, Pastor Gaffney, Philadelphia Community Church, Tabernacle of Prayer, Arnold and Ma Thornton, Gregory Jones Sr. and family, Newkirk family, Tay, Toya, Tora, Keysha, Shell, A, Melissa, Tidewater Community College, Morris Publishing, Horace C. Downing Branch Library, Audubon, the Oaks, Berkeley, Park Place, Devereux, Webbtown, the Jungle, Old and New Projects, West Haven, Fairview, North End, Seven Cities, and all my brothers and sisters locked in the system (hold your heads.)

Special thanks goes out to all those who helped with the compilation, marketing and the promotion of this book. Time or space would not permit me to list everyone who's been instrumental in my life. Those of you know who you are so I thank you much the same.

Author's Note

This autobiographical work was composed to depict scenes and events from in and around the author's life. While the situations and language in some areas may be considered graphic or explicit, they are real. Names and some events have been altered to protect the innocent...and the guilty.

The relation of this story is in no way an endorsement to the reader to participate in like actions. These situations have been portrayed to demonstrate the perils and distress associated with things such as promiscuity, drug dealing and abuse, gambling, alcohol, guns, crime and other ills that have been accepted by society.

The reader is encouraged to read this novel from an objective point of view, without judgment or preconceived notions from similar works. The main character's thoughts, actions and words are those of the author. Some of these ideas have changed while attitudes towards certain concepts remain the same.

In creating this book, the author had the unique opportunity to examine his entire life from a third person perspective. In doing so, he was able to perceive his strengths and weaknesses, successes and failures, talents and faults. Reliving the history, the author encountered certain times where his behavior and mindset was even appalling to even himself.

However, the writing process has served as a therapeutic medicine in assisting the author with confronting many of the issues listed above. The author does not shy away from the reality of these conditions in his life or the lives of others. He hopes that his work will be a deterrent to those who are not yet involved in criminal activity. He also hopes "Brushes with Death" will be an inspirational motivation to induce those entrenched in the lifestyle to digress from the course of destruction.

While the world endures violence, famine, poverty, disaster, genocide and a host of other problems, the author holds the idea that these calamities can be solved with one act: love. Love for the Creator, our fellow man, and lastly our own self should cause every human to react with maximum effort and charity to reduce any and all inhumane conditions; first in their immediate environment and then the world beyond.

My challenge to the reader is to examine the state of the characters in this book with the mindset of love. The author asks the reader to consider someone who they know that may be engaged in a similar struggle and figure out a way to intercede or help them. People sometimes just need a small bit of help or a show of concern to jumpstart a healing or recovery process.

My goal is to shed light on those who have been considered outcasts and show that no one is a lost cause. The author has entertained some of the greatest minds ever in prisons and on the streets. The author was once one who felt like no one cared or there was no hope. Fortunately, the author had those in his family and circle of friends who took time to invest love into his life. I am a testament to the power of this love and through this book, it is intended that the love shown to me, will be imparted to all of those who read, via the loving spirit in which it was composed. Thank you in advance for assisting your fellow fallen man,

Richard Taylor

Table of Contents

Prologue:
....12

Chapter 1:
    Dice Games
....17

Chapter 2:
    Central
....50

Chapter 3:
    Party Time
....93

Chapter 4:
    Scarface
....125

Chapter 5:
    Locked
....161

Chapter 6:
Murder
....177

Chapter 7:
Back on the Grind
....210

Chapter 8:
Back to the 'Boro
....226

Chapter 9:
Warning Signs
....249

Chapter 10:
Great Escape
....271

Chapter 11:
Calm before the Storm
....295

Chapter 12:
A New Life
....316

Chapter 13:

Death in the Flesh
....340

Epilogue
....367

"This, know also that in the last days perilous times shall come. For men shall be lovers of their own selves, covetous, boasters, proud, blasphemers, disobedient to parents, unthankful, unholy, without natural affection, trucebreakers, false accusers, incontinent, fierce, despisers of those that are good, Traitors, heady, high-minded, lovers of pleasures more than lovers of God; Having a form of godliness but denying the power thereof: from such, turn away."

2 Timothy 3:1-6

"But these, as natural brute beast made to be taken and destroyed, speak evil of things they understand not, and shall utterly perish in their own corruption; and shall receive the reward of unrighteousness, as they count it pleasure to riot in the daytime. They are spots and blemishes, sporting themselves with their own deceiving while they feast with you; having eyes full of adultery and cannot cease from sin; beguiling unstable souls; hearts exercised with covetous practices; cursed children. Which have forsaken the right way and gone astray, following the way of Balaam, who loved the way of unrighteousness; but was rebuked for his iniquity; the dumb ass speaking with a man's voice forbade the madness of the prophet"

2 Peter 2: 12-16

Prologue

October, 2008
Virginia Beach, VA

Slick limped out of the hospital at 8:30 Saturday night. He called a cab to the Oceanfront hotel he was at a day earlier. When they arrived at the beach, he paid the fare and struggled to exit the vehicle. After getting both legs on the concrete, he pushed himself up with his arms. The weight against the ground caused sharp pains in his pelvis and he buckled.

"You okay," the cab driver asked.

"Yeah, I'll be fine," Slick answered, pulling himself up from his knee. "I can make it to this car right here. Thanks a lot though."

Slick regained his balance as the taxi drove off. He tried to walk normally, but couldn't control his legs. With his arms Slick moved each leg, dragging himself the fifteen feet to the rental car. He gingerly removed the keys and opened the trunk. He reached under the spare tire and felt for the bag. The cocaine was still there. He grabbed the dope, closed the trunk lightly and headed for the stairs.

Slick moved as fast as he could. The nerve damage in his groin didn't afford a full range of motion. He held the railing tight, laboring with each step up the three flights to his room. After five grueling minutes, he made it to the door. He checked the key to see if it still worked. It did.

The smell of death was still in the room. A chill came over him as he looked at the blood stained carpet. Bloodied clothes and shoes lay in disarray around the room. Black dust clouded the walls from the fingerprinting. A bullet shell remained in the spot where it was discharged, overlooked by detectives. Slick's mind reeled as the scene from the previous morning spun like a movie in his head.

After latching the chain, Slick's first destination was the closet. He shuffled over to where he had the five thousand dollars stashed. He found the stack of paper on the inside of his leather coat. He stuffed the drugs in the same coat while assessing the room.

He looked at his possessions strewn around the room. He made a futile attempt to gather them, but the pain was unbearable. The wounds were fresh. The doctors had just removed two of the bullets three hours earlier. Against their advice, Slick left the hospital without further treatment. The detective he spoke to earlier told him that he would be back in the morning. Slick decided that he would avoid charges by disappearing at the first opportunity.

Slick labored to the bathroom to examine his wounds. White flesh still hung loosely out of the nickel sized holes in his hip, thighs, buttocks and pelvis. Blood and puss oozed from the center of the sores. Slick replaced the bandages, before pulling his pants back up.

Since he had snuck out of the hospital, Slick didn't receive any prescription for pain. With the morphine already worn away, Slick turned to the other substance he knew would numb the pain. Oblivious to his circumstance, Slick sat on the bloody baby's blanket and opened the bag of cocaine. He took four large toots and waited for the drain.

When the high came, everything was fine, or so he thought. His mind began to race. Where's Italy, he wondered. Oh no, the blood. Was she hit too? He called Shea, the mother. Still, there was no answer. Where are they? Are they alright?

The more he sniffed the faster thoughts came.

The pain is leaving. I can move around better. Okay, what now? Yeah, call all my peoples and let them know I'm back. I gotta get this money. I still gotta lotta dope to move. I'll be fine.

Slick got on the phone and called his customers. Less than an hour out of the hospital, Slick was back on the road making drops. He conducted business like the previous morning had never happened. He went to various spots, barely able to get in and out of the car. It was no longer Slick that controlled himself. The drugs and lifestyle had become his master, not letting him quit.

While he was out, he stopped at Shea's. His desire to see the baby was heightened by the drugs. When he got there, no one was home. He called her friend.

"Shea's fine," Tonesha said. "Her and the baby are safe. She just wanted to have some time to get over what happened."

Slick hung up the phone. Damn! She gonna take my baby. I done messed up for real this time. What now, back to the beach? I got to get that stuff out before morning. Need cigarettes, and beer.

Slick made it back to the hotel. His intentions were to pack his things into the car and rent a room elsewhere. His apartment would be ready in the morning according to the owner. If he could make due until then, he could settle into the new environment.

The urge for cocaine told him otherwise. The desire to get high trumped his every notion. With beer and cigarettes, Slick remained at the crime scene and continued to sniff. He sat on the bed all night, reliving the nightmare of the previous morning. Money, sex, guns, coke, blood, Italy, prayer, Jesus, life, death…

The images came and went all night until the sun came up. With the daylight, he grew more paranoid but still couldn't leave. The cocaine had him stuck. He peeked out the window constantly, as worry and fear consumed him. He didn't want to face the world in his present condition and preferred to escape reality through coke.

At ten o'clock that morning, Slick was aroused by a knock at the door. When he peeked through the curtain, he saw four Virginia Beach police officers staring into his face.

"There he is. Come on out Mr. Richardson," a short white officer said still knocking. "We just saw you, so we know you're in there. Let's not make this hard."

Slick didn't panic. After what he'd just survived, jail was nothing. He closed the curtain and walked over to the closet. He stashed the bag of cocaine back inside the coat. With a calmness that betrayed his drug use, Slick opened the door and greeted the officers.

"Yes officers. How are you guys doing this morning?"

"We're fine. How are you?"

"Well I'm making it," Slick said with a grimace. "What do y'all want? Y'all need some more information or did you catch them yet?"

"No sir," the lead officer said. "That's not why we're here. If you would, please turn around and put your hands behind your back?"

"For what?"

The officer stayed silent until getting Slick fully cuffed and then responded. "You're under arrest for possession with intent to distribute cocaine."

"What y'all talking about," Slick protested. "I already told the detective that dope wasn't mines."

"I understand all that Mr. Richardson, but we have a warrant and I'm just doing my job."

Slick was escorted from the room and transported to the Virginia Beach jail. When the magistrate, denied him bail, Slick made an appeal because of his wounds. The official explained that because of the charges and his criminal history, the law didn't allow bond. Slick was then booked and admitted to the medical ward of the jail. Slick was given a bottom bunk and entered the room of sick offenders with caution.

Slick had been to jail plenty. He'd been to jail in three states and seven cities previously. This time however was different. As he lay on the bed he couldn't believe what had happened. The death that he had been begging for had come to visit him. And after all of the shots, he still was able to walk away. The scary part was that he knew that same death would be waiting for him when he returned to the streets.

Slick was amazed that he survived. He had been in tough situations before, but this last incident had humbled him. At the mercy of a gun and on the verge of death, he realized that he wasn't a super hero; that life was fragile. He was shaken to the point of almost giving up. He couldn't understand why or how he survived but he knew there had to be a reason. With this in mind, he reflected on how he'd come to this point.

Seven years earlier, he had moved to Virginia with hopes of avoiding jail time and the streets. Ironically, years later, Slick found himself involved in the same foolishness that he'd tried to escape. He thought about the events and times of previous years that led to the present chaos as he lay on his bunk.

1
Dice Games

August, 2003
Virginia Beach, VA

"Yo, I'm making short term goals, when the weather folds…just put away the leathers and put ice on the gold. Chilly with enough bail money to free a big willy… high stakes I got more at stake than Philly…"

The words from JAY-Z's classic Reasonable Doubt, thumped through the Sony speakers atop the wicker stand in Slick's two bedroom apartment. The rhythmic vibration of the baseline from "Can't Knock the Hustle" mixed with the aroma of marijuana, creating a euphoric atmosphere for the young hustlers crowded around the Aztec rug in the center of the floor. Life-sized posters of Bob Marley, Al Capone, John Dillinger and Malcolm X covered the four walls. The iconic images of Tony Montana and Alejandro Sosa radiated from the silent sixty inch flat screen monitor that sat in the corner, adding to the aura of gangster life already prevalent in the loud home.

The black leather couch and love seat had been turned to meet at a ninety degree angle, forming a half square around the men, who had no use for the chairs, as most were squatting on the tips of their toes or on one or two knees, eyes glued to the floor. Occasionally, one would arise and exit the house, only to return momentarily, after making a pluck (a sale of any number of drugs to a paying customer).

The glass table, which served as a lamp stand, was littered with Backwood cigar droppings, empty bags of weed, and ashes scattered about, as anxious players missed the ashtrays while focusing on the game. The dark brown carpet grew darker as German lager soaked into the fabric, seeping out of Heineken bottles tipped over by arms, feet, or elbows. Any other available space on the floor was arrayed with automatic pistols, revolvers, extra clips and cell phones. Nobody feared a thing as Mary J. Blige's soulful voice pierced the air.

"So until that day then, I'm the one whose crazy…Cause that's the way that you making me feel…I'm just trying to get mines, I don't have the time…to knock the hustle for real…"

Slick stooped down and picked up the three small dice one by one with his left hand and methodically transferred them to his right. He scanned the men's eyes, hands, and their money as they tossed combinations of tens, twenties, and fifties onto the ground. Then, Slick lifted his arm at a ninety degree angle, fist nearly touching his ear, all the while shaking his forearm vigorously. He tilted his head to the right, listening to the crackling sound of the dice, which to him was tantamount to the 1996 rap song that blared through the speaker.

When Slick felt that he held the dice comfortably in a rhythm, he took a step forward, bent down and tossed the dice softly into the air. "Big six," he yelled.

As the dice bounced off the carpet, the players angled their necks to view the results. The first one twisted and rolled to rest on a one, just as the second spun and stopped at a deuce. Despair came over Slick after envisioning a three or a two on the remaining die.

"Ace him now," yelled Flash. The remaining die landed on a six. A sigh of relief emerged from Slick, while his opponent, Flash, let out an expletive of frustration.

Determined, Slick gathered the stones and repeated his routine, re-energized by another chance. As he closed his eyes, he pictured the outcome of a four, five, six, bent down and let fly. The dice landed on four, three, and six.

"Y'all see that? Yeah, I think y'all seen it! I'm just a block away from 546th street. Get them stacks right for daddy," Slick teased.

"You can't strike," stated K J, a chubby, sleuth-foot cat with braids. "Go 'head and ace so I can get my buck!"

Slick looked down at the two fifty dollar bills lying in front of K J's purple and yellow Air Forces. The Nikes matched perfectly with the 1971 Fran Tarkenton throwback jersey he wore. Slick added up all the bets and realized that a strike on this round would net him a profit of nearly four-hundred bucks. He glimpsed at the Scarface movie and saw the globe. Closing his eyes, the slogan ran across the back of his eyelids..."THE WORLD IS YOURS."

With extra motivation and the greed that is characteristic of so many gamblers, he scooped the dice and prepared for his next roll. This time however, Slick held his right arm to his side and locked his elbow in place, so that his arm was perpendicular to the floor. He shook the dice gently in the cup of his hand with his palm facing forward. When he got the feeling, he placed both feet together and bent his knees until his hand was three inches above the ground. He then flicked his wrist and rolled the dice precisely three feet in front of him.

The multi-colored objects came to rest within two inches of each other. Before the numbers on the dice could register, Slick knew from the chorus of four letter words and deep breaths that his roll had been a success. When he realized that the red, blue and green dice showed five, four and six, Slick called out, "C-Lo," and gave a fist pump, like MJ in ninety-eight when he won the championship.

"Don't nothing move but the money," Slick murmured, proceeding from left to right to collect his winnings. "You know the game don't stop! Let me get that Akbar," he said to the quiet, but fierce dude with braids. Slick grabbed the eighty dollars that lay next to Akbar's wrist, adorned with a diamond white gold bracelet.

Next, he moved to Kwan, who mischievously tried to retrieve twenty of the sixty dollars he had wagered. "Don't play with my change yo," Slicked warned.

"Judge said try 'em all," joked Kwan.

"Yeah, but he meant all of 'em but me nigga," Slick said.

Even though Slick knew Kwan was playing, if he had not been aware he would have been short on his take. These guys shot dice nearly every day, but money was still money and nobody wanted to lose. So whenever someone could get over they would try. If they succeeded it was all good. If they got caught it wasn't a big deal. But a person still had to be on their P's and Q's.

Next, Slick moved to Spray, a real livewire, sporting freshly twisted dreads. When Slick picked up the forty dollars, Spray reverted to his normal routine of asking for his money back.

"Lemme, let me, let, let, lemme get a kickback, Slick".

Slick just shook his head in denial and laughed to himself about Spray's stuttering episode. He didn't stammer naturally. Only when he got excited and hurried, did his words run together.

Slick continued towards K J who kicked the money just as he tried to grab it. K J had money but was extremely tight and always agitated to lose. Flash, who was the youngest but most mature, handed the money to the winner respectfully. Lastly Boss, a small time weed man gave a perplexed look as he watched Slick confiscate his fifty dollar bet.

After collecting the spoils, Slick added the bundle of money to the pile of green already in front of him. He counted out twenty-five twenties with the precision of a bank teller and then confidently placed the access wad of cash in his back pocket. The other players gave looks of disdain and disgust as Slick called the rules for his new bank.

"Five-hundred in the bank; push pay, trips double, fifty or better, anything off the rug ain't good. Bet's got to be down before I roll!"

"Come on with that fifty or better shit Slick! You can't do that," Boss complained. He was frustrated because he couldn't afford to lose as much as some of the others and was fearful of going broke.

"My house, my bank, my rules, you ain't gotta shoot if you don't want to nigga! If all the money down, I'm gone!"

Boss rose from his knees and stretched his arms. He mumbled a few inaudible words and retreated to the couch. He dug into the pocket of his oversized Akademik jeans, retrieved a quarter-ounce of green, and proceeded to roll a blunt. Flash tossed him a dime sack and instructed Boss to twist him up one too.

Flash was a boss; a true G. Although only eighteen, his demeanor and character displayed an authority equal to Alexander the Great, Napoleon or Genghis Khan. When one looked in his eyes one could see pain, anger and wisdom all at the same time. The tattoos that covered his arms and neck honored deceased family, friends, children and street codes. The youngest of three boys, he lost his mother early in high school and was left to fend for himself. Although he lived with his grandparents, they were aging so he gravitated towards the streets. He soaked up the game like a sponge and at seventeen already had an apartment with his girlfriend and their daughter. While most of his peers were fascinated with clothes and jewelry, he was focused on stacking money to the ceiling, in the refrigerator, and anywhere else he could put it. He commanded respect from anyone he encountered and more often than not, he got it.

Slick prepared for the next round of bets. Before he rolled, he went into the kitchen, a few feet away to get the pint of Hennessy on the table. Without flinching, he unscrewed the top, tilted the brown liquid up to his lips and took a huge gulp. Swishing the liquor in his mouth for the taste effect he extended it to his opponents who quickly accepted and passed the bottle amongst themselves. "What a rush" he thought as he swallowed and felt the stinging in his insides.

With the bets in place, Slick took a casual role and the dice did not yield a point. After two more throws of the dice there was a knock at the door.

"Don't answer it," K J said. "I got my money down and I'm losing two-hundred. You can't stop the dice now!"

"Boss," Slick yelled out. "Get the door for me yo!"

"What you think this is cuz? Do I look like Benson to you, nigga?"

Slick glared at the man. "Come to think about it, you do," he said, drawing laughs from everyone.

"I'll get it," Spray said, heading for the door. "Boss, you lazier than my baby momma!"

"Whatever nigga," Boss retorted. "You look like your baby momma!"

More laughs rang out as the two friends went back and forth with jokes.

"Spray, your feet smell like you crush corn chips for a living!"

"Boss, you look like you got your little brother hair on, that tight ass afro rolled up on the back of your neck!"

"Boy, you need to brush your teeth more than twice a month, yellow mouth monkey," Boss came back.

"You need to wash more than twice a month, smelling like last week's garbage."

"Both of y'all look like two high school janitors in the face," Ski said as he came through the door with Worm.

Ski could joke for days. He was short, fat, and dark-skinned with a receding hairline, which is likely the reason he was good at joking, having to retaliate as people insulted him. He was also a loud mouth and considered soft by most of his peers. Additionally, he wasn't much of a hustler either, always playing middle man, or trying to muscle in on or steal other people's clientele. His most profitable hustle was breaking in people's spots or setting up robberies, which is why he always had to be watched, even among "friends". What he did do well, however, was chase girls and party at the clubs. He had a few broads but the majority of them were saddled with low self-esteem.

Worm was a different story. He was a hustler in every sense of the word. At about five foot eight inches and a hundred and forty pounds, he acquired his name from the features of his face. His eyes were puffy and black around the bottom, therefore giving him the resemblance of a cartoon character, namely a worm. He also sported a two and a half inch beard, which had become common with the emergence of Roc-A-Fella artist Freeway. Despite his appearance, it in no way affected his ability to make money. He sold whatever; hard, soft, pills, weed, you name it. If he didn't have it, he sure knew where to obtain it. His attire always remained neat and ironed, which was a testament to his old school values. He was said to still possess sneakers from the tenth grade. He was Slick's age, so therefore they had a mutual respect for each other.

"It's wicked on these mean streets…none of my friends speak…we all trying to win. But then again…Maybe it's for the best though, 'cause when they saying too much…you know they trying to get you touched…"

As the new guests settled in, the dice game was set to resume. JAY-Z's dark lyrics to the "D'evils" blared through the speaker. Slick rolled the dice. Two, two, and four were the numbers. Akbar was the first one to shoot.

"Crush that four cuz," K J encouraged his friend. He and Akbar were closer than any of the others because they lived closer. K J also held contempt for Slick and always rooted against him.

Akbar rolled the dice with his left hand and screamed, "Six now!" The dice didn't take heed. He regrouped and tossed the stones once more.

"Fall to the four I say," said Slick with emphasis. "Let me see some threes on your knees!"

"Never that," Akbar said as he picked up the one, two, and five.

He shook the dice, kissed them, blew on his hand and slid the dice on the carpet. Three, five, three were the numbers on the dice and the winner let out a shout of elation as Slick handed him the fifty dollar bet.

"I told you that four was nowhere," Akbar yelled.

"That's gravy," Slick told him. "Somebody will fall, right Kwan."

"It won't be me," stated Kwan as he grabbed the dice. BZZZZZ, BZZZZZ, BZZZZZ, BZZZZZ.

Slick felt his cellular phone vibrating against his thigh. He had been wondering when someone would call since his phone generally rang off the hook. He looked down at the caller identification, all the while keeping an eagle eye on his opponent. Kwan would steal from God. He rolled the dice and failed to point.

Slick felt aroused as he noticed who was trying to reach him. When he thought of Ashley, he remembered the caramel complexion twenty-year old that he had met when he worked at Ticketmaster. She had given him rides home and they developed a business relationship when he was selling weed. As time progressed, he found a cocaine connection. Slick was astonished to find out that the pretty brown thing with the small waist and fat bottom played with the white girl occasionally. He had not gotten the panties yet but he could sense that it was only a matter of time before they came off like crack in the eighties.

"What's popping ma-ma," he asked after he flipped the 750i open.

"You daddy," the sweet voice on the other end of the phone replied. "What you up to right now?"

"You know me, getting this money in the dice game. I'm at the crib though. What's up with you? Nah, Kwan, let me get my dough! I saw that deuce!"

"What you talking 'bout Slick man. I rolled a two, three, and a four! Didn't I Spray?"

"Hold on baby," Slick told Ashley. He then looked at Spray, who looked away not wanting to get involved.

Everyone in the room knew that Kwan had lost. "Quit playing and give me my scrill nigga."

Kwan sighed, picked up the fifty dollar bill and threw it to Slick. To many, that would have been a sign of disrespect but Slick understood the game and was content with getting the money. He did not get emotional win or lose. His motto was "easy come, easy go."

"Yeah shorty, I'm back," Slick said to Ashley, as Flash grabbed the dice. "I got to watch these cats ma. But what up though, you coming through?"

"Yeah, I'm a go get Tina and grab some beer and we'll be over there. Give us about twenty minutes."

When she mentioned Tina, Slick knew it was on. He had met Tina through Ashley but the two had engaged in a few episodes in Ashley's absence. When Tina got drunk and high, she threw caution, along with everything else she had on, to the wind. She was down for whatever. Slick was already making plans to shut the dice game down before he hung up the phone.

"That'll work. Just hit me when y'all get outside."

"I will. I know you got something for me right."

"No question," he replied.

"We'll see you soon then."

"Yeah," Slick said and hung up the phone.

Flash had rolled the dice a total of five times without pointing. Slick tried to refocus but all he could think about was Ashley and Tina in compromising positions. He could care less about the dice game now. He wasn't even upset when Flash rolled a four, five, and six to C-Lo, taking the bank. Slick happily gave him the seventy-five dollar bet and waited for the others to roll to the four.

Akbar passed him one of the many blunts in circulation. Slick took a long inhale on the half-finished marijuana cigarette and held the smoke in his lungs for five seconds. He exhaled just as K J rolled a four to push the point. K J cursed as he had to pay the host again. Spray rolled last and scored a big six on the dice. He jumped up and down laughing, happy to receive the fifty dollars from Slick.

"You can buy the bank back for fifty," Flash propositioned. Slick shook his head, already determined in his mind to lose twenty more dollars and quit. He knew the dice games could go on for hours, even days straight. A man had to be careful or he could forfeit his winnings in a short amount of time. Slick had experienced the scenario, as his compulsive and addictive nature had caused him to falter on several occasions. He would use discretion today, he resolved, while taking a seat on the couch next to Worm and Boss.

Reaching in each of the pockets of his Roc-A-Wear jeans, Slick pulled out the various amounts of cash that had been won in the dice game. As he separated and organize the different denominations of currency, he felt the envious glares from some of the men in the room. He was aware that a few of them disliked him, not only because he wasn't from Virginia, but also because he had his hustle to a science. He had made several connections during his year's stay in Virginia Beach, but he also treated his customers like family, with respect.

Most of the others regarded their customers as fiends and beings lower than human. Slick learned early on that people were the source of your business, not the money. Consequently, most of his clients introduced him to their friends who became regulars as well. Many were seated on the high end of society. Slick dealt with a contingency of doctors, lawyers, bankers, business owners, club owners, bondsmen, and numerous other professionals. Their patronage kept Slick's lifestyle on a level that was equal to theirs.

After counting the cash, Slick realized he was still five-hundred dollars short of recouping the two thousand dollars he had lost the day before. Including the grand with which he'd started the game Slick wrapped a thick rubber band around the folded paper for security. Then he deposited the twenty-five hundred dollars into his right rear pocket.

He then shifted his mind to the four and a half ounces of raw uncut cocaine that was stashed in the storage room of the apartment complex hallway. Tallying up the figures mentally, Slick concluded that he could easily gross seventy-five hundred off the remaining product, breaking it down into grams, eight-balls, and quarters, depending on how the business came. He then considered cutting the dope to bring in an extra grand or two, but decided against it, knowing it would be detrimental to business. He liked to keep the product pure for his customers, not to mention he sniffed it himself. Thinking of getting high at that very moment, he restrained himself, kicked back and took in the sounds of Biggie on "Brooklyn's Finest."

"Where the hoes at," Ski asked, interrupting Slick's mental reverie.

"Slick, Kwan, and Akbar got 'em all," spouted Spray, as the saliva that spurted from between his teeth validated his nickname.

"Yeah Akbar," Worm said. "Call them freaks from Twin Canal we had at the room that night."

Akbar ignored Worm, focusing on the task of beating Flash's three in the dice game. It wasn't until Akbar rolled three fours that he snapped out of the hypnotized state.

"I aint stuttin' them whack broads. Let me get this money right now, those chicks can wait," Akbar exclaimed as he accepted the eighty dollars from Flash.

"Slick, what's up with them cokehead bitches you had jumping off over here the other night? I know they stay ready," Boss inquired thirstily.

"Ain't nothing popping off right now. I'm not dealing with that headache today," Slick replied, as he pondered the actions of Red and Melissa, the black and white girls to which Boss referred.

Red was a light-skinned, gorgeous, beauty, about five feet two inches, a hundred and twenty pounds with thick red lips, swollen thighs, and a round backside that was soft as baby doo-doo. Melissa was a pale Caucasian brunette, with big brown eyes, shoulder length hair and a butt that would make the average black girl jealous. Both women came from good homes and were genuinely kind and sweet under normal circumstances.

Unfortunately, the two had debilitating cocaine habits that caused them to act in ways completely out of their character. Once the chemical entered their system, they couldn't stop, and they would do anything to keep the supply coming. Slick knew that and took advantage of their needs by satisfying his wants.

What the three of them often engaged in while under the influence would rival any pornographic film in circulation. Slick often felt guilty about exploiting the ladies in such a manner, but when he was high there were no reservations in his heart about the actions. It was only after did his conscience would afflict him and he would experience shame and regret. "It's just the life we live," he would emptily justify to himself.

"You can't cuff them hoes cuz," loudmouth Ski shouted. "Let the boys get some of that fire head they got?"

Slick shook his head in disgust. He perceived that the boys really were co-dependent of each other. They hustled together, rode together, dined together, got motel rooms together and screwed girls together. If one of the boys got something individually, the whole crew felt entitled to whatever it was. Slick was always his own man so he couldn't understand the concept they lived by. He dealt with the youths despite their conflicting views because he had invaded their neighborhood and set up shop, and also because he didn't have anything else to do for entertainment.

BZZZZZ..., BZZZZZ..., BZZZZZZ..., BZZZZZ...,

Slick heard the vibration of his cell phone against the glass table. Feeling the groove from the music, weed smoke and alcohol, he flipped his phone open without checking the caller identification.

"Yo," Slick greeted the anonymous, but soon to be familiar caller.

"Hi Buddy... What you up to my friend," said the voice.

"I'm chilling, got a few dudes over here shooting some dice. You know me. What's up with you?"

"Well, me and the wife just dropped the kids off at the movies to see Shrek. We were just leaving the liquor store right around the corner from you, and were wondering if we could stop by and say hi?"

"Of course," Slick retorted. "Just call me when you get outside."

Slick hung up the phone before the caller could reply. He knew the identity of the man when he spoke his first syllable; Toby from the rim shop. Toby and his wife Fee-Fee had opened a detail shop at the beachfront two years earlier. They were introduced to Slick by their employee, Tone, who was introduced to Slick by the white girl Melissa. They employed another young white man named Jay, and all four of them spent money with the hustler on a regular basis, sometimes daily. However, conflicts did arise from the paranoia that cocaine caused.

Toby was somewhat of a henpecked husband. Whatever his wife proposed to do was basically done without question. That led to insecurity on his part and the authority was handed over to his wife.

Fee-Fee would come by at times alone and score product from Slick. She would hide the fact from her husband and send him to get more drugs later. Evidently, he caught on to her schemes and approached Slick petitioning him not to serve Fee-Fee without him.

This request put Slick in a peculiar predicament, because he was a drug dealer, not a marriage counselor. If Toby wanted her to refrain from making ill-advised purchases, then he would have to enforce that rule between he and his wife. There was no way Slick could refuse Fee-Fee if she continued to solicit his services and that is exactly what he told Toby. Eventually, they must have come to some sort of an agreement because the discussion never occurred again.

"Shoot something," Flash implored, attempting to lure the host back into the game.

"Alright," Slick agreed, reluctantly dismounting the couch. He withdrew the knot from his pocket, snapped the rubber band, and slipped an Andrew Jackson from beneath the Hamiltons. As soon as he dropped the money on the floor, Flash rolled a six to win. Ignoring the limit he had set for himself, he unconsciously placed two more twenties on the ground.

"Bet forty this time!" Slick demanded, as he noticed a spirit of anticipation in the bank holder's eyes. Slick knew he was treading on dangerous ground because of his degenerate gambling habit. Flash rolled the dice.

BZZZZZZ.., BZZZZZZ..., BZZZZZZ..., BZZZZZZZ...

Saved by the bell.

He looked at the phone. It was Grim, another one of the boys from the Pine Gardens apartment complex, which was next to Slick's complex, Thalia Oaks.

"Where y'all at," Grim asked, after Slick answered.

"We at the crib!"

"What y'all niggas doing, shooting," asked Grim.

"Yeah, come on through and lose some of that guape!"

"Alright, nigga me and B gon' come through there."

"Bring me some squares when you come," Slick asked.

"Yeah," Grim complied. Click, the phone hung up.

Grim and B were brothers. They were originally from Elizabeth City, North Carolina but had migrated to Virginia with their mother at an early age. Grim, the elder, was tall, slender, brown complexioned with shoulder length dreads. He was the only one of the men with enough sense to apply for a gun permit. Since he was licensed, he could carry his weapon legally and never separated himself from his chrome forty-five. He had four kids with four baby mammas. The stress he had to deal with was evident in his facial expression as he always showed a look of discontent.

B was only nineteen but he had a lot of wops(customers). Though he made a lot of dough in the streets, he spent amost of his profits in the malls, clubs and on women. He was involved with a lady that was older than he, and it seemed that she was always stretching him to the limit. That was primarily the reason that he was in a continuous struggle to maintain his level of money and status in the game. These brothers did relate well to Slick, however, because he originated from North Carolina as well.

BZZZZZ...BZZZZZZ..., BZZZZZZ..., BZZZZZZZ...

The hotline rang again as Flash managed to roll a two, two, and five on the dice. Slick allowed everyone else to compete while he answered the phone.

"Slick, we're outside!" Toby said.

"Okay, I'll be out there. What you want me to bring you?"

Toby conversed with his wife, "What you want to do Fee-Fee, a 'teenth, an eighth, what?"

After a brief pause Toby indicated that he wanted an eighth of an ounce which was equal to three and half grams. Slick would charge them two-hundred dollars. He instructed them to wait about five minutes and then enter the hallway.

Kwan and Boss, who were eavesdropping on the telephone exchange, interjected their desire to participate in the sale.

"Let me throw in on that," asked Boss, who didn't even sale coke, but occasionally distributed small amounts of crack.

"Yeah, Slick, I got some girl in the car," added Kwan, who was known to dabble in a little soft from time to time.

"I got it yo," Slick confirmed as he headed for the door to retrieve his stash.

"Shoot to the five, Slick. You know you got forty down," Flash yelled just as Slick grasped the doorknob. Slick almost forgot about the money he had betted. It was such a hard point he decided to hold off until he made the transaction.

"I'll be right back," Slick informed, as he opened the door.

"You can't hold up the ga...."

The heavy metal door slammed shut before Flash could get his words out. Slick entered the storage room through the entrance just at the right of his door. He bypassed three storage cages, where his neighbors kept bicycles, camping equipment, coolers and all manner of stuff. He then opened the door to the utility room where the trash containers were kept. He reached above the fuse box and felt for the Ziploc bag full of the rocked up cocaine that he could smell before he located. He maneuvered through dust and insects until his pinky finger came to rest on a plastic bag containing the toxic substance that his body was now craving for.

Slick pulled the treasure down from the sky and placed it on the black garbage container. He then stepped on the wooden sidebar connected to the wall to get a better view of the top of the box in order to locate his digital scale. He snagged the gray calculator sized device from the edge of the surface, stepped down and positioned it an inch from the drugs. His nose began to moisten and drip as he unzipped the bag.

BZZZZZ...BZZZZZZ...BZZZZZZ..., BZZZZZZ...

"Hello!" Slick answered the phone in frustration.

"Poppi, we're just leaving the store and wanted to know if you wanted something?"

The irritation subsided as he recognized the sweet but firm voice of Ashley on the opposite end of the phone. "No pumpkin, I'm straight. Just bring your little tail on over here, pronto," he commanded.

"Hey daddy, I miss you, can't wait to see you," screamed a husky voice in the background. He immediately discerned the tone of Tina's words and grew excited that she was able to come.   "You know I miss you too, so y'all broads hurry up. I'll be outside when you get there," he replied.

Urgently, he reached in the bag and broke off a chunk of the shiny fish scale that his connect always provided. He pressed the on button and waited for the scale to calibrate. As soon the digital numbers displayed double zeros, he dropped a portion of the product on the surface.

Four point eight grams was the weight of the rock. He picked the matter up and broke it in half. He deposited half on the scale and the reading amounted to two point four. Perfect. Despite the fact that Toby wanted an eight ball and Slick's measurement was more than a gram short, his product was so good and their relationship was so friendly, that he could essentially give them what he wanted to and there would be no questions asked. Some days, when he felt particularly generous, he would give people the correct weight. Other days, he wouldn't use the scale at all. He would just use his own eyes.

Feeling pressed for time, Slick reached in the garbage can and grabbed a plastic grocery bag. He ripped off a piece of the top and enclosed the dope intended for Toby and Fee-Fee. He repeated the action and wrapped the other half of the dope in the same manner. Before closing the Ziploc bag, an irresistible urge overtook him. He had to have it.

Slick knew from experience that once he started it would be an all-night affair. Undeterred, he took out his wallet and removed his Virginia State identification card. He tilted the bag, so that the hard rocks rolled to the side and the powdered cocaine stayed at the bottom. He dipped the card in the dust, removing it carefully as not to waste any, pressed his left pointer finger against his left nostril, and poured the substance down the nasal passage of his right. A deep snort ensued.

Frozen for about ten seconds, he repeated the process only this time switching hands and nostrils. He swallowed hard, as the toxic element drained down from his nose to the back of his throat. The whites of his eyes began to get smaller as the pupils in the middle of his brown eyes expanded to three times their size. His ears stood at attention as the voices in his house that were once inaudible, penetrated the walls. He then took two more snorts only to be interrupted by the vibration of the phone. He ignored it. Cocaine could sure negate every sense of responsibility and obligation of the user.

Slick regained his senses. He needed a cigarette immediately. Sniffling and snorting, he returned the bag and scale to their hiding place. Closing the door to the utility room, he retraced his steps through the storage room, out into the apartment hallway. He bypassed his own door and exited the front door of the apartment building.

Fixing his eyes on the densely populated parking lot, he spotted Toby and Fee-Fee on their work truck, which was decorated with their company logo, Wheels-R-Us. The blonde-haired woman and the round faced man with a buzz cut replaced looks of impatience with expressions of glee, as they noticed Slick approaching. The Marlboro light tobacco smoke filled the interior of the vehicle, as the pair exhaled and discarded their cigarettes out the window. The smiles they wore as he got to the car were a testament to their addiction to drugs.

"What's up buddy," Toby asked, extending his hand for a shake.

"Y'all," Slick replied as he grabbed Toby's rough right hand, placing the small bag in his palm simultaneously.

"Here you go honey," Fee-Fee said flirtatiously, handing the folded green money to Slick as he accepted it with his left hand. He automatically slipped the revenue into his pocket as there was no need to check the amount. No one ever dared to short the man with the golden eggs.

"I hope you don't have a house full of those thugs in your place man," Toby inquired with a look of concern. He had always disliked the boys Slick gambled with because they were young, wild and disrespectful. He constantly cautioned the dealer about the content of his company and left abruptly whenever they were present. Truthfully, Slick knew he was right, but sometimes he couldn't resist the temptation of hosting dice games or going out with the young men. He felt that they kept him sharp, on his toes.

Slick just gave Toby a smile in response to the statement. "Just call me when you need me and I'll be around," Slick said in departure.

"Okay. Tomorrow is Saturday, so we'll definitely be getting in touch with you. We're gonna do a little partying at the crib. You're welcome to come by if you like."

"For sure, just hit me up," Slick answered. The couple pulled off with Fee-Fee waving frantically out the window.

They were always inviting the young man to their place. They had a nice house in a prestigious neighborhood and he had visited a few times. Slick did not feel comfortable, however, because it seemed Fee-Fee was always making vulgar and provocative remarks around him. He was aware that some married couples indulged in a fad called "swinging", but he had never seen it first hand, nor did he want to become involved. Nothing good would come of it. First of all, his morals would in no way allow him to do that. His father, a Pentecostal preacher, had instilled in him to never covet or lust after another man's wife. Also, adultery was forbidden in the Ten Commandments. Secondly, Slick knew that if he ever penetrated the thin white woman, it would be the beginning of the end for their marriage. As the saying goes, "Once you go black...!" Loud music invaded his mind.

"Many men...wish death upon me...Blood in my eye dog and I can't see...Lord I don't cry no more, don't look to the sky no more...Have mercy on me...Have mercy on my soul...somewhere my heart turned cold..."

Gritty lyrics from Fifty Cent's "Get Rich or Die Trying", blasted from Ashley's four-door Honda Civic as it careened around the corner of the parking lot. Slick turned around just in time to view the sedan as it pulled into the empty space eight feet away from where he lingered on the sidewalk. He could tell that the girls were entrenched in the melodrama of the lyrics. The way their heads bobbed, necks gyrated, and their hands moved in a motion that suggested that they were directing an orchestra.

No sooner than the vessel came to rest, the driver shifted the gear to park, halted the engine, and cracked the door, emerging from the car. Her passenger followed suit and both frisky young women sauntered over to their target in a way that accentuated their hips and waists.

"Hey baby," they said in unison, as they threw their arms around Slick in a group embrace and planted a kiss on his large lips, side by side in a three way show of affection. The cocaine in his system resurfaced in his throat as he took another deep breath, chasing the drain.

"Alright," Slicked warned. "Don't start nothing y'all ain't ready to finish!"

"Boy, we always ready. The question is can handle what we ready to do," Tina replied jokingly.

"I'm built for whatever," Slick informed while walking to the car to collect the beer. When he reached the car, he was none too surprised to find Ashley's favorite brand of malt beverage, Icehouse. He didn't particularly care for her choice but when he snorted cocaine he would drink anything that would curb the crash.

After shutting the door, he found the girls already in route to the apartment building's door. He took time to examine the women as they proceeded to his house.

Ashley's petite figure was accented by black spandex. He could see the print of the small thong protruding through the fabric. The purple shirt that covered her torso, extended to form a v shape formation midway down her back. The snug fit ensured that wherever she went, the nipple rings implanted in her small breasts would be on display.

Tina's attire was just as enticing. The jean skirt that she wore ended in the middle of her giant, chocolate thighs. The pink velvet boots with four inch heels came to her knees, giving her the appearance of a Las Vegas strip call girl. The pink halter top stopped at her navel, where a red star and crescent belly ring covered the hole, adding an extra flare of seduction to the flatness of her stomach. The matching jean jacket covered her arms but could in no way come close to hiding her voluptuous, large double-d chest.

Slick evolved from his mental utopia of lust to open the door to the apartment building. He was not surprised to find the girls standing at the threshold of apartment 102, as the noise and excitement from inside, transcended the walls and seeped into the hallway. They did not want to enter unguided and be subject to all manner of advances and vulgarities from the young men.

Slick opened the door and escorted the guests into the midst of the lively room. The attention of the thugs shifted from the grind of the game to thoughts of grinding on the chicks. The demeanor of most of the men changed from confident and assured to wanting and insecure. They looked at Slick with expressions that suggested "Me first" or "Can I have one." None of them spoke, except for Worm and Ski, and there words were barely understandable. Feeling the tension in the room between the women and their admirers, Slick led his girl toys back to the bedroom. Providing them with a gram of white to entertain them, he clicked on the television and promised to be back in a couple of seconds.

"Hurry up Pa-pa," Ashley requested. "And bring us a beer when you come," she added. Tina grabbed the remote control and switched the channel to BET as Slick was about to exit the room. He caught the excerpt of Jaheim's hardcore ballad, "Put That Woman First," as it exhumed from the tube.

"If it wasn't for the makeup on my shirt, still I'd be chasing skirts now…I could remember…and if it wasn't for the fight last night, you smashing out my headlights…I could remember…but silly me, silly me…tell me how could I ever forget to be…"

BOOM, BOOM, BOOM, BOOM, BOOMP!!!

The door vibrated thunderously. Grim! Slick thought as he eased towards the door.

"You gon' shoot the dice or what man," a voice evolved from the commotion. As he let Grim and B in, Slick remembered the forty dollar bet he had in Flash's bank and realized they had been patiently waiting for almost ten minutes. He gave the two brothers a pound and readily accepted the Newport's he asked Grim to bring. He opened the pack of cancer sticks with the urgency of S.W.A.T. team members defusing a bomb on a New York subway. He fished a lighter from his pocket and feverishly lit the cigarette he so desperately craved.

As the nicotine entered his lungs, Slick unwillingly moved towards the three dice that lay on the floor. He picked the dice up and rolled them nonchalantly not interested in the money that was on the line. The cocaine had him moving a hundred miles per hour and that's exactly how his opponents liked it. He picked the dice up again and rolled a four which was a failure to the five. He paid the money that he owed and unconsciously reached into to his pocket for more money to bet.

"What the world you do with them hoes, Slick," Kwan asked loudly.

"They probably back there getting snorted out," Akbar suggested.

"They ain't trying to trick nothing," K J asked.

"Breathe easy, they don't get down like that," Slick corrected.

"Not with nobody else but you nigga, you keep feeding them that booger dust and then they do whatever you say," Boss explained.

He did have a point, Slick thought in agreement. Unlike K J and Kwan, Slick never grew fond of the idea of paying women for sex. He preferred to spend time with them and if they did indulge in coke or any other drugs, he would gladly oblige. He understood that when most girls got inebriated they tended to get horny and want to have sex anyway. Most girls understood that when Slick got high he was going to want to engage in some form of pleasure, be it oral or standard. Nevertheless, there were rare occasions where he had to exercise his option of withholding the product in order to ensure compliance from the female subject. However, this was not the norm as he had a steady flow of female companions, many of whom didn't defile themselves with drugs or alcohol.

Kwan and K J, on the other hand, were treacherous. They figured since they had money to burn, all members of the opposite sex were obligated to comply with their solicitation for lewd and lascivious acts. They were attended trick parties regularly, where scantily clad ladies pranced around and presented themselves to anyone who would compensate them for the use of their bodies. Many of the girls were beautiful enough to compete in Miss America pageants, which left one to wonder why they would engage in such a degrading profession. Slick had come to learn through his experiences, that a lot of women loved to be treated in a demeaning manner, such as the two that occupied his bedroom presently.

BZZZZZ.... BZZZZZZ.... BZZZZZZ...BZZZZZZ.

Here we go again, Slick thought as he examined the screen on his mobile phone. He recognized the number of Gino, a short, fat Italian dude with a Napoleon complex. He was the son of a powerful mob boss and was well taken care of by his father. He was known to get drunk in clubs and pick fights with bouncers who were twice his size. He also wrecked several of the expensive cars he had been spoiled with and constantly accumulated infractions with the law. Other than that, he was generally a cool guy and Slick sometimes hung out with him.

"Gino," Slick greeted the caller with excitement, once again making his customers feel needed.

"Hi Slick. What you got going on," Gino inquired.

"What's your bet," interrupted K J who had just acquired the bank from Flash with a C-Lo head crack.

Slick answered the question by dropping one of the fifty dollar bills he'd received from Toby and Fee-Fee. Easy come easy go, he reasoned, as he exceeded his limit thoughtlessly.

"Slick, where's the beer at," a voice resounded from the back room.

"I'm at the crib," Slick responded, turning his attention back to the phone. "Alright, I'm coming right now," Slick yelled to Ashley, juggling three conversations at once.

"Four to you, Slick," indicated K J, referring to his point.

"Okay, me and Brock are coming through and we need a quarter," Gino declared.

Slick gathered the dice and rolled. "Just call me when you get outside," he said. He hung up nervously, as the dice stopped on a dime. Two, three, five, the dice read, nothing.

"Tell them hoes to come out here and get naked, back there hiding," Ski said.

Slick ignored him and took the last drag of the cigarette that he barely had a chance to enjoy. He picked up the dice once more and rolled with confidence. Three fives appeared magically on the tops of the dice. He smirked at K J, who flung his purple Yankee fitted hat on the floor in anger, before handing Slick his hundred-dollar prize.

"Life is good," Slick joked, before withdrawing from the next round. He maneuvered through the gang of men towards the kitchen, where he had placed the beer. He tore open the box and snatched three bottles out of the case. He then retrieved the cognac from the floor and transported all four bottles to the back room where the ladies were.

"Dang nigga, we was like where this nigga at. You just neglecting us ain't you?"

Ashley gave Slick an enticing glare, as she lifted the dollar bill that held the coke to her nose and took a small toot.

"Yeah," Tina chimed in. "Ain't you tired of playing with your friends yet?"

"Oh yeah, y'all act like y'all ready to play or something!"

"You'll never know if you stay up there with them all night," Ashley added, taking another snort and passing the plate that held the candy to Tina.

Slick turned his wrist to gaze at his silver Movado watch, with the diamond encrusted black face. The time was six fifteen. He instructed Tina to fix him a bump before he left the room. He leaned over and ingested the small dose of powder as she caressed the back of his neck. As the dosage took effect, he peeped at the alluring woman while she ran her tongue across the front of her pearly white teeth, tasting the cocaine on her gums. He assured them that the game would be over and the house cleared by seven o'clock as he left the two ladies in their drug controlled state.

"Let me go back there with you next time," B requested as Slick re-entered the front room.

"You got enough broads don't you playboy," Slick flattered him.

"Where they at then," B shot back.

"Probably out there in Chesapeake, somewhere. Wherever you be at," Slick guessed.

"Whatever nigga," B mumbled. "I'm a find out how you be getting all these hoes sooner or later."

Slick eased back to the dice circle, energized by the recent snort and the drain he felt in his throat. He felt like a super hero and was ready to commence his quest for more paper.

"Let me buy that gun Flash," Worm asked the young O.G.

Flash shook his head without even looking up. In a further act of refusal, he carefully positioned the chrome three- fifty-seven, six shot magnum so that it touched the material of his black Marithe Francois Girbaud jeans.

"I'll give you three hundred for it," Worm propositioned.

"Five and it's yours," Flash said seriously.

Worm cursed and dropped the matter. He knew in his heart Flash would never sell a gun unless he absolutely needed the money. If anything, Flash would buy every gun that was in Worm's possession before he would part with one of his own.

Before Slick could rejoin the competition, his source of income alerted him to the call of duty. BZZZZZ... BZZZZZZ... BZZZZZZ... BZZZZZZZ.... It was Brock.

"Yo," Slick answered abruptly.

"Yeah Slick, me and Gino's outside. Hurry up though because the police are in the next parking lot."

"What are they doing," Slick asked with concern.

"Well, it was two of them, facing each other, talking. They're probably just on patrol."

Slick thought for a minute and instructed the two men to come inside. He realized he had to go to the stash spot because he didn't have the seven grams needed for the quarter sale. He waited for a few moments until there was a knock at the door. The peephole confirmed that it was his two clients. He let the men in and told them to wait in the front room. The other young men tried unsuccessfully to market their drugs while Slick walked to the door.

Slick exited the apartment cautiously. He knew that he had a warrant stemming from an incident the week before. One of his playmates, Koko, a straight up hood chick from Norfolk, had gotten upset one morning when he would not give her any more coke. After he denied her, she asked for money to catch a cab home. It was six o'clock in the morning and they had been up all night snorting, drinking and fornicating. He told her to wait and said he would get her home after he got a few hours of sleep. Undaunted, the intoxicated woman insisted that she be accommodated immediately and continue to badger Slick.

Finally he gave her two dollars for the bus and she exited the apartment. Slick arose from the bed, buck naked to escort her out. She left, only to return minutes later as Slick was in the bed, almost sleep. The girl proceeded to bang and kick on his door. He resolved within himself to ignore the chaos, regardless of the disturbance it was causing his neighbors. Finally, she adjourned to his bedroom window, where she banged and eventually broke the window. That was the last straw.

Slick got up, still unclothed and opened his door. Koko came in, and in a drug fueled rage, he grabbed the woman, pulled her inside and slammed her on the ground.

"You want to come in, you in here now!" he yelled as he stomped the woman with his bare feet.

She screamed, but her cries went unheeded as the young man punch and kicked the girl in her face, back, ribs, and stomach. He then bent down and choked her, pulling her up by her neck.

"You wanted to come in so bad, now you staying in!" he informed, while he dragged her to the master bedroom. He threw her in the room, shut the door and placed a chair under the knob, securing his captive, or so he thought.

Slick proceeded to his bedroom and laid down, his heart beating from the three grams of cocaine in his system. Before he could relax, Koko somehow escaped from imprisonment and sprinted out of the door, screaming that she would call the police. He gave little merit to the threat as they had been involved in violent altercations before. He was surprised when the police knocked on his door thirty minutes later. He had monitored the law enforcement through the peephole, until they grew discouraged and left. Since then, he had taken no thought in the matter.

"Ah shoot!" Slick exclaimed as he stumped his foot on the door jamb leading to the utility room. He took a look down at his royal blue Timberland boots and noticed the white streak that decorated the one hundred and fifty dollar shoes. At least now, they match the jersey more, he thought, referring to the 1964 royal blue and white Johnny Unitas Colts throwback.

He finally got to the stash and before he prepared the merchandise for distribution, he took two more scoops of the white horse into his nostrils. He then dipped his pinky in the bag and rubbed his tongue, numbing his mouth. This time he didn't the use measuring device, but simply broke off a chunk of rock that he was sure amounted to no more than five and a half grams. That would be their quarter-ounce today. He grabbed a piece of plastic and wrapped the rock in such a manner that it looked more than what it was.

Reentering the house, he asked the patient men into the kitchen. Gino and Brock made remarks of the outlandish statements some of the dice players made in Slick's absence, as the dealer presented them the work.

They twisted it and turned it between the two of them, and as usual Gino asked, "Can I get it for three this time," negotiating fifty dollars off the standard price.

"Three twenty," Slick countered as the sly Italian added another twenty to the three Benjamin Franklins he had closed in hand.

With the deal complete, the three men exchanged pleasantries and walked outside. The sun was going down and there was a refreshing breeze to combat the late August heat. Slick noticed the birds descending in and out of the pine trees that encumbered the grounds of Thalia Oaks. The white clouds in the heavens formulated various images of animals and other objects against the backdrop of the blue sky. The intake of the soothing scenery was disrupted by the revving engine of the 2001 candy apple red Acura TL, with the front-end smashed. The newly supplied occupants gave waves and nods to their dope man, as they sped off to their destination.

****

Slick was drained. It was nine o'clock and he had been gambling for almost ten hours straight. His back hurt, his knees ached, and his fat bankroll had been reduced substantially. He had sold nearly a whole ounce and squandered the majority of his profits on the red, blue and green dice he held in his hands. His nose hurt and he yearned for another hit of the cocaine, which was partially responsible for his money mismanagement. He had disregarded several business calls in an attempt to recover his losses in the dice game. His female company was complaining of the lack of attention. When will I ever learn, he pondered to himself, tossing the dice in the air expecting to lose?

"Deuce," Kwan announced, at the same time extending his hand to collect his winnings from the beleaguered man.

"Just quit Slick," Grim advised sympathetically.

He knew it was the correct move and in turn retired to the refrigerator to grab another beer. Searching through the cardboard box he was able to unearth the last twelve ounce bottle. He popped the top and passionately guzzled six ounces in one swig. He walked towards the back to check on the girls, but before he made it there was an authoritative knock on the door.

"Oh shoot. Y'all be quiet, the police at the door." Slick relayed, backing away from the peephole

A scramble ensued that resembled a goal line fumble between the Bears and Packers. The men grabbed guns, weed, phones, and money and stashed items in their drawers, backpacks, and even under Slick's couch. The host continued to peer through the peephole and calm the guests down all at once. He knew the law would not break the door down for a simple domestic violence warrant, but he was adamant about making sure all contraband was completely out of sight.

All of a sudden, Boss, the one man with the least to lose, made a dash out of the back storm door. No sooner than he got his foot on the concrete, a voice called from the shadows.   "Where do you think you're going?"

Boss literally jumped back into the apartment. He turned around, locked the door, and retreated to the kitchen. The officer peeked through a slight opening in the curtain and observed the room full of criminals. They watched the official by the light of the badge, gun, and handcuffs glowing in the darkness.

The standoff lasted for approximately four or five minutes, which seemed like an eternity. There was no doubt in anyone's mind that the dice game was over. It was just a matter of time before the apartment contained only the owner and his two female visitors, if they even decided to stay.

Eventually, the officers vacated the hallway and left the premises. Everyone felt a sense of relief as two more blunts of marijuana circulated through the uptight room. Slick decided to wait a few more minutes before sending one of the coked up girls to scout the outside area. Tina volunteered.

Upon her return and verification that the coast was clear, the nine gentlemen departed amid conversations of going to the club, shooting dice elsewhere, finding some freaks and getting motel rooms. Slick was just happy to have avoided jail momentarily and plopped down on the ash stained couch facing the back door. He thought about the unproductiveness of his lifestyle and the reality of his upcoming confinement. He was perplexed by the desire to change his living conditions, while simultaneously loving the fun and excitement that the game provided.

He was reminded of a scripture his father used to expound on when he was a child. It was in one of the books that Paul wrote. It spoke of the will to do right but not having the ability to accomplish the task. The author stated that the good that he wants to do, he doesn't, and the evil, that he would prefer not to do, is exactly what he does. What a wretched soul am I, Slick thought as he related to the problem the writer was having.

He lit a cigarette as Tina and Ashley entered the room holding a twenty dollar bill full of cocaine.

"You alright poppa," they asked with false concern.

"Yeah but I need y'all to do me a favor," he directed.

"Anything you want," they submitted.

"Clean this mess while I take a shower and I'll leave y'all a little something to play with until I'm done."

The girls instantly sprang into action. They picked up bottles, cleared tables and grabbed the vacuum. Slick got up and went straight to the bathroom. He stripped naked and turned the hot water on in the shower. He then sat on the toilet, fighting the urge to open the two gram package of dope in his jean pocket. He checked the temperature of the water spouting from the gold shower head. It was just beginning to heat up. Unable to restrain himself, he let his hand flow into the pocket where the cocaine lay, removed it and opened the bag. He crushed a half a gram up by rubbing his fingers against the outside of the plastic. He took two large scoops, using the house key on his chain, snorted them and stood up. Looking in the mirror, he noticed how fatigued he looked. He was fed up with this destructive habit.

His eyes surveyed the granite counter top that surrounded the sink. The gray surface was covered with Johnson & Johnson baby powder, baby lotion, Degree deodorant, Crest toothpaste, and a variety of expensive cologne. He had spent over four-hundred dollars for the bottles of Curve, Coolwater, Isse Miyake, and Joop. For some reason his eyes gravitated to the motivational plaque his mother sent him as a housewarming gift. He overlooked the content of the message and concentrated on the small words Jesus spoke at the bottom of the frame. He took them in.

"Come unto me, all ye that labor and are heavy laden, and I will give you rest. Take my yoke upon you, and learn of me; for I am meek and lowly in heart: and ye shall find rest unto your souls." Matthew 11:28, 29

The words had little effect on Slick as he pushed them from his mind and took another toot of the coke. With his nose filled, he entered the steaming shower. The water hit his face just as the cocaine dripped into his throat, igniting the euphoric feeling he craved. With his mind frozen, he tilted his head back, closed his eyes, and recited the words to Mobb Deep's "Out for the Gusto."

"I'm yawning while I wake up to the early morning gunfire…another day another scar to acquire…Hopped out my bed, tried to break my alarm…took a shower and then I strapped on my firearm…Grabbed my Pelle Pelle cause I wanna look fly when I die…."

The rap music had captivated Slick since he was fifteen. It was embedded in his soul like the scriptures he quoted as a child. He had no idea how the words that he spoke from rap songs he recited affected his life. The understanding of the wicked powers transported through some music was unknown to his distorted mind. He couldn't comprehend that every word that came out of his mouth would bring forth fruit, good or bad. However, he would soon reap the harvest of the many negative statements he had prophesied over himself throughout the years.

Completing his cleansing, Slick stepped out of the shower onto the gray throw rug covering the ceramic tile. He pulled the customized towel, with the initials T. R. from the silver rod. He commenced to dry his body, ridding it from all the grit and grime accumulated throughout the day. He lifted his left arm and rubbed the towel under his shoulder. He repeated the action with the towel in the opposing hand and raised his right arm.

He stopped when his eyes met the nine millimeter bullet wound that scarred the front of his right shoulder. He then took a moment to examine the reciprocal hole in the back of the same shoulder. In an instant, he drifted back reminiscently to the circumstances surrounding the shooting that occurred in Durham, North Carolina seven years earlier.

The graphic scenes replayed clearly in his mind as if it were yesterday....

2
Central

October, 1996
Durham, NC

"A young wild, beautiful love child…you like 'em thug style link rocking, the mink copping…Hit you on the sink, a hundred dollar drink popping…the head that make him take you shopping…a fowl doctrine…"

The smooth lyricism from Nas rode the pop track of "Black Girl Lost" like a jockey on a thoroughbred horse in the Kentucky Derby. Eighteen year old Slick sat alone in the dorm room of North Carolina Central University smoking blunts back to back, bobbing his head to the music. He was zoned out, bagging up quarters, halves and ounces of the last pound of marijuana he had for distribution.

Engulfed in the weed smoke and music, he was oblivious to the repeated knocking at his door. The pager he used to communicate with customers vibrated on the desktop next to college textbooks that went equally neglected. His only priority at this point in life was to get money, as evidenced by the lack of food in the refrigerator, lack of decor in the room and the abundance of ill-gotten cash locked in his closet. He hurriedly bagged the green buds in preparation for the influx of business expected during the homecoming weekend.

"Yo, Slick. What you doing in there man? Open the door," a voice resounded through the only window in the room that overlooked the basketball court in the center of the horseshoe shaped dormitory.

Slick recognized the deep voice of Spook, a senior who he'd known since his days playing ball at the Boys Club in Goldsboro, North Carolina. Spook had been the closest acquaintance of the freshman since he arrived at the school in August. He served as a tour guide for the younger man, introducing him to clients, girls and showing him the lifestyle of a college student. He stuck to the young player closer than a brother and was with him every day. They smoked, drank and ran trains on girls together. Slick was always excited to see him, because of his sense of humor and the fact that he always kept something going. He always had a story to tell. Slick removed the moist towel from under the door and cracked it a few inches for Spook to enter.

"What up big bra," Slick asked, offering the weed stuffed Dutch Master Cigar to his friend.

"Man, I been paging you for an hour," Spook exclaimed as he accepted the reefer and gawked at the mass of marijuana cluttering Slick's bed. "Damn cousin. You sitting in here like O.G. Bobby Johnson from South Central," he joked, adding his trademark laugh that resembled the chuckle of a witch in a haunted house.

"Nah, man just trying to get this money up before I go to the basketball game tonight," Slick replied. "You going?"

"Yeah, that's why I was trying to hit you. My man Mike from New Bern want a ounce, and the light skinned dude that sell mix tapes is trying to get a half. You straight, right?"

"Where they at now," Slick asked, hoping he didn't miss the money.

"They at the student union waiting on me right now. I knew you was in here, so I told them I'd be right back. You trying to walk with me?"

"Nah, I have to finish bagging and I'm waiting for somebody to come through," Slick said, handing Spook the merchandise.

"Who, Crystal," Spook guessed with the distinct laugh.

Slick shook his head in denial.

"It must be Ursula then."

Slick even had to smirk at the mention of that name. "Nah, yo, quit playing."

"Alright then, tell Layla I'll be back in a few minutes," he said as he closed the door behind him, laughing the whole time.

"Whatever man," Slick yelled through the door. He thought about the women in chronological order.

Crystal was an extremely unattractive girl, who Slick had sex with one night while in a drunken stupor. The incident was subsequently exposed and a lot of people would not allow him to forget it. Slick was disgusted with himself initially, but after remembering how good it was, he was disappointed that he didn't endure the ridicule and keep her in rotation. Instead, he dissed her in such a way that she may have been emotionally scarred for life.

Ursula, on the other hand, was introduced to Slick by Spook. She scored weed from the hustler nearly every day and sometimes they got high together. On more than one occasion, the three of them had engaged in partying that started innocently enough, but ended with the two men exploiting the body of the drunken girl in every shape, form and fashion. She seemed to like being tagged teamed in that manner

So did Layla. She was an undercover freak. One would never suspect that she would participate in the orgiastic acts that were prominent on college campuses. Nevertheless, anytime the young studs requested her company she didn't hesitate to comply. Day or night; rain, sleet, hail or snow, she was bout it like Master P and them.

Slick's daydream was interrupted by an anonymous knock on the door. He stuffed the mass of felony charges into a pillow case and tossed it in the spare closet. The peephole revealed another close friend of Slick's, Blake, who was actually his second cousin. They had known each other in high school, but didn't begin to associate until Slick arrived at Central.

Blake was uncommonly reserved for a college student. He was more focused on his schooling and future goals, than partying and chasing women (not to say that he didn't have his share of fun). His stern demeanor and logical reasoning presented more of a father figure to the freshman than a friend. Blake knew about Slick's activities, but neither condemned nor endorsed them. He encouraged the young man to make the right decisions and maximize his potential. He had too many relatives serving long stretches of time to become involved in any illegalities. Slick respected him a great deal for that decision and tried to follow Blake's advice.

"What's up folk," he said entering the smoke filled room.

"Chilling," Slick stated with reverence.

"You need to light some incense in here. I can smell the trees halfway down the hall. What's wrong with you boy," Blake rebuked.

Slick didn't bother to answer. He obeyed the inferred order and pulled two cherry sticks of incense from the pack on the dresser. Lighting them, he tried to make light conversation.

"Where Ta-Ta at today," he asked, alluding to Blake's girl.

"I don't know. We ain't speaking right now," he said in a distressed tone. He lifted one of the pre-rolled blunts on the desk along with a lighter and burned the end. He took a long pull and exhaled three seconds later with a sigh of comfort. "She came over last night unexpectedly and caught a girl in my bed," he confessed.

"Wow," Slick said. "I know it was ugly over there on Canal Street huh?"

"You don't even know the half," he replied with a solemn look. "You know how crazy she is. She went haywire. Swinging, kicking, screaming, throwing; all over the place. I had to yoke her up. It was serious."

"What the other girl do?"

"She got her ass on out of there while she still could. I had to hold Ta-Ta down while she slipped out the kitchen door. And guess who let her in," Blake asked rhetorically. "Spook, I can't believe that nigga!"

Blake and Spook shared the two bedroom house off campus and had been roommates since they were freshman. Though they were opposite in several ways, they were able to coincide without much conflict, notwithstanding this situation. All in all, it was evident that Blake was still in control and he and his girl would soon be back together soon as if nothing ever happened.

Despite his portrayal of strength, Slick suspected that his kinfolk needed a bit of mental refreshment. With that in mind, he suggested a quick trip to the liquor store to purchase a bottle of his favorite liquor, Hennessy, or Hen-rock, as it was dubbed. Blake agreed and waited for Slick to tie up the royal blue and white Penny Hardaway's, and slip on the matching Nautica coat. The two left the small room, which reminded Slick of the many jail cells he'd been in. They walked into the hallway, advancing to the lounge area near the exit of the building. As Slick pushed open the door leading to the outside he heard a familiar voice yelling his name.

"Slick, wait up," exclaimed the youth, approaching fast from the resident assistant's office. "Where ya'll finna go?"

Slick observed the well-dressed student as he walked up and extended a dark brown hand. The bright orange Timberlands covering the man's feet, testified to his eccentric nature, as they complimented the orange polo jacket with the hat to match. The purple Tommy Hilfiger sweater covering his stout chest added flavor to the already loud outfit. That was Polo's style since junior high school, Slick remembered as they exchanged a firm hand shake, contorting and gripping their fingers in a lock, before letting go.

"We just going to the liquor store real quick before the game. You want to ride with us," Blake asked.

"No thanks fellas. I got to meet Candy at the library at seven and I'm almost late," he explained with a worried look.

"Yeah, you better move on, before your mama come looking for you," Slick teased.

Polo nodded in agreement. "You know how that girl is."

Slick marveled at the young player's lack of backbone. He was cool and they grew up together but they were built from a different mold. While both were extremely intelligent, that was where the similarities ended. Where Slick held the wham, bam, thank you ma'am creed close to heart, Polo was more of the long term, committed type. While Polo catered to and sought to please his lady friends, Slick lived by Tupac Shakur's infamous code of M. O. B., (Money over Bitches). When Slick was on the block at the early age of fifteen, Polo had yet to jump off the porch; preferring his mother's companionship, to that of thieves, murderers, con artists and perpetrators of all sorts of debauchery. Before the weekend was over, though, Slick would experience things that would make him rethink the path he'd chosen in life.

"Don't suck too much face tonight," Slick told his childhood mate, holding up the peace sign while exiting the building.

The cold November air stung the face of the cousins, as they walked down the hill to Blake's car. Reaching the white Maxima, the two hopped in the warmth of the whip, escaping the fierce night wind. When Blake turned the key to the ignition, the booming base of Notorious B. I. G.'s "Warning" violently intruded the thought process of both students.

"It's the ones that smoke blunts with you, see your picture, now they wanna grab they guns and come and getcha...I betcha Biggie won't slip...I got the Calico with the black talons loaded in the clip..."

Slick's delusion into Biggie's problem was interrupted by the sight of Spook treading up the hill leading to the dorm. When they stopped in the middle of the road, Spook approached the car. He lifted the door handle and plunged his six foot two inch frame into the back seat.

"What's up Spook," Blake greeted his roommate.

"I can't call it. Everything is everything."

"So you got everything for me," Slick asked, referring to the weed sales.

"Yeah Slick, I got that for you. Mike said his cousin just came in and he need two more." Spook handed his protégé the money from the transactions. "I ran into about five more people that were looking for you on the yard. Asia, Micx, JC, and Rafiq; they said they hit your pager up like two or three times apiece."

"Ah man," Slick expressed in frustration, feeling for his pager. "I left it right on the table!"

"I just told everybody to meet us over there in twenty minutes, cause you know the game is about to start."

Slick checked his calculator watch. He only had fifteen minutes until he had to meet a few customers that he'd given a predetermined time. "That's straight," he said as Blake pulled into the ABC store.

Slick handed the driver the money for the liquor. Blake and Spook left the car and entered the store. Slick watched his mentors browse the shelves and select different brands of alcohol. When they reached the counter, he noticed the Seagram's Gin, Earnest and Julio brandy, Hennessy, and Goldschlager.

As his friends returned to the car, Slick thought about the money people were waiting to give into his bosom. With a breath of satisfaction, he slowly absconded deep into the words of the Brooklyn Bad Boy's monologue....

" They heard about the pounds you got down in Georgetown...now they heard you got half Virginia locked down...Damn! Niggas wanna stick me for my papers... Damn! Niggas wanna stick me for my papers...."

Slick inhaled the words deeply into the space of his mental lungs. When Blake dropped him and Spook off at the four story dormitory, Slick could not fathom the prophecy the song foretold upon his near future. The only concern on his mind as he entered the building was if he had enough supply for the thirteen potheads that awaited him in the lobby.

After the last patron left, Spook closed the room door and secured the towel that was used to keep the strong odor of marijuana smoke from penetrating the hallway. Slick calculated and arranged his profits with the concentration of a restaurant manager at the close of the business day. Spook finished licking the tobacco paper, indicating that he was through rolling the last of three blunts that the men decided would be enough to smoke in route to the game.

After separating the seventy five one dollar bills he intended to pocket, he folded the remaining stack of currency and moved to the locked closet on the right side of the room. Administering the combination, he removed the lock and submitted the day's take inside the pocket of a yellow and blue Bear bubble jacket. He also checked the other places in the closet that he sporadically hid his money. Knowing his cash was safe, Slick shut the door and replaced the lock.

"I know there gonna be some chickens at the game tonight," Spook said, lighting the blunt at the end that was loosest. "And they having the concert tomorrow. I can't wait to see Foxy and Lil' Kim on stage. And you know Mobb Deep and M. O. P. gonna rock that joint!"

Slick took a large swallow of the brown liquid that filled his cup. The savage gulp relieved the container of half the contents. Slick could care less about the games or the parties that defined life on campus. He just wanted to make money and meet chicks.

"We gonna see what it is they gon' do tonight," Slick conferred, standing up and viewing himself in the mirror. "Matter of fact, it is about that time. You about ready," Slick asked, looking at the clock radio that showed seven fifty.

"Yeah, but let's finish the blunt first though," Spook countered.

"Blow me a gun then," Slick asked and chuckled at the foolishness of his request.

Undeterred, however, Spook obliged the request by positioning the lit end of the cigarette towards his face. Tightening his grip, Spook opened his lips and placed the fire in the interior of his mouth. With his jaws expanded and tongue curled, he blew smoke into the mouth and nostrils of Slick, who had moved to within two inches of the man's face.

Slick inhaled the white air and felt the THC forcefully enter his cranium. He then retreated, trying to retain the massive amount of smoke confined in his lungs. After a second or two, unable to maintain, Slick excreted the toxic substance in a debacle of coughs, wheezes, gags, and chokes. His eyes watered and his head spun, as he attempted to regain composure and control over his breathing.

"Ha, ha-ha-ha, ha. Aah, ha, ha-ha-ha-ha-ha!" Spook doubled over in an uncontrollable fit of laughter. "You 'bout to die over there ain't you. Aah, ha, ha-ha-ha-ha!"

"Let's go," the struggling young man said between coughs.

"Alright, hold up. Ha-ha-ha-, hee-he-he-ha-ha." Spook continued.

Slick ignored the joker and retrieved a washcloth, his toothbrush and toothpaste in preparation to freshen up before the game.

"I'll be back," he stated, as he opened the door, and left for the bathroom.

"You sure you can make it. You need some help bra," Slick heard Spook say as the door closed behind him. He heard the ghostly laugh in the distance as he rounded the corner to the bathroom. "Ha-ha-ha- hee -ee hee, ha."

Slick washed his face thoroughly with warm water. He then lathered the toothbrush and brushed the utensil forcefully against his teeth, jaws and gums. He picked at the blackheads on his face that represented his battle with acne. As he brushed with his right hand, his left hand pushed yellow clumps of oil and dirt from the pimples on his light skin. Washing his hand of the smelly substance, Slick then rinsed his toothbrush and his mouth of the gritty tasting paste.

Heading back to his room, he spotted a man knocking on the door directly across the hall from him. From the looks of the guy, Slick was certain that he wasn't a student. Many people from the outside came into the dorm on a daily basis, many of whom were there to see people like himself and the older student that lived across the hall named Rob.

Rob was a career student. He originated from New York and Slick was told that he had lived on campus for about five years. One thing that the two had in common was their profession. Rob sold weed also, but in lesser quantities. His customers could purchase no more than dime bags from him, whereas Slick sold as many as four ounces at a time. So if someone patronized Rob with a hundred dollars they would get ten dimes, a little under a half-ounce. Contrarily, Slick's people would get twice as much for the same amount of money. That kept his customers happy and returning. Rob did have a higher grade of product, however, therefore keeping a steady queue of customers himself.

At this time however, Rob was absent from his post. Slick observed the man's persistent knocking and saw an opportunity to sell the last two ounces he had. He caught the potential buyer's eye in passing.

"What's cracking," Slick engaged, trying to lure the man for business.

The prospect turned his head slowly and gave the universal head nod in response. He then refocused his attention to the door in front of him. Before entering his own room, Slick glanced at the man quickly through his peripheral vision. He noticed the attire that the man wore, all black with a matching fatigue army coat, hat and boots. The man peeped nervously over his shoulder as Slick shut his room door.

Spook was at the dresser, pouring a cup of brandy. Slick replaced the hygienic materials and grabbed his coat, keys and royal blue Dodgers baseball cap completing his ensemble. "Let's rock," he said to Spook, watching him demolish the drink like Ned the wino from Good Times. Spook contorted the muscles of his face as the combustible liquid burned his esophagus. Slick opened the door and the two men walked out.

Ahead of them, Slick spotted the man walking away slowly in disappointment. Slick seized the moment and beckoned to the all-black figure. "Yo, you trying to get some smoke?" Slick held his hand to his mouth in a puffing manner.

The visitor turned around and his eyes expanded to the size of fifty cent pieces. He shook his head yes and approached the two friends while looking over his shoulder.

"What you trying to get," Slick asked, when the man reached whispering distance.

"Um... I don't know. You got an ounce?"

Slick's heart pounded within his chest cavity. This transaction, if successful, would put him at his goal for the week. "Yeah, come on." Slick turned around and escorted the newfound client to the door. He entered the room, followed by the dude, with Spook bringing up the rear.

"How much you want for it," the stranger asked.

Feeling generous, Slick decided to give the man a discount. "I normally be taxing a yard, but I'll let you get it for eighty."

Slick noticed the surprised look he had anticipated. Most people in the dorm would charge one-twenty-five for twenty eight grams, if they would sell an ounce at all. Slick was different, however. He was from Goldsboro. He found in his short time in Durham that the prices he was used to were foreign to most.

Slick did not feel anything out of the ordinary as the man took out five twenties. He proceeded to his work study desk to fetch the hand held scale and the sandwich bags stored in the top drawer. The weed was already on his person, tucked in the top half of his underwear to avoid detection if searched.

He listened as Spook and the customer made small talk about Jersey, where Spook was born, the surrounding neighborhood, and the Durham club scene. Slick learned from the chat that the man's name was Bunn, and he was from Mcdougal Terrace, the large housing project east of the dormitory.

Bunn's place of residence should've been a red flag. Doing business with people you don't know was clearly forbidden in the code of the streets and opposed everything that Slick learned while selling crack on the block. However, he was feeling uncommonly loose from the massive amounts of liquor and weed he'd consumed since his classes dismissed at one o'clock. Also, the underclassman had a mind frame of invincibility, stemming from the hardcore rap he digested in his brain. The fact that several students had been robbed by suspects who fled to Bunn's project was nowhere in Slick's psyche, as he walked over and presented the greenery.

"Here you go, my nigga," Slick said, interfering with the conversation the two taller guys were having. "That's straight for you?"

Bunn shook his head in satisfaction as he fingered the bag, moving the contents from side to side. "Yeah, that's good. Matter of fact let me get your number, so I can hit you when I need some more."

The suggestion of repeat business was all Slick needed to hear, as he tore a sheet from his science notebook and scribbled his pager number. After adding his name, Slick handed the man the homemade business card and kept his hand extended in expectation of the money.

Bunn examined the handwriting and verified the number by reciting the numbers slowly back to the weed man. "Yeah, you got it, just call me anytime," Slick said reaching for his money.

The uncertain buyer looked Slick in the eye, while holding the money towards him. As Slick reached for a third time, Bunn retracted the money once more and asked if he had an additional ounce.

Growing impatient, but also oblivious to the intentions of Bunn, Slick withdrew the last package of weed from his top drawer and sat it on the dresser. Spook, who had been sitting, arose from the bed to get the lighter that was on top of the dresser. He lit the second blunt of Mary Jane, equally unaware of the mayhem that was about to unfold.

"There she is; the last one. Just give me one fifty and take it all."

"That'll work," the man said as he counted the same five twenties and turned them over recounting them. That subtle mistake of buffoonery should have alerted Slick to the danger. Instead, he just stood there like a rock group, with his third eye blind.

"Let me give you my number too," Bunn stated as he moved closer to the door, blocking the exit.

Slick gave him a piece of paper and watched him scribble a few illegible characters on the note. Bunn handed him the illegitimate contact, while at the same time getting Spook's attention as he puffed on the reefer.

"Whoa cousin, that's a hot joint you got on there. Where you get that from," Bunn inquired, referring to Spook's lime green and black Mecca coat.

"My sister brought it back from Philly last year," Spook replied proudly. "We go up there at least once maybe twice a year."

"Shit man, that joint is fire," Bunn complimented, cleverly setting Spook up. "Let me see the back of it again."

Genius!

Spook turned his back to the man and displayed the reverse of the jacket, while readjusting the leaf that held the blunt together. With Spook's back turned and Slick needlessly attempting to read the numbers on the paper, Bunn gave Spook a hard shove in the back, sending him sprawling onto the bed.

Hearing the commotion, Slick picked up his head in time to see a black thirty-eight revolver in mid-air falling towards the hard floor. Click-itty clack, clack, click, clack! The pistol hit the ground. Before Slick's nauseated mind could react, the robber scooped the pistol and put the barrel of the small gun against his acne plagued forehead.

"Don't move," were the words Slick heard as he entered into a trance, dreamlike state. The pressure of the cold steel impressed against his face, quickly made it apparent that this event was live and in color. Slick took careful heed to the order as he noticed the shakiness of the gun holder.

How could this be? Slick couldn't believe that he had been entrapped in such a fashion. He was no stranger to holdups, but in times beforehand, he had been on the other side of the gun. He thought of the age old saying that said what goes around comes around. The many devious crimes he'd committed flooded his spirit as he imagined a small golden bullet leaving the little black hole, ending his short life.

"Where it's at," the perpetrator demanded, recklessly waving the murderous weapon between the stunned victims.

Spook had managed to stabilize himself on his back, frozen in fear. He gave his friend a look of confusion followed by a silent request to comply without resistance. Slick understood the helplessness of their plight and decided it was better to surrender and live to fight another day. Reaching in the pocket of his Guess jeans, he carefully pulled the wad of ones out. The size of the knot, he thought, would surely pacify the wily thief.

"There it is man. That's all I got," Slick insisted, keeping his eyes glued to the erratic gunman. "Just don't shoot me," he pleaded, holding the seventy five ones out.

Bunn aggressively snatched the money from Slick's shaking hand, all the while keeping the thirty-eight targeted on his head. He then stuffed the money and the marijuana from the dresser in the interior of his army issued jacket. Satisfied with his spoils, the robber backed towards the door and twisted the knob, with the gun still raised.

As Bunn opened the door, Slick focused in on the hammer of the revolver as it tilted back. Slick braced for impact as the man's finger squeezed the trigger, releasing the hammer.

Slick was not able to distinguish which noise he heard first; the slamming of the door or the empty click of the handgun as it failed to discharge. Relieved, Slick prayed a silent "Thank you Jesus" and then foolishly rushed after the culprit.

Bursting through the side door exit, Slick studied the night angrily. He scanned the grounds for a glimpse of the fleeing felon. Peering down the block in the direction of the infamous projects, he saw a shadowy figure scampering down the road. He unwittingly pounced over the steps and sprinted down the sidewalk. Realizing that he was unarmed, Slick came to a halt after running about thirty feet. Charge it to the game, he wisely advised himself and returned despondently to the scene of the crime.

Spook was still in the room when Slick walked in with a dejected smile.

"I knew something was wrong with that dude when I first saw him," Spook stated. "You see how jumpy he was. He just kept fidgeting and looking around. We should've known. And you see how he tried to bust off going out the door? He was scared to death! We slipped up for real this time, though homey."

"What's so bad about it is that that strap was empty," Slick exclaimed. "That cat had to be on that boy or something to pull that stunt."

Spook continued in a nervous rambling frenzy. Slick just shook his head in disbelief. He realized he did have some consolation, picking up the half full bottle of Hennessy. With no regard for his liver and kidneys, he took an alcoholic swallow of the liquid that left nothing in the gold and burgundy labeled bottle but air.

With a few more regrets concerning the holdup, the young men gathered themselves and left for the homecoming festivities. North Carolina Central would be playing Winston-Salem State University in a battle of black colleges that reminded Slick of the black on black crime that was so frequent in his line of work.

****

Slick awoke Saturday morning still discombobulated over the previous night's occurrence. The first thought on his mind was getting another more weed to start recouping the two hundred and fifty dollar setback. He instantly got up and called both of his connections.

First, he paged Lisa, a sexy, sultry local girl who was introduced to him by Spook. He had dealt with her on a few occasions and was impressed with her prices and product. She worked for a dude, but she always came to see him personally, delivering the drugs directly to his door. Slick tried to talk her down on every transaction but she would not budge, just as she wouldn't on his sexual advances. She was all business and no nonsense, the reason why Slick liked her. Hearing the phone ring, he instinctively assumed it was her, because she was always punctual.

"What's up Queen B," he asked, not bothering to confirm her identity.

"Yo," was her one word reply, exhibiting her less is more philosophy.

"What's going on baby, your boy need to holler at you, ya feel me?

"Well it ain't nothing right now. It might go down later on. Soon as I hear something I'll let you know, page you or something."

"Aight," Slick said disappointedly, placing the receiver back on the hook.

Reluctantly, the young man picked up the telephone and dialed his other option, a long time student named Sean. Even though he was not an on-site resident, the weed supplier was a part time student. He attended mainly for the purposes of providing mid-level dealers like Slick merchandise to distribute. Slick dealt with him with reservations, after Spook had connected the two. He preferred to deal with Lisa, however, because Sean once shorted him four ounces on a pound. After numerous threats and calls, the man did correct the shortage. However, Slick was still sour from the episode and only used Sean as a last resort.

After twenty minutes of waiting, it became evident that Sean was not going to return the page, so Slick racked his brain for other options. The fact that he was new to the area left him with no choice but to wait for Lisa and hope that she would be able to come through.

Meanwhile, he decided to call Kay, a fellow freshman from Texas. She was a short, pecan complexioned girl, with green eyes and auburn colored hair. She was not attractive to Slick, however, because of the manner in which she carried herself. The whites of her eyes were always bloodshot red from the tremendous amount of weed she smoked. She also walked and talked like a guy, with only the slightest hint of femininity. She was a regular customer of his, and had invited him to visit Fayetteville with her. The city had a large flea market that sold jewelry and Slick was eager to flash some cash.

"Hello," a grungy, sleepy voice answered on the other end of the line.

"Rise and shine soldier," Slick said authoritatively. "What is you doing still in bed on this fine Saturday morning?"

"Uh, I don't know. What time is it," the girl asked in a state of confusion.

"Man, it's almost twelve o'clock. What did you do, go out last night?"

"Yeah, me and Elaina went to the Power Company. Hold up, who is this anyway," Kay asked, showing signs of coherence.

"This is Slick, who you thought it was? And what are you doing hanging out with my future baby mama? I didn't tell her she could leave campus," Slick joked concerning Elaina.

"Whatever nigga, what's the deal though? Are we still going to the Ville today or what?"

"You know it, sleeping beauty. That's what I'm calling you for. What time we gonna be out," Slick asked curiously.

"Let me get up and take a quick shower and I'll be ready to roll. Make sure you got something for the ride."

"You know where some is at, because I got rid of the last little bit I had yesterday." Slick intentionally failed to disclose the robbery.

"Call AG. He said he would have some today," Kay said, growing more alert with every sentence.

"Alright, I'm a get at him right now. Just call me when you're about to leave your room." Slick hung up the phone.

Slick arose and went to the bathroom to wash his face and remove the morning breath from his sticky mouth. After the game the night before, He and Spook had retreated to the Canal St. apartment, to guzzle beer, and languish over the stickup with Blake. They drank until the early hours of the morning, until Blake finally took Slick home. Slick had gotten to the room in a drunken stupor, falling asleep without removing his high priced sneakers. The refreshing cold water from the rusted faucet served as a hot cup of coffee, removing the cobwebs from his brain.

After replacing his rag and toothbrush, Slick journeyed up the stairs to the fourth floor residence of Algernon, popularly known as AG. At a lanky height of six foot two, he had the skin of an Ethiopian and the mouth of a sixth grader with bad teeth. The silver braces covering the yellow teeth added further to AG's adolescent demeanor.

AG was another five year student who sold weed part time. He didn't need the money as he was an only child and systematically supported by his parents He regularly copped an ounce or two from Slick and subsequently divided it into smaller quantities for resale. On some occasions, however, he did have a supply from an unknown source and at times like this Slick was fair enough to give him business.

"Who is it," a muffled voice yelled from the other side of the room door, after Slick had knocked repeatedly.

"Slick yo, get up out of that bed!"

After a brief wait, the door slowly opened amidst the sound of tape separating from the surface of the wall. Some students would surround the frame of their doorway with duct tape to keep the smell of potent weed from escaping, thwarting the attempts of resident assistants to catch smokers in the act. AG appeared at the door in gym shorts, a tank top and Nike flip flops.

"Slick, my man, what gives me the pleasure of a visit so early in the morning?"

"I came to see what you working with. I'm about to take a ride to Fayetteville to do a little shopping," Slick retorted.

"Word, you know that's where I'm from. Shoot, I ain't doing nothing today. Do you mind if I ride with you?"

"Not for real. But I'm riding with your girl Kay, so it's up to her." Slick knew that the girl really didn't care and in reality it was up to him. Kay was a rider and basically did what she was told.

"Oh yeah, that's not a problem. Remember, I brought her to you when I didn't have any goods. And speaking of tree, you normally keep something twenty-four seven. What's going on Slick," AG asked confused.

"I got robbed," Slick replied nonchalantly.

"What," AG exclaimed.

"Yeah, I got caught slipping and a nigga came strapped up. But you know me. It ain't nothing."

"When was this," the upperclassman asked.

"Last night about eight," Slick said sensing that AG wanted to know more.

As AG went into his laundry hamper retrieving a half-ounce of lime green reefer, Slick sat down in the rocking chair and began to relay the incident. The man looked on with disbelief as Slick retold the story like he was in a state of hypnosis.

"Yeah man, you got to watch yourself. I've been here for a minute and it's a lot of cats that come in here just to rob students. Just be careful from now on," AG told the younger man.

Slick received the advice with an open heart as he reached in his pocket and pulled a twenty from the fresh stack of money he'd withdrew earlier from his closet. He offered it to AG in an unstated request to buy a dub sack. AG in return pulled a small digital scale from under his bed and placed a small amount of weed on the device. After weighing the trees, he dumped them in a sandwich bag and handed them to Slick.

"I'll be downstairs in my room, but I'm gonna call Kay and tell her you plan to ride out with us," Slick said.

"Okay," AG agreed. "I'll be down there in a minute. If she comes beforehand just give me a ring and I'll be right there."

Slick left and descended down the four flights of stairs, pondering how he would get more drugs to sell. He had forgotten to inquire about AG's connections and wondered if Kay knew anyone that would supply him. He reached his room, still in a disheveled state of mind. He concluded that the blunt he was about to smoke would stimulate his thinking and solve all of his problems.

After breaking down the buds, he licked and split the last cigar from the box of Dutch Masters. Slick ceremoniously placed the greenery proportionately throughout the wrapping. Dipping his nose closer to get a final smell before enclosing the weed, he twisted the cigar with the precision that it took the tobacco company to make the original. Not waiting for the saliva to dry, he hastily put fire to the end of the homemade cigarette and took several hungry puffs, in an attempt to expedite the high. No sooner than he obtained the desired effect, was Slick's phone ringing. It was Kay.

"Hey dog, I'm gonna be outside in about five minutes. I'll meet you in the lobby," the girl said, sounding excited. "Oh yeah, AG called and said asked if he could go. I said yeah, because I don't know where the flea mall is at and I know he's from there. That's cool, right?"

"Yeah, that's not a problem," answered Slick. "Matter of fact, I already spoke to him. I meant to call you myself, but I got high and forgot."

"You better not had smoked it all Negro," she said.

"Nah, I got you," Slick said smoothly and hung up the phone.

Slick gathered his wallet, pager, school identification and coat and placed them on the bed. He then quickly slipped into a pair of navy blue Tommy Hilfiger jeans and complimented them with a beige, red, and blue Tommy shirt. Jumping into a pair of beige Timberlands, he admired his outfit in the mirror and gave a head nod of approval. Putting the items on the bed in his pockets, he then grabbed his coat and keys and hit the door.

Slick nearly bumped heads with AG as he bounded around the corner. "My fault homeboy, you ready to bounce," Slick asked.

"Yeah, she already out in the lobby waiting," AG replied. "I was coming from the room and saw her sitting on the couch."

"Let's do it," Slick exclaimed heading towards the young co-ed, as she arose from her seat. He gave her a fist bump, similar to the way he would greet one of his homeboys.

"We got to stop at the store and gas up. Plus I need some cigarettes. Then we can hit the road. How long of a ride is it anyway," the girl asked AG.

"It's only about an hour, hour and a half, depending on how you drive," AG answered. The three departed to the two-door hatchback Geo Metro that was parked in the fire lane at front of the dormitory.

"We might not be going nowhere if you keep parking in tow away zones," Slick jested to the dense girl.

The three students entered the vehicle and settled into their seats, Slick preferring the backseat. The engine started with a loud noise, and then quieted as the motor warmed. Kay inched the car away from the curb and the travelers started their journey.

Kay pulled into the parking lot of the Seven-Eleven and stopped at the gas pumps. She reached her hand into the backseat, requesting the gas fair that Slick had promised.

"Grab a box of Garcia Vegas and a Corona," Slick commanded, as AG instructed her to buy him a pack of gum and a Heineken.

The girl followed all of the orders and returned to the car with the goods. She slid them in through the window and continued to the back of the vehicle to fuel the tank. Slick gave a cigar to AG and the two potheads speedily twisted blunts.

Slick placed his production on the seat and immediately started to roll an additional cigar, to prevent further distraction during his therapeutic hiatus. The THC filled smoke encompassed the compact car, even before Kay reentered. The three sat at the gas pump and passed the marijuana around twice before leaving. The ignition key turned, initiating the factory tape system that came with the vehicle. Tupac's aggressive lyrics from "Blasphemy" permeated the speakers.

"My family tree consists of drug dealers, thugs, and killers…struggling, known to hustle screaming fuck they feelings…I got advice from my father, all he told me was this…Nigga, get off your ass, if you plan to be rich…"

Slick absorbed the harsh words while popping the top of the Mexican beer. He took a long swallow from the twenty two ounce bottle, savoring the coldness as the beverage caressed his dry throat. The alcohol affected him instantaneously, sending his mind into a whirlwind of anger, regret, disappointment, and despair. He had not left the streets of Goldsboro to become engulfed in similar circumstances. Nevertheless, he concluded that his life was what it was. He declared to himself that he would continue the outlaw lifestyle he had chosen. With that affirmation, Slick drifted off into a drug and alcohol induced sleep that would last until the group reached the destination.

■■

Slick awoke to the sound of his name and slight nudges from AG and Kay upon his knee. His eyes opened to behold the massive, warehouse like flea mall. His spirits quickened, knowing that he would soon be ornamented with jewelry. Nothing exuded the persona of a successful hustler more than link chains, gold rings and bracelets. The anxious young man ejected from the car in such a hurry, he nearly forgot his friends as they stood stretching their limbs, stiff from the seventy-five minute drive.

"Slow down," AG shouted in a tired voice. "The gold ain't going nowhere. At least, not until you get there anyway."

Slick slowed his pace to wait for his companions. "Y'all better put some pep in your step, 'cause your boy is in and out. I ain't got time to be up here all day."

"Well, you go ahead and we'll see you when we see you," Kay said, as she and AG continued to walk at a slow pace.

Slick arrived at the entrance within a minute. He walked into the large shopping palace that was everything he thought. The high ceilings displayed the exposed rafters. The lighting was reminiscent of an NBA basketball arena. The bustling noise of energetic activity reflected the thousands of shoppers milling around in search of a bargain. Booth operators, thirsty for blood, announced their presence with the fervency of auctioneers executing estate sales. The atmosphere was ripe for Slick as he spotted one of the many gold jewelry dealers in the busy mall.

"Hey, my friend," the man greeted Slick in an Indian or Arabic accent. "What may I do for you today?"

Aware of the tie down tactics of many salesmen, Slick declined to reply immediately, giving the impression that he did not want to be bothered. "Nothing much, I'm just looking, that's all," Slick finally said after the uncomfortable moment of silence. After the rejection, the resilient merchandiser promptly moved to another section of the counter to entice another onlooker.

Freed from the unwanted distraction, Slick was able to examine the contents of the counter with more clarity. He noticed the different styles of chains and charms that the man had for sale. Some chains were rope, some were link. Some were short, some long. Some were fourteen karat, some twenty-four and some ten.

He then turned his eyes to the rings. The foreigner had a variety of finger wear, ranging in design from square, triangle, circular and pentagon shaped. Star and crescent, crosses, Jesus heads and handguns were just a few of the symbols that were embedded into the frames. One particular ring solicited his attention. The exterior of the ring formed a pentagon pointed upward. Inside the house-like figure was the image of a man, holding a walking stick. By his side were two dogs looking up toward him. Slick entered the item into his mental inventory, marked the booth's location and then searched the immense room for the next jeweler.

"Hi, you like wear jewelry," said a small Asian man with thin glasses and thin pieces of hair draped across the top of his balding head. "I something for you. Come, take look," the man said in broken English.

Slick allowed himself to be accosted by the frail man in an act of pity. He was soon elated, however, when the man raised a four foot Cuban link chain that looked larger than the holder. Slick was captivated by the long necklace and instantly knew that he would be wearing it within an hour. The Asian was a mind reader as he discerned Slick's thoughts.

"Nice, huh, you like?"

Slick gave the man a look of disinterest. He was foretold by AG that the jewelers kept an eye out for big spenders and the price would be rendered accordingly. The best thing to do was to walk away and return later, showing minimal concern for the item.

"It's okay," Slick said slowly. "But it's a little too big for me."

"I have smaller," said the determined jeweler as he searched for and found a smaller link. "See."

Slick gave a partial glance at the twenty inch rope chain the salesman held up. "No that's alright. I don't want anything," Slick denied, with a frown and wrinkled eyebrows. "Thanks, though," he said in a false farewell, walking away.

Slick browsed around for a charm to attach to the forty-eight inch chain. He inspected a few booths but nothing appealed to his taste. When he thought all hope was lost, he found himself on the opposite side of the Oriental man's booth looking at a charm that was identical to the ring he saw earlier. The only difference was the size, being five inches long and three inches wide. Ruby like gems encrusted the cane and the man's robe. The thickness of the charm was also an asset as he suspected the weight was at least fifteen to twenty grams. This time the young hustler didn't wait for the owner's help. Instead, he applied the stealth approach method and surprised the unaware merchant from behind.

"Hey," Slick yelled frantically. "Tell me how much that weigh." Pointing to the object, he leaned over the counter aggressively, demanding a response.

"This," the startled man replied.

"Yeah that. How much you want for it? Thirty dollars," Slick said, asking two questions simultaneously, answering one.

Confused, the man recovered and resolved to answer the former question first. He produced the digital scale he used to measure gold. He dropped the charm on it and invited Slick to look. It showed seventeen and a half grams.

"What about that chain you showed me. How much was that," Slick switched. The man sidestepped to the opposite counter where the chain lay, keeping his eyes on the youth the whole time. He then switched the charm with the chain upon the scale, and displayed the results again.

"Sixty-five grams. I sell for four- hundred fifty. You want right now."

"Four-hundred and fifty," Slick shouted in a tone of exasperation that put the small man on edge. "No! No way! That's too much! How much you want for that one," Slick said pointing to the charm with a look of anger upon his face.

Disturbed, the small Asian removed a calculator from beneath the counter. He punched numbers slowly and wrote a few figures on receipt paper he from the cash register.

"Tell you what I do for you," he said with care. "Since you customer, and you buy, I give chain and charm for special price, five hundred."

Slick threw his arms up in a display of frustration. "Look," he said pulling out a wad of twenties. "I have money. I will give you three-seventy five for both of them, chain and charm. If you don't want it I'll go somewhere else," Slick said counting the money. After reaching three-hundred and eighty, he put the rest back in his pocket. He then looked intently at his opposition.

"No. No. Can't do that, not enough money for me," the merchant denied softly. Slick turned and walked away without speaking another word, knowing full well what was about to occur. Before he reached twenty-five feet, he heard a light voice calling out. "Mister, mister, please wait. I have better price!"

Slick stopped and turned towards the defeated man. He approached halfway and then stopped. The Asian man beckoned him to keep coming with a gesture of his hand, while looking around the mall.

"I'll give you both for four-hundred. Please, no lower."

"I got him," Slick said to himself as he handed the man the three eighty that was in his hand. The man punched in the digits on his register and commenced to counting the money. After counting three times he looked up at Slick, who gave him an innocent look.

"That's all I got," Slick said raising his hands in the air, palms upward.

The man shook his head in unbelief, put the money in his cash case, and smiled. "Thank you. You drive good bargain," said the jeweler, bagging the jewelry.

Slick received the items and returned the thank you as he walked away victoriously. He then located the spot where the matching ring was. He approached the jeweler and asked him for the ring and a bracelet.

"I give you the ring for thirty and the bracelet for thirty," offered the yellow toothed Arabian.

Slick thought about the price and realized that even if he bought both he would still be under his predetermined budget of five- hundred. Therefore he browsed the man's counter for additional merchandise. He found a square shaped gold nugget ring and a circular shape ring with a dollar sign embroidered on the top. He applied the same bargaining tactics as before and obtained all four objects eighty dollars. With his budget accounted for, he ended his spree and set out find his colleagues.

After a brief search, he found the two window shoppers at a booth with paintings and pictures of African culture and scenery. Having twenty dollars to spare, he purchase a painting of an African lion chasing a gazelle through an Ethiopian desert. His friends eagerly awaited their acquaintance at the register, impatient to see what type of jewelry he'd collected.

While walking to the car, he displayed the items. AG and Kay admired the ornaments and commented on their beauty. Slick accepted the compliments with gratitude and placed the gold into the bag, concealing his own excitement. The three walked hurriedly to the car, ready to celebrate the successful trip. The two blunts of reefer would serve as the catalyst to begin a night of partying.

While in route back to the university, the three engaged in light philosophical conversation induced by the introspection that occurs after smoking marijuana. Each individual asserted their theoretical opinions on life, love, God and a diverse scope of other topics that have perplexed the human species since the beginning of time. Ultimately, Slick grew tired of the vain talk and once again drifted off into an Eden of peaceful thoughts until he was once again in dreamland.

■■

"And that nigga that was down for me resting dead…switched sides, guess his new friends wanted him dead…Probably be murdered for the shit that I said…"

The serenity of Slick's sleep was broken by Tupac's "Against All Odds" as he found himself once again on the dreaded college campus. As he ascended from Kay's car in the early part of darkness, he was taken aback by the sight of the dormitory. The large resident hall suddenly reminded him of a prison. He had been in a few jails and some of them were actually bigger that the dorm rooms. Nevertheless he was here for a purpose, even if he didn't know what it was at the time. Reluctantly, he gathered his goods and said good night and thanks to Kay.

"I'll call you tomorrow," she replied, riding off into the night bobbing her head to the music.

Slick opened the door of his room and closed it anxiously. He removed the pager from his hip that he'd ignored for lack of product. He then methodically emptied the contents of each bag upon his bed. He was fonder of the chain and charm combination than any other of the pieces. He examined the charm more closely and finally came to the realization of what it represented. Lazarus.

Lazarus was a Biblical figure in the New Testament when Jesus walked the earth. He was known to the people as a leper, covered with sores. He would sit at the gate of the city and beg for food, while the dogs would come and lick the wounds that covered his body.

In time Lazarus would die and go to heaven and many people who passed him by died and went to hell, the place of eternal fire. Now, Lazarus was on top and the people that he used to beg from, now pleaded with him to bring them water from the heavens. This testified to the redemption of God to those that may suffer despite living righteously, in contrast to the punishment of God upon those who live in comfort on earth, but are evil in heart.

Slick developed a newfound sentiment towards the chain that was bought in an act of vanity, as he thought about the bible passage that his father had preached about in his youth. He now had a revelation of what the dogs were doing at the man's side. He had no inkling, however, that within the next twenty four hours he would have his own wounds that needed attention. Unaware of the danger about to unfold in his life, Slick prepared himself for his shower and the concert that would be the highlight of his weekend, or so he thought.

■■

"To all the killa's and the hundred dollar billa's...for real niggas who ain't got no feelings...I got you stuck off the realness...we be the infamous...you heard of us...official Queens Bridge murderas...the Mobb comes equip for warfare.."

Slick moved among the crowd of college students as they bounced, danced and shouted to the performance of the Mobb Deep's "Shook Ones". The mayhem reminded Slick of his younger days when he saw people engaged in a similar scene. The difference then was that the people were worshiping God in church. Now instead these teens were idolizing the people, lyrics and the lifestyle associated with hip hop. Nevertheless the music was invigorating and Slick found himself entranced in the glorification of the violence, murder and sex that the rappers promoted. His head bobbed and fist pumped in the air as an act of solidarity with the content of the music. Little did he know that the violence perpetrated in the song, was soon to manifest itself in his life.

Slick awoke early Sunday morning, again feeling the effects from a night of drinking, smoking and partying. After the concert, he and a few of the boys from school went to the after party at Durham's premiere urban nightclub, the Power Company. The events following the group's arrival were still foggy to Slick as he tried to distinguish the blurry figures on his alarm clock that read two fifteen p.m.

Excerpts of miniskirts, broken bottles, circulating blunts, fighting, gunshots and high pitched screams summarized the night. Slick looked at his blood stained shirt and jeans and remembered Spook's man Mike. He was plastered and had been harassing a girl who was leaving with another man. After repeated warnings, the man called his five of his homeboys over to handle the beef. The men pummeled Mike until Spook, Slick and Mike's roommate Noland came to the rescue. The last thing Slick remembered was Mike leaving in the ambulance.

The brief recollection was interrupted by the heinous growl of a stomach deprived of food. Slick ceremoniously completed his morning routine, culminating with the adornment of the newly purchased jewels over the brown Champion hooded sweater, matching his Gortex boots. With his rugged look, Slick made his way out the dorm, across the yard, to the student cafeteria.

Upon entering the cafeteria, Slick absorbed the quiet scenery of the building. He noticed the unusually scarce crowd. Most students were probably still recovering from the weekend. The people that were present were fraternizing in a relaxed manner, laughing, joking, and talking between bites of the much maligned cafeteria food.

Slick had no inhibitions whatsoever about the meal today, considering his stomach banging against his back with each breath. He made it to the serving line to inspect the contents. His eyes gleamed with satisfaction when he saw the cheesy lasagna, topped with chunks of Italian sausage. The server dipped the meal onto the tray just as Slick was accosted by a voice from his rear.

"What's up Goldsboro," said a familiar voice. The speaker slapped Slick on the shoulder, causing him to turn around.

Slick whirled to see Eric, a fellow freshman with whom he played cards, smoked and did business. "I can't kill nothing and won't nothing die," Slick replied in a smooth southern tone.

"After you eat, if you ain't doing nothing, we gonna be gambling in the student union. We playing tonk, twenty a hand. You down?"

Slick's testosterone level rose when he thought of gambling. He had been in love with the five card game since his days in high school. He'd spent many hours honing his skills playing with the legendary Willie Simmons on the drug infested corner of James and Pine streets in Goldsboro, NC. Three or four days would past before the sixteen year old Slick would return home hopelessly broke or with his pockets stuffed with dirty money.

"Yeah you know it. I'll be there as soon as I finish," Slick replied. "But yo, you know where I can get some smoke from? I need a pound, or a half-pound to hold me until my peoples get right."

Eric looked confused by the question. He was usually the one questioning Slick about product, so the unexpected request astounded him. Slick knew that Eric sometimes sold weed, so he inferred that he had a connection. What he did not perceive, however, was the grudge that Eric held against him for taking advantage of him in a previous card game.

"Yeah, I can call my man. I'm for sure he got it, 'cause I just talked with him earlier. Matter of fact, you can go with me when I go get mines. What you want?"

"Just tell him I want a half. I' ain't going no higher than four hundered," Slick insisted, one step ahead of the negotiation process.

"That should be straight. Just meet me in the union. He ain't gone be ready until about seven o'clock though."

"Alright, I'll be there. Just bring some money to the table," Slick commanded jokingly, as he walked toward his seat.

Slick could feel the stares and glares of the young men and women as he passed through the aisle of tables. He was then comfortable that the weekend journey was a success, accomplishing the intended goal, attention. He navigated through the sea of winking eyes, head nods, and handshakes, arriving at a small round table and sitting down alone, just as he liked it.

Halfway through the meal Slick began to ponder the stupidity of the man he'd just spoken with. Slick noticed early on that Eric was a follower. He also was insecure because of a deformity. The ring and pinky fingers on both hands didn't extend fully and were fixed in the folded position. Nevertheless, he still donned a persona that he was the man and attempted to fit in with people who really didn't want him around.

Also Eric was not very smart. He had challenged Slick to a game of tonk a few weeks earlier in the lounge. With tonk being a game requiring math skills and quick logic, Slick knew he had a sucker. Even the games Slick didn't manage to win he'd quickly manipulate the slower thinker into believing that he did. It paid off great until a nosy bystander alerted Eric and advised him to quit. Slick laughed within himself over the antics as he got up to discard his tray and head over to the union. He could not foresee that Eric's revenge would be no laughing matter.

When he got to the student union, Slick entered the game room with the confidence and authority of a king ascending to his throne. He had never lost any money in games played in the lounge and everybody and their momma wanted to beat him. The table where the big timers gambled was flocked with spectators. Slick maneuvered through the crowd and drew the attention of the gamblers.

"I got forty dollars for a seat if somebody gets up now," Slick said, jokingly but serious.

"Get out of here with that Slick," said Kevin, an ex-student who no longer attended but loitered about campus searching for card games and marks. "You know you ain't giving up no money just to sit down."

"Why not," Slick retorted. "Only thing that's gonna happen is I'm a win three times that amount when I tonk out the first hand!"

"Man you can have this bad luck seat for free. I ain't won a hand in thirty minutes," said Barry, another older student who still attended but was taking his time graduating.

"Come on, sit down," he said with a smile, displaying corrective braces.

"Yeah let me get some of that good weed money you got nigga," yelled Peaches, a loudmouth, heavyset dyke chick with braids. Slick disliked her clamorous nature. She was a nice person in other regards, but she was obnoxious and boisterous at the card table, which made for a bad game.

Slick sat down ignoring the comment from Peaches. He situated the red deck of cards and started to shuffle them. "Who deal is it?"

"Yours," mumbled Jerry, a quiet forty year old con man who posed as a student to hustle on campus, even though he was banned from school grounds. He was the most seasoned of the gamblers and presented Slick with the most formidable challenges.

Slick shuffled and mixed the cards with the versatility of a Las Vegas black jack dealer. After counting the cards he sat them down to his left for Kevin to cut.

"Cut 'em thin to win," said the card shark.

Slick looked at the man with discontent and dealt the cards carefully, not wanting to misdeal on the first hand. Each player retrieved their five cards and studied them intensely. After the three players plucked from the deck and discarded, Slick examined his hand. His five cards totaled twenty-one. Analyzing the five, seven, and six everyone dissed, he figured the players were depending on high cards to spread. He smiled sheepishly as he laid the cards face up on the table.

"Twenty-nine," Slick said, giving the opponents false hope.

"Oh, I got you! I got you! Nine, eighteen, twenty-three, twenty-five, twenty-seven," said Peaches, failing to count Slick's hand. "Pay me. Pay me double!"

Slick watched with a reserved calm as Jerry and Kevin counted his cards.

"Seven, fifteen, nineteen, twenty, twenty-one," said Jerry adding Slick's cards. "Nah, Peaches baby, he only got twenty one. He won."

The two older men slipped the winner two twenties under the table. Peaches, always sore to lose, stood up irately. "He can't do that. He got to call his hand correctly. Nah, I'm not going for that!"

"He can overstate his cards but he can't undercount. That's the rules," Kevin assured the woman. With no other recourse, the girl unzipped her purse and tossed a twenty dollar bill across the table at Slick.

"Come on girl. You know you can't be showing the money. You going to get us all kicked out," stated Kevin, even though Slick was the only one at the table who had a legitimate concern as a student.

Peaches answered back in a mumbled discourse of expletives as Slick gave her a menacing puppy dog looked. She returned a middle finger to Slick, just as Spook's voice invaded the air.

"You stay up to something don't you boy?

"Just trying to get it how I live. Where the drinks at," Slick asked of Spook, knowing he always kept a bottle close by.

Spook answered by flipping open his coat like he was Hustle Man on Martin. The subtle move revealed the top portion of Spook's favorite, Paul Masson brandy. Slick made an equally discreet request for a cup and Spook left the room and appeared minutes later with a cup of ice. That was all Slick needed in order to concentrate on destroying his competition.

An hour and a half later, Slicks spirits were high. He was up about three-hundred dollars, full of liquor, and had met a cute red bone sophomore. Eric also had just entered, indicating it was time to score. Before leaving, Slick coldheartedly teased the losers, especially Peaches, who had been antagonizing him all game.

"Nobody don't want your fat, sloppy, self," Slick degraded. "You already lost all your money. Now you need to go somewhere and lose some weight."

The victim of the insult was already ill because she was losing. Slick's derogatory statements didn't help. Onlookers could see the girl reaching a boiling point. Her knees were shaking up and down, her mouth was curled as she bit her lip and her eyes stared blankly at the two cards in her hand. Slick dissed a card to the edgy woman.

"Tonk," Peaches yelled, standing up and slamming her cards on the table. Rolling her neck and pointing her fingers within an inch of Slick's face, she continued to taunt. "I told you nigga, you ain't shit. Give my money, yeah, nigga what now?"

Standing up, Slick reached in his pocket to pay Peaches when her finger poked him in the eye. Inadvertent or not, Slick was too lit to ask questions. He instinctively backhanded the girl in the face.

This act ignited a melee in which the girl attempted to swing on Slick but one of the bystanders restrained her. Slick tried to move toward the girl, while being held by Spook. In the midst of the chaos, Peaches somehow got free and charged Slick, wielding a box cutter.

"Slick," Spook alarmed, trying to prevent the assault.

Slick turned to see the girl's arm coming down and Spook diving between him and her. He put his hand up in defense and fended off the wild blow, just as Spook grabbed her arm. Only when he heard the object hit the floor did Slick realize the danger he was in. With campus security in route Spook and Slick slipped out the back exit, with Slick motioning to Eric to join them.

"Shorty damn near cut your head off," Spook said as the three men walked into the dormitory's lobby.

"Man I didn't even see a knife. Only thing I know is if I would've got to that broad, it would have been no doubt if she was a woman or a man," Slick said. "What's wrong with her, out there causing all that commotion?"

"Yeah, that's a crazy bitch," Eric added. "But look though, I'm a go to my room and ask my roommate to take us to grab that. My folks said that four hundred was alright too. Just meet us in the lobby in about fifteen minutes."

Slick agreed and he and Spook went down the hall to Slick's room.

"Do you want me to go with you," Spook asked, just as an afterthought.

"Nah I'm alright. I'll be straight when I come back, so just spread the word."

"Okay. I'm gonna be in JC or D's room. I got some hot lyrics I wanna lay down. Just come through when you get back."

With that, Spook left the room and Slick prepared for his mission. He removed the lock from his makeshift safe, and counted the designated amount of cash, arranging the bills face up in the same direction. He then considered the jewelry around his hands and neck. Something deep within urged him not to sport his shine. He unhooked the large chain and slid the rings off of each finger, placing them in his desk. Grabbing a brown Avirex jacket, he hit the door with the mentality of a businessman going to meet a new partner.

When Slick reached the lobby, he spotted Eric, his roommate Lowell, and Damien, a fellow freshman and weed head. They waited in anticipation for the dealer. When he made it to the door, his accomplices merged in stride with him, destined for the long blue Delta eighty-eight that Lowell drove. Slick and Eric got into the backseat, Damien road shotgun.

"You got the right address and everything," Slick asked. He always liked things to go smoothly when conducting business.

"Yeah, right here," Eric stated, looking down at words noted on a white scrap of paper. "It's on the west end, about fifteen minutes away."

Slick felt no qualms about the west end, despite the area's reputation for murder, robberies, and all sorts of crime.

He had been in sticky situations before and regarded them minimally as regular hazards of the lifestyle.

He also was relaxed by the smell of marijuana that Damien had lit. The four students journeyed to their destination in a silent cipher of smoke, with Eric knowing full well the possibility of only three returning.

"Here it is!" Eric pointed to a five story brick building that resembled the housing in Cabrini Green projects. "Pull up right here by the sidewalk."

The driver eased into the parking spot directly facing the building. The structure was equipped with a breezeway that opened at the left side and ran straight through to the right side of the building. The breezeway was not visible from the front, however. Only the side of the building, full of windows and brick were in view.

"He know we coming, right," Slicked confirmed as he and Eric exited the car, walking towards the side.

"Yeah he waiting on us right now," Eric answered with his head down.

The two men strolled towards the left side of the building and disappeared around the corner. Slick ignored the feeling that told him to retreat as he studied the bushes at his left side. The two approached the entrance and made the turn into the small breezeway. They arrived at a door marked 102 and Eric raised his hand to knock. Before making contact, he stopped and looked at the paper.

"This ain't it," he stated, with a confused expression.

This lack of surety should have been an indication of peril for Slick. The fact that Eric should've known the exact location, if he dealt with the man on a consistent basis, never registered. Instead of backtracking to the car, Slick followed Eric out of the breezeway and made a right heading to the back of the building, away from where they came.

"It's around this way," Eric said softly, leading Slick around the corner into a field. The guide kept walking until they reached of the end of the building when a voice sounded from behind.

"Hey!"

Slick turned to see a large man in all black, standing at the opposite corner of the building. "That's him," Slick asked Eric, suddenly realizing the position he was in.

"Yeah, that's him," Eric answered, walking towards the man.

Slick followed Eric like a sheep being led to slaughter. His instincts pleaded with him to turn and run. However, his invincible, ready for whatever mindset encouraged him to proceed into an obvious ambush. When they got within ten yards, the all black figure turned his back and about faced quickly, revealing a shiny silver nine millimeter.

"Get down, Get down," the robber demanded. He charged the men, with the pistol pointed directly at Slick.

Eric immediately knelt to one knee and slowly placed the other on the ground. He then put his hands above his head and lay prostrate on the grass. He glared up at Slick, who beamed back with a murderous look. Eric knew at that moment Slick knew he was guilty. In a ploy for mercy he shook his head. Slick stared silently, swearing an oath of retribution through clenched teeth.

"Get the fuck down nigga, don't play with me!" The robber reached for Slick, grabbing him by the hood of his coat.

Slick stood still and stared defiantly at the gun holder. He looked the man directly in the eyes as he felt the gun press against his ribs. When Slick continuously ignored the commands, the six foot four, three-hundred and sixty-pound man swept him to the ground with a violent leg whip. Slick stopped the impact with his hands before buckling under the thief's huge frame. Pinned under the weight, Slick felt the barrel of the gun against his right shoulder. He then glanced at Eric, who was watching through the creased hands over his face.

BLAAAAAWH!

The loud bang shattered the quiet of the night. Slick's heart raced from the surprise of the gunshot so close to his ears. He felt nothing as the shooter's deliberate movements distracted him from the burning in his shoulder. Slick noticed the blood trickling down his wrist as the robber searched for his jewelry, something he'd been forewarned of. After realizing he'd been shot, the will to retain the cash quickly dissipated.

"The money is inside my coat pocket. Just don't kill me. Don't shoot me again, you can have it," Slick pleaded, suddenly fearing for his life.

The culprit rummaged through the bloodstained jacket until he located the clump of currency. He then continued to scour the man's neckline, hands, and wrist in an attempt to find the jewelry that Eric had assured would be there. The lone bracelet that Slick failed to remove was snatched by the robber who was obviously displeased with the take. This action certified Slick's belief that he was set up by the middle man. He gave Eric a menacing look as he lay on the ground still undisturbed.

"That's it. That's all I got man," Slick relayed, feeling the burning pain in his shoulder intensify.

"Shut up. Shut up nigga," the robber commanded, stripping the wounded man of his jacket. Slick lay frozen in expectation of what would happen next. The man stood up, cocked another round in the chamber, and took a few steps back. While Slick watched the blood flow freely from the top of his white T-shirt, the strong man began to drag his body out from the light into the darkness of the bushes. Slick had the premonition that his bloody death was imminent, so he did the only thing he knew that would save him.

"Lord my Father in heaven, I come to you in the name of Jesus, asking you to forgive me for all of my sins…" Slick prayed whole heartedly.

The robber interrupted. "Shut up. Be quiet"

"God I know I have done wrong and I repent of all that I've done that was not pleasing in your sight," he continued.

"Shut up nigga. I'm telling you," The gunman demanded, taking off Slick's shoes and jeans.

Slick cried to the Lord more earnestly. "Lord I plead the blood of Jesus over my life and against the devil and all of his forces. Forgive this man for he knows not what he's doing. Forgive him Lord, in the name of Jesus…"

The assailant grew angrier. "Shut up nigga…If you don't shut the fuck up right now, I'm telling you," the man said removing the bloody white shirt, jeans and shoes, leaving Slick clad in only his boxers. The assailant then walked to the spot where he'd fired the gun and picked up the shell casing and bullet. This collection of evidence indicated that this was not the man's first robbery. Slick prayed in the distance.

"Lord, Father I pray for your grace and mercy. Spare my life Lord Jesus. Send your angels down from heaven in to protect me. Thank you Jesus, Thank you Jesus, Thank you Jesus."

"Get up, get up and shut up," the efficient felon instructed Slick, still ignoring Eric on the ground. Slick stood up and looked the man in the face. "Don't look at me. Turn around." He pointed the weapon at Slick's face.

Slick turned away from the man fully expecting a bullet in the back of his head. He felt the sting of the cold chrome against the bottom of his neck, conflicting with the hot itch that inflamed his shoulder.

"Run," was the command given by the robber. Slick took off, trotting slowly, anticipating a few slugs in the back. The anxiety ended when Slick rounded the corner of the building, passed the breezeway and sprinted through the parking lot. He ran passed the Oldsmobile towards a corner store across the street. He was numb to the harsh asphalt scraping against his bare feet. The blood that had flowed minimally before the sprint erupted profusely as he barreled through the convenient mart's doors.

"Help, help me! Call the ambulance! I've been shot," exclaimed the half-nude Slick running towards the Iranian clerk.

The few shoppers in the store looked at Slick with alarm when he rushed behind the counter. The clerk, who was equally startled, unveiled a .45 caliber cannon, when the bloodied victim drew near.

"No, don't shoot! I'm already shot! Please help me sir," The cashier waved the gun at Slick, unsympathetically motioning him from behind the counter. Slick backtracked with his hands raised and came to rest on the floor in front of the door.

"Somebody help him. Somebody, help my baby," pleaded a large black elderly lady, holding a loaf of bread and a black pocketbook. "Lord Jesus, help him. Please don't let him die Lord!"

Slick lay on the floor spouting blood for what seemed an eternity. After fifteen minutes, the door opened and Slick saw a figure enter holding what looked like a video recorder. His intuition proved right when a camera lens was inserted a few inches from his face and then retracted to view the full length of his body. Feeling exploited, Slick scolded and cursed the cameraman.

"I'm sitting here bleeding to fuckin' death, and you stick a camera I my face. Where the hell is the ambulance at or y'all just gonna film while I die?"

As the wait for EMS continued, the bell of the door rang again. Slick saw Eric approach and his insides boiled with anger.

"I didn't know! I promise! I didn't know man," screamed the co-conspirator, leaning over his victim.

Energized by vengeance, Slick leapt from his back to his feet in one motion. "Fuck you! I'm a kill your ass, nigga. Don't give me that shit like you ain't know. I swear if I ever see you again," Slick threatened.

Before he reached his target, Eric was out of the door and down the street. Slick tried to exit the door and give chase but was restrained by the newly arrived police officers.

The small affray weakened the gunshot victim even more. Slick collapsed onto the floor amidst the noise of ambulatory sirens pulling onto scene. After twenty minutes of bleeding, the rescue squad finally had the blood drained man stabilized. They supplied him with oxygen and intravenous fluids while securing him into the ambulance. Before the doors closed, the officers asked Slick whom he'd like them to contact. With fleeting strength, he yelled out the only people he felt that ever loved him, his parents.

"Mr. and Mrs. Lee Richardson…919…735…7991," were the last words uttered by Slick. He knew, however, that his life was still in danger and wanted to ensure eternal rest for his spirit in case he didn't make it. Drifting in and out of consciousness, Slick focused his mind on the heavens and prayed silently…

"Lord Jesus, I know I am not worthy of your forgiveness. I know that I have sinned and fallen short of your glory. But Lord Jesus I know and have faith in the fact that you were crucified to pay the cost for my sins and through your blood I have redemption. So right now I confess those sins and repent of them and receive your forgiveness now and forevermore. I commit my spirit into your hands Lord, and I receive Jesus Christ as Lord and ruler over my life. I thank you and I praise you for saving me in Jesus name, Amen! Amen! Amen!"

With the comfort of the sinner's prayer finished, Slick relaxed and put his fate in God's hands. He realized that his prayer was effective when he woke up in the hospital three hours later, surrounded by the doctors, and most importantly his father, mother and sister. With a peace that passed understanding, he smiled at his parents to let them know he was fine. Then in an act of gratitude towards his Lord and Savior, he lifted a final "Thank you Jesus" in silence, and then drifted off into a calm sleep as the morphine took effect.

3
Party Time

August, 2003
Virginia Beach, VA

"Slick, what are you doing in there," a girl called from the bedroom.

The daydream of his college days was disturbed by Ashley's voice. Slick snapped back to reality and remembered the pair of ready for whatever playmates that occupied his bed.   "I'll be out before you know it," he responded, double checking his nose to make sure it was clean. He opened the bathroom and was greeted by one of his favorite melodies.

"Ooh, my first mistake was…I wanted too much time…I had to have him morning, noon, and night…If I would have known then…the things that I know now…"

En Vogue's "Hold On" resounded from the small radio atop the black and gold chest of drawers in front of Slick's bedroom window. The remake of Michael Jackson's hit, ushered in a sensual mood, as Slick emerged in a plush Carolina blue Nautica bathrobe, with matching slippers.

His brush cut Caesar displayed three hundred and sixty degree waves, manufactured by extensive brushing and Murray's grease. He located the durag stored in his night stand and positioned it on his head. Without the use of a mirror, Slick pressed the nylon fabric firmly against his skull and wrapped the strings around twice, tying the ends in a bow at the top of his neck. This procedure ensured that the circular motion of his hair would be preserved.

His two female counterparts, Tina and Ashley, were sprawled comfortably across his king-sized bed, with their shoes and boots scattered across the floor. The black, eight foot tall pillars stood at attention, guarding the corners of the four foot high Sealy mattress set. The green, blue, yellow and red plasma lamps, in conjunction with the five foot mirrors on the walls and ceiling, gave the room an exotic decor. The three by five foot black framed painting of the pyramid and the all seeing eye, cuffed in large dark brown hands in the midst of the Masonic square and compass, glowed in the colorful strobe lighting of the dimly lit room. The content of the portrait alluded to Slick's personal quest for truth. As an existentialist, he loved being alone and treasured the isolation of his thoughts and ideas.

The five foot by nine foot gray hardwood bookshelf that bordering Slick's bedside was his solace. Hundreds of books lined the seven shelves, attesting to his avid pursuit of knowledge. Literature from Frederick Douglass, Richard Wright, James Baldwin, Donald Goines, Iceberg Slim, Eldridge Cleaver, and Huey Newton, accompanied philosophical works by Marx, Lenin, Socrates, Plato, Nietzche, Freud, Malcolm, Garvey, Mao, Confucius and several other great thinkers. Biographies of Jack Kennedy, Dale Carnegie, Martin Luther King Jr., Che Guevara, Mussolini, Dalai Lama, Gaddafi and other influential people, complimented the inspirational works of Smith Wigglesworth, Watchman Nee, T.D. Jakes, Joyce Meyer, Rick Warren, Joel Osteen, and many others. This varied collection stimulated and challenged the mind of the reader, who was already seeking ways to change his life.

Meanwhile, he still had the luscious ladies on the sky blue comforter at his disposal. He joined the two on the mattress while trying hard to ignore their shallow conversation.

"He's always calling me," Ashley complained about an ex of hers. "I'm like dude, you don't get it. I'm not fooling with you anymore. It's like he can't read between the lines. I think I might have to paint him a picture, send him an e-mail or something."

Tina giggled while finishing the last line of cocaine on the CD case. "You shouldn't a never gave him none of that bomb pussy you got. That nigga probably be at home fantasizing, jacking off and all that," Tina teased.

"Girl, you know that cat would be doing that right in front of my face sometimes. Be all drunk and stuff, trying to get his little man to rise to the occasion. It was so pathetic. I had to leave him alone," Ashley justified.

"Yeah, that sound 'bout like that nigga Tito from Green Run. You remember him, used to be good in football. That clown would be so would be so high, he watching flicks, asking for head, trying anything to get right. I just used to sit there and laugh at him. I'm butt naked and this nigga sitting there stuck," Tina agreed to their similar experiences.

"I don't know what's wrong with niggas these days. No wonder they advertising all that Viagra and shit. I guess they really need it," Ashley added.

Slick couldn't relate. He never had that issue. Anytime, anyplace, anywhere, it was lights, camera action. Even as he opened up the bag of cocaine that caused impotence in many, he knew that the ability to perform was all in the mind.

Dumping the remaining amount onto the CD case, he could feel the mass of his manhood swelling with just the idea of Tina's tongue doing magic. He chopped the rocky dope into a fine pile of dust and scooped up a nostril size toot with the end of a straw. He poured it into his left nasal passage and then inhaled with the force of a chronic sinus patient to procure a drain. He leaned his head against the headboard as his brain released dopamine, causing the high.

"Y'all, ain't nothing but some hoes," Slick interjected. The words exited his mouth between hard swallows as the coke dripped into his throat.

"We know that, so what you gonna do about it," Tina confirmed.

"And what do you think you are nigga? All them broads I see you with, coming in and out of here. You can't even talk," Ashley sassed.

"Nah, see, them is just customers, that's all." Slick continued in his eastern North Carolina drawl. "Business is business. Anything less is uncivilized. You gotta to understand that."

Ashley gave a look of disbelief. "Slick, I know two or three broads that you banged personally, when we was working at Ticketmaster," Ashley accused.

"What you talking about girl. I ain't touch none of them strumpets!"

"What's that short, brown skinned thick chick from New York, with the gap tooth name? Shanique, Yanique, one of them. And then, that stuck up chick with the glasses and the loud mouth that was messing with the supervisor, Joel. She was sexy as hell though," Ashley added.

Slick noted the compliment that Ashley gave Kimmie. He knew a lot of girls were able to critique others without sexual innuendos. To hear it from Ashley however, was a shock. He was aware that Tina was interested in lesbianism, but he didn't know about Ashley. He hoped that Tina had already conquered her and turned her out.

"How in the world do you figure that," Slick denied. "You might need to check your sources." He placed the drugs at the foot of the bed between the two foxes.

"You know bitches can't keep they mouth shut about something good. They had your business all over the break room, and the bathroom, and the sales floor. Not to mention the parking lot," Ashley expounded. The two girls laughed and gave each other high fives before feeding each other doses of the illegal medicine.

"You can't believe everything you here in places like that. Things are not always as they appear," he reasoned, standing firm in his denial.

"Slick you know you be pounding them whores. No sooner than they come out they clothes, you have them bent over like a Jane Fonda workout video," Tina joked.

All three friends let out a burst of laughter, knowing that the metaphor was true. Tina knew from experience.

"I need some brew. Ashley, you'll go to the store and grab a twelve of Heinekens please babe," Slick asked in the form of a command.

"Yeah, I will. I need cigarettes anyway. Let me hit the girl before I go, though." Ashley arose from the bed and grabbed her keys and purse. Tina handed her the cocaine and she took four snorts, two in each of her wide nostrils. "You gonna ride with me baby," she asked Tina.

"No, I'm gonna just chill with Slick until you get back. I'm too high to move. We'll be right here though."

Ashley's light brown eyes squinted in anger towards her friend. She sensed the connection between Slick and Tina. She could smell the passion and lust in the air. "Tramp," she thought, as she laid the CD case on the mattress and plucked the twenty dollar bill from Slick's grasp.

"Make it quick too," Slicked smirked, arising from the bed also. He pimped over to Ashley and gave her a hard smack on her rear as she left the room. She looked over her shoulder with delight at Slick's gesture. What a freak, he thought as he opened the dresser, removing a pair of black Polo briefs and a large pair of Tarheel gym shorts.

The front door slammed, while Slick slipped the underwear over his bare feet, followed by the basketball shorts. He undraped the robe and hung it on the door. He gave himself a once over in the mirror, admiring his upper body. Tina's phone rang as he headed to the bathroom.

"Hello," Tina greeted, with her eyes fixated on Slick. She didn't know why, but the young man turned on her fire like Rick James.

Slick ignored her conversation, while rolling on the baby fresh scented Degree. Next, he grabbed the lavender baby powder and poured generous amounts on his chest and upper back. He then rubbed baby lotion on his arms, legs and feet, removing the dry ashy feeling. Slick completed his hygienic task by brushing his teeth and rinsing with mint flavored Listerine. He exited the bathroom at the same time Tina was ending her conversation.

"Okay…. Okay then….Alright. I might call you back tonight. It depends on what time we leave. If not, I'll just get up with you another time," Tina said, flipping her cellular device closed.

"Who you was talking to girl," Slick asked in a forceful but kidding manner. He walked over to the bed and stood over her, waiting for a reply.

"Nobody daddy," she answered in an adolescent tone of voice.

Slick grabbed her firmly by her jaw and cheek. "Don't let me catch you on that phone again! Do you understand me?"

"Whatever nigga," Tina answered in a harsh laugh, slapping his hand away. She then sat up on the edge of the bed and aggressively fondled Slick's groin area. "Don't let me catch you on your phone no more! Now what," she said groping the man's genitals.

Slick moved closer without saying a word. He pulled her newly relaxed hair downward causing her face to rise in submission. She let out a squeal of satisfaction in response to the rough foreplay that was common between the two. He then grabbed the back of her head, above the neck and pulled her mouth to his torso.

"Stop Slick," Tina mumbled, falsely resisting.

"Shut up slut," Slick said through a closed mouth with a muffled voice. "Don't act like you don't know what time it is!"

Tina gazed up at the young thug, as he pressed her head against his freshly cleaned body. She tried to resist but couldn't bring herself to keep her mouth closed. She unveiled her five inch tongue through the crevice of her plump lips, unleashing it on Slick's stomach in a hurricane like motion. The whirlwind of licks and strokes made the rod in Tina's hand expand to dramatic proportions. She gave a seductive giggle when she felt the growth.

"Damn Slick! You ready and I ain't even did nothing. Calm down!"

"Girl you know how I love how that tongue work. Don't even trip," Slick said, positioning his self on the bed beside her. He then lay back with his left leg dangling from the bed and his right around Tina. She accommodated by crawling over the right leg, coming to rest on her elbow at his side.

"Come here," Slick commanded, leaning his head back in expectation of pleasure. Tina obeyed by laying her head on the right side of his chest. She then commenced to rub the tip of his left nipple softly with her thumb and forefinger. "Ah girl," Slick said, as he rubbing her head.

"You like that daddy," she asked, before placing her lips on Slick's right nipple and sucked softly. "Huh? I know you do! You don't have to talk. Just lay back and relax."

Slick caressed the back of the girl's head vigorously as the passion in her mouth grew more intense. Tina slid her hand up and down his upper body while she arranged herself on her knees. She then brought her head up to the left side of his neck, giving it a lick before flicking her tongue back and forth on his Adam's apple.

"God knows," Slick exclaimed. "Where you been at all this week?"

"Waiting on you, Poppi," she answered, sticking her tongue down the canal of his ear.

"This is what I've been missing in my life lately."

"Don't worry baby," Tina said as she licked his large lips. "I'm about to make up for lost time right now."

Slick said nothing as Tina's saliva warmed his earlobe and neck. He removed his right hand from her head and placed it on her back motioning towards her thick round bottom. She arched her back making it easier to reach.

Slick's manhood leaped in excitement when his palm squeezed the Tina's soft backside. She instinctively lifted the small skirt up to her hips. Slick gasped in astonishment when he realized Tina was not wearing undergarments. He felt around expecting to find at least a small thong, but was amazed to find her loins completely bare.

"Surprise, surprise," yelled Tina. "I let it breathe all day just for you, daddy!"

"You're terrible girl. You know that," responded Slick. He gave her a strong slap against her naked romp.

"Aaaiih," Tina exclaimed joyfully, as Slick rubbed the spot he assaulted. "You know I like it like that. Spank me again daddy, please!"

Slick happily obliged the request by striking the center of each cheek twice more violently. He then rubbed the softness of her bottom as she lowered her head to his navel.

"Yeah, daddy, make it hurt so good!"

The blood continued to rush into his shaft when Tina stuck her tongue inside his bellybutton. Her right hand slowly drifted to the location of his enlarged weapon. The main vein in his prostate throbbed erratically after Tina secured a vice like grip through the flimsy shorts. She began to stroke with maximum effort while Slick's right hand journeyed from her butt to her inner thigh. The heat from her midsection set the tone for what was to come. His hand ended up against her labium. Slick stroked the moist area with his pointer finger, causing Tina to wiggle in rhythm.

"Yes, daddy, right there! Pop it right there!"

Slick began to insert his forefinger in and out her quickly, rubbing his middle finger in a circular motion around the outer layers of her vagina. She tightened her hold upon the man's organ. Both participants began to move their pelvic areas in synchronization with the other's cadence.

Slick had seen enough. He moved his left hand from the girl's hair and lowered it to the rim of his gym shorts. With his thumb, he slid his garments down until the hair above his package was exposed. His impatient partner assisted by grabbing the back his boxers and yanking the material down. Slick arched his back and raised his buttocks, making the transition from clothed to nude more feasible. When the shorts reached his thighs, Slick's rock hard member sprung from the bondage, striking Tina in the face.

"Ouch daddy, you almost let it hit me in the eye," Tina cried. Still she took the organ and rubbed it lovingly against her cheekbone.

"Well, it's your fault," Slick said easing his left leg from the tangled cloth that stuck at his knee. "You got him all worked up and now he got a mind of his own. You done woke up a monster!"

"Is that so? Let's just see if I can put him back to sleep then!"

With that comment, Tina looked up and gave Slick a provocative stare. He braced for the inevitable act of fellatio from the ebony goddess. Before he could situate himself, Tina took the liberty of inserting the top half of his penis into her mouth. She clamped down with her lips and ejected it from her mouth all in one action denoting the sound and of someone sucking on a lollipop. The blood pumped furiously throughout his erection as if his heart was in his testicles. Slick jammed his fingers inside the walls of the loosening vagina, causing Tina's butt muscles to clench.

"Daddy, please. Not so rough," Tina pleaded falsely.

Slick respected the request and softly flicked the fingers back and forth with a speed that made Tina quiver. She returned the pleasure by replacing him into her hungry mouth and bobbing her head in an up, down and sideways pattern. She tilted her head to a ninety degree angle, resulting in the imprint of Slick's weapon through her jaws. Slick could feel the saliva from her throat forming a puddle as it dripped onto the carpet of his pubic hairs. Tina gagged and choked as she tried to force the entire length into her mouth.

"Don't hurt yourself," Slick said with a slight laugh.

Tina removed the object from her shiny lips. She gaped at Slick with a hint of determination and proceeded to swirl around his meat with the side of her tongue. Slick gazed at the girl weaving her head about his midsection, trying hard not to explode. The erotic exchange was prematurely interrupted by a knock at the door.

BOOM, BOOM, BOOM, BOOM, BOOM, BOOM!

Slick and Tina ignored the initial distraction even though both knew the door had to be answered. Tina continued in her game of hide the sausage while Slick tried desperately to free himself from the sexual arrest.

BOOM, BOOM, BOOM, BOOM, BOOM!

Tina reluctantly loosened her grip. Pulling her jean skirt down to her thighs, she stood up with curse words streaming from under her breath. She rolled over to the foot of the bed, while Slick adorned his shorts and underwear. Slick winked at Tina as he sat up and swung his feet to the floor.

"It ain't like we can't let her in," he informed, standing and staggering towards the front door.

"Yeah, you're right," Tina agreed as she straightened her frizzled hair, trying to restore some sense of dignity. "Let her little freaky tail on in."

Slick opened the door to find a frustrated look on the Ashley's face.

"Damn! What in the hell y'all two doing in here. You had your head so far up her ass, that you couldn't hear me banging on the door," Ashley said pushing past Slick's half naked body.

"I'm not you," Slick retorted, placing his hand on her jiggling backside as she walked by. She grabbed his hand and thrust it away.

"Get your filthy hands off of me, you nasty dog. I don't know where them things been," She walked towards the refrigerator with the beer.

Slick trailed her into the kitchen and took the twelve-pack of Heinekens. He removed three of them and sat the rest inside the cooler. He then followed her toward the bedroom and sat the drinks on the dresser. He noticed Ashley's jealous indifference as she deferred to look at Tina while setting her pocketbook and keys on the floor beside the bed.

"I've got to use the bathroom," Ashley said as she unzipped the front of her spandex pants. She left the room swaying her petite hips sway from side to side. The door made a loud thump when she secluded herself inside the toilet.

Tina caught Slick's frozen admiration for Ashley's sexy body. "You want some of that, don't you?"

"What you think, shorty," Slick replied rhetorically.

"Me too, I'm a go 'head and get it poppin' when she come out. You saw how jealous she was. That hoe is bound to do anything not to feel left out."

Slick grew more anxious with the prospect of a first time ménage with Tina and Ashley. He disguised his eagerness by leaning back on the bed with the cool confidence of Ron O'Neal in the 1970's flick Superfly. His attention was soon directed to the cocaine on the night stand. Grabbing the case, he scooped a load with the long nail of his pinky finger and held it up to his friend. Imitating his big screen hero, he extended the coke to Tina.

"Want a blow," Slick said.

Tina answered by bringing her nose down to meet his finger and inhaling the caustic substance. Slick then fixed him a similar dosage and laid the drugs on the floor beside the bed. He rubbed the back of Tina's neck while massaging his own organ, enticing the girl to do the same. She happily consented by once again stroking his manhood. Slick grabbed her breast with a fist full of passion. The unfinished liaison was just about to resume when Ashley burst open the bathroom door and propelled into the room.

"Let me hit the powder, shit. My nose is burning for some reason," Ashley said, rubbing her large snout. Slick gave a nod, indicating the location of the drugs on the carpet. He noticed that the top of Ashley's stretch pants remained unzipped when she knelt down doggy style to get the drugs. Slick gave a subtle nudge to Tina, motioning towards Ashley. Tina understood her cue and got up from the bed. She then waltzed over behind her friend, giving Ashley a slap on the backside, causing her to flinch.

"Girl, you getting kind of fat back there lately, ain't you," Tina complimented. Ashley seemed oblivious to the advance as she sunk her head down into the pile of cocaine. After taking the snort, she raised her nose in the air to absorb the drain. "Slick what you think," asked Tina, while grabbing the elastic of Ashley's loose pants. This act revealed the purple thong that was submerged between the girl's buttocks. "You can do something with that, right? I don't know about you, but I'm 'bout ready to take this pussy! You down for it or not Slick?"

Slick rolled over to get a better view of the happenings on the floor. Tina stood over Ashley and held the back of her pants, while Ashley stayed frozen upon her knees. Slick reached over to Ashley and rubbed her face. She moved her head sideways, allowing her lips to contact his fingers. She opened her mouth and licked the tip of his pinky.

"Yeah, I think she is about ready too!" He continued to move his hand around Ashley's mouth, as she sucked each one.

"Come here girl," Tina demanded, snatching Ashley closer to her body.

Ashley complied with a slight laugh while shooting Slick a look of enticement. Tina grabbed her friend beneath her underarms, lifted her up and hurled her face down upon the bed. She then straddled Ashley's backside like a rodeo bull rider. Slick joined in on the affray by yanking the victim's ponytail. Her face jerked towards him and he was happy to see her smiling with her eyes closed. He then knew that his most recent fantasy would become a reality.

"You like that, don't you trick." Slick said quietly. Ashley responded in silence, grinding her pelvis against the bed and Tina's open thighs.

"Hell yeah she do! You like it rough too huh," Tina interjected. She lifted herself off of Ashley and gave her bottom another love tap. Ashley let out a high pitched scream that resulted in another erection for Slick. Tina sensed Ashley's cooperation and started to pull the spandex from Ashley's legs. Ashley assisted by raising her midsection and wiggling her hips.

"Umm, umm, umm, look at that pretty ass." Slick admired the perfect body as the pants were lowered. The only thing left was the thin purple thong which further enticed Slick's lusting eyes. "I got to have some of that right there!"

"Come and get it then," Tina insisted. She rolled over to the mattress on Ashley's right side replacing Slick.

He stood up on the side of the bed, positioning his self behind Ashley. Tina placed her hand under Ashley's shirt and caressed her back. Slick complied with the order to finish undressing Ashley. He dropped the pants to Ashley's ankles and she consented by removing her right foot, leaving the black material dangling from her left ankle. In a swift kicking motion, Ashley freed her remaining foot. Slick's erection grew instantly as he watched Tina's hand move from Ashley's back to the thong, sliding it to the side.

"Smack that fat ass one time for me, Slick. You know you want to," Tina instructed. She also knew how much Ashley liked to be violated and manhandled.

WHAP! Slick obeyed the command.

"Damn, I love that sound," Tina exclaimed. She lifted up her own shirt, revealing her breast and rubbing her nipples. "Spank it again for me! Do it harder this time!"

Slick grabbed Ashley by the thighs and scooted her forward so that her entire body was on the bed. Tina grabbed Ashley's hand and moving it towards her exposed breasts. Ashley twisted to the left to face her aroused friend.

WHAP! Slick struck the girl's bottom with twice the force as before.

"Ooooh, sssst!" Ashley extended noises of pain and pleasure. She squeezed the flesh of Tina's chest in reaction to the sting penetrating her skin. Tina provided soothing by rubbing the spot in which Ashley was assaulted. Ashley moaned in gratitude.

WHAP! WHAP!

"Yeah, daddy, that's it. Spank that monkey," Tina exclaimed. "I like it. Does it hurt real good ma-ma?"

Ashley ignored the question and continued to suffer the in silent joy. Tina lowered her face towards the girl's butt cheeks while Ashley poked her bottom in the air, begging for more. Slick massaged Ashley's romp while Tina began to lick the flesh not covered by his fingers. Slick removed his hands and placed them on Tina's head, guiding the motions as she licked her friends behind. Then, in an act of utter vulgarity, Tina spread the buttocks of her friend and stuck her tongue directly inside of her anal canal.

"Ooh, yeah, ooh, oh! Yes right there. Lick it, slut! Deeper, lick it!" Ashley broke her prolonged silence with a moans and groans. Slick looked on in disgust as Tina's head bobbed up and down. Her tongue moved furiously, in a flurry of back and forth flicks against Ashley's anus. Ashley began to thrust her tail up and down in an effort to increase penetration and contact. Tina lifted her own skirt and allowed Ashley to rub between her moist legs. Ashley unconsciously started to pat her middle finger against Tina's clitoris. Even though the scene was distasteful, Slick could not restrain the urge to participate in the perversion. He fondled himself in excitement.

"Damn bitch," Tina yelled. The bulge in Slick's gym shorts caused Tina to burn with passionate fervor. "Give me that, Slick! Let me hold it! Put it in my mouth!"

Before Slick could oblige, Tina took Slick's male organ and inserted it into her mouth. She slurped upon the flesh while jamming her fingers in and out of the Ashley's vagina. All three participants made exclamations of joy as they pleasured each other in different ways.

"Get all of it! Yeah that's right swallow it," Slick coerced, while Tina tried to fit the body part entirely into her mouth and down her throat. She gagged in failure, vomiting spit onto the bed spread.

"Good god. It's too much! Smack me in my face with it," Tina demanded. Slick swung his body, causing his penis to smash into Tina's jawbone. "Harder. Hit me with it," Tina begged. She grabbed it and began punishing her face between sucks and licks.

"I want it! Give it to me! Put it inside me!" Ashley requested penetration after seeing the fun that Tina was having. She backed herself up to Slick and grabbed for the man's posterity.

"Hold up shorty. I got you," Slick stated, contemplating the need for protection. He ran his hand under the girl's tail to her pelvis, feeling the juices that had accumulated inside her. He decided against using the condoms in his nightstand. There was no way that he could justify this negligence no matter how wet and fresh that Ashley was. The alcohol and drugs had made it too easy for the normally cautious man to become careless.

With his erection at full blast Slick to tapped the rock hard organ against the firm butt of the girl. His manhood bounced off the surface like a two year old on a trampoline. Tina continued to suck as Slick readied himself to mount the young stallion.

"Let me put it in for you, daddy. Please, let me do it," Tina asked persistently.

"Just get it in me. I don't care who does it. Just do it," Ashley requested with impatience.

Slick succumbed to Tina and allowed her to control the process. After sucking the man for about twenty seconds, she positioned the stick at the entrance of Ashley's love hole. Ashley shook vibrantly, feeling the head of the penis up against her. Tina massaged Ashley's clitoral area before squeezing the missile into the launch pad.

"Ah yes! Oh, give it! Get it!" Ashley emitted expressions of ecstasy as Tina and Slick maneuvered the cock inside her. She spread her legs and arched her back to aid to the abusers of her body. Tina opened Ashley's butt cheeks to get a better view of the penetration. Slick pulled out and pushed in, only able to get a third of his manhood into the tight passage. Tina assisted further by letting large amounts of saliva drop from her mouth onto the genital area of both partners. She then began to rub the fluid in and around the Ashley and Slick's genitals.

"Get in there! Get all the way in that thang, boy! Pump it. Bang it." Tina gave commands to Slick in her eagerness to see her friend violated. "Yeah, that's it daddy. Dig it out!" Slick pumped harder as Ashley's walls loosened.

"Yeah, get loose! Throw it back! Act like you want it," Slick yelled, gripping Ashley's buttocks, pulling her into him with every thrust.

"Uh huh, that's it! Come on! Give me all of it," Ashley exclaimed. She contorted her body downward allowing Slick to go deeper. Tina moved to the front and took off Ashley's top. The two women began to kiss and rub each other's breast while Slick still plowed from behind.

"Suck my nipples! Yes! There you go! Harder!" Tina pulled her friends hair and smacked her face while Ashley tried to stuff the whole breast in her mouth. Watching the girls lick each other, Slick's libido increased and he tried to punish his victim even more.

"No, no! Don't! Stop Slick! That's it! No more! I don't want it," Ashley screamed. She felt Slick entering her second level. Her legs shook vigorously and she knew that an orgasm was near. "No let me… let me turn over. Tina, come here. Let me eat you. Bring it here," she said between pants. She then fell forward, pushing Slick out of her with a shove to his midsection.

"No ma'am! You can't get away that easy! I ain't even half way finished with you yet," Slick grabbed Ashley by the hips and turned her sideways, opening her legs into a v shape. Tina assumed the same position, facing Ashley in the opposite direction. Both girls started to perform oral sex on each other. Slick watched the sixty–nine until he could restrain himself no longer.

"Hold up shorty. Let me see that for a minute" He pulled Tina away from Ashley's crotch by her hair. He then smacked the wet faced girl in the mouth with his member before plunging back into Ashley.

"Ah shit!" Ashley reacted. She attempted to inch away but Slick held tight to her waist while pounding away.

"Beat it like you hate that bitch, Slick! Yeah, that's it nigga!" Tina still gave orders while fondling both participants. She then reached around to Ashley's backside pulling it closer. "Let me see that butt hole of yours. Let me play with it." Ashley lifted her tail off the mattress, permitting easy access to her anal canal. Tina took her moist middle finger and pressed it into the girl's forbidden entrance.

"Aaiih! Easy! Easy, yes, that's it." Ashley clinched her muscles to brace for the infringement upon the natural use of her body. Tina managed to shove her middle finger two thirds of the way inside the space reserved for expelling feces. Ashley moved in a rhythm that collaborated with Slick's ravaging and Tina's sodomy. "Oh yes! That's it. Oh yeah! Lick my clit. Tina, suck on it! Please!"

Tina placed her head down to execute the order. The deed nearly brought Ashley to an orgasm as she experienced stimulation from three parts of her body. Tina lifted her face in order to breathe. "Stick it in her butt, Slick. That's what she likes. She wants it. Don't you, trick?"

Ashley nodded in acceptance. Slick was shocked by the demand. He had enlisted in anal sex before but he never liked to enter a woman in that way. He always felt base and low afterwards. He knew in his heart that he shouldn't defile his or her body in such fashion. Nevertheless the passion and coarseness of events that already transpired made the sodomy of Ashley permissible in his delusional eyes.

"Turn over," Slick told the girl. Ashley returned to the mattress face down with her tail in the air. Tina continued the sexual assault upon her companion by sustaining the friction against her swollen clitoris. She then gathered a sizable amount of saliva on the tip of her tongue and spewed it into Ashley's crack. She held the buttocks open as she worked the thick white substance around the area, providing a lubricant for the already rock hard Slick. "Yeah, you ready for it ain't you? Here we go," Slick said rubbing the tip of his penis against the girl's swollen anus.

"Let me see it again," Tina asked handling Slick's man like it was a pot of gold. She stuck it into her mouth as if she wanted to taste the mixture of his semen and her fluids. Slick thought of how nasty and crude a girl had to be to indulge in fiascos of this sort.

Who was he to judge? He reasoned that he was just as guilty being the catalyst for the whole episode. His moral and ethical values subsided when Tina drew him in with the wonder workings of her tongue. "I think it's ready now," she said. She then crawled to the top of Ashley's head and slid under her torso with her legs spread eagle.

Slick noticed the nodding motion of Ashley's head as she gave her friend cunnilingus. He then spread Ashley's cheeks placing his erection on the edge of her entrance. The two pushed against each other in order to align themselves. After several attempts, Slick found the head of his penis secluded inside of the girl's rectum. He pushed slowly, concentrating on his goal of climaxing instead of the perversion of what he was doing. Ashley squeezed the muscles of her canal, pulling him deeper into the depths of oblivion. Slick continued to press until her anus began to make squishing noises that resembled the sound of conventional intercourse.

"Oooh, Oooh! Yes. It feels so good! It feels so right, Slick." Ashley spread herself with her hand to further increasing the diameter of her hole. "Pump it baby. Get this tail!" Slick pumped harder as prompted. Their skins made slapping noises as his pelvis banged against her buttocks.

"You in there now, ain't you daddy! Oh yeah. Dig into it. Dig into that booty, nigga! Stick your tongue up in there tramp! Don't be shy! Lick this twat! You know you love it!" Tina gave commands, receiving gratification from Ashley's mouth. She gripped her friend by the hair and mashed her head into her vagina in a suffocating manner. Tina then lifted her legs so that her knees were at her chest and her butt in the air. She cuffed her thighs to hold herself easily in that spot. "Lick my booty girl. Taste my tail."

Slick was equally amazed when Ashley carried out the same wicked deed that Tina had performed on her. Both girls were now certified whores in Slick's eyes and his main objective was too ejaculate as soon as possible and rid himself of them. He pushed himself off of Ashley much to her dismay.

He then lay on the bed and watched Tina pull her friend up to her face, French kissing her. The two indulged in a tongue wrestling contest that induced Slick's need for orgasm. Normally, the cocaine would not sanction his sexual release until an hour or two. However, on certain occasions he did possess the ability to ejaculate on demand, no matter how much drugs he had ingested.

"Come here, girl," Slick said. He grabbed Tina by the arm and pulled her close. "Ride that thing like you did before. You know cowgirl style!"

The chosen one smiled in adoration of the man who chose her to bring him to climax. She crawled over on top of him and began to stroke his organ. "Whatever you like, you know I'll do it," she said seductively. She began to mount the host before stopping. "Hold on," she said. "Come here Ashley and suck him off before I ride this horse."

Ashley complied with no resistance. She meekly went to Slick's genitalia and started the fellatio. Tina escorted her head in up, down and sideways movements. The ferocity of her efforts nearly caused Slick to explode in her mouth. He had no doubt in his mind that Ashley would not have cared.

In fact, that is exactly what she wanted to happen. Slick rejected Ashley's objective by pushing her head off of him.

Tina understood the unspoken command and straddled Slick, squatting on both feet. Her arms provided balance while her vagina hovered over Slick's penis in mid-air. With excellent precision, Tina slid herself halfway down upon the stiffness. Slick cuffed her butt cheeks and guided her motions. She began to bounce up and down on the man, rocking back and forth. Slick synchronized his thrusts with Tina's rhythm. She leaned her body forward to obtain maximum penetration. Slick lay back and enjoyed the enthusiastic grinding of Tina upon his manhood.

"Ride that stick. Get it girl." Ashley overcame her disappointment to cheer for her sporting mates. She sat Indian style to Slick's right, with three fingers crammed inside her vagina, fornicating herself. She then joined in the orgy by leaning in and blessing Slick's right nipple with gentle kisses and sucks. His toes curled up as the sensations given by both women brought him to the verge of ejaculation. Tina continued to ride with unbridled fervency.

"Get it daddy. Get it. Give it!" Tina pumped hard as if she was the man and Slick was the female. He laid there motionless, trying to conjure up the orgasm he so desperately wanted. Ashley arose to bestow a sloppy kiss to Tina's breast and then advance to stick her tongue deep into her friend's welcoming mouth. After about five more minutes of the bumping, grinding and watching the girls spit swap, Slick's eruption was inevitable. He gave one hard pump that sent Tina hobbling off of his wood.

"Here it go ya'll! Come and get it! Aaah! Aaah," Slick screamed in ecstasy. Tina regained her balance and lowered her head towards Slick's penis. The creamy white semen spewed out of the hole just as Tina wrapped her mouth around the top of the vessel.

"Um, um, um," Tina mumbled as Slick squirted twice more onto her face while she came up for air. Ashley then wrestled the organ away from her friend and rubbed the object on her mouth and across her face as Slick shot three more loads into the air.

"Yes daddy. Give it all to me. Let it all out," Ashley said in satisfaction. The excretion continued to ooze out as both girls concurrently sucked and licked, trying to swallow every bit of semen possible. Tina stuck her tongue under the man's testicles to retrieve some of the wasted semen. Ashley kept attacking the opening in an attempt to taste more of warm milk-like matter.

"Yeah daddy, I like it all in my mouth. I just love the way it taste on my tongue!" Ashley praised. She noticed the stiffness that remained in the semi-erect vessel. "Let me ride it! You did save some for me, didn't you?"

Slick pushed Tina's head aside and allowed Ashley to straddle him, facing the opposite way. Ashley quickly inserted the weapon inside of her and began to grind profusely against it. Slick tried to maintain focus but eventually lost interest as his goal had been achieved. After a few minutes of lethargic sex, Slick ordered Ashley off, much to her chagrin.

"That's it for now ladies. I've had enough. Get up," Slick told the girls. Both Ashley and Tina followed the command and sat upright on the bed. Slick stood up immediately and headed straight to the bathroom to cleanse the filth from his body. The naked girls paid minimal attention to his exit. They were too busy feeding themselves more of the powder that had fueled the orgy.

Slick turned the hot and cold knobs allowing the water to become warm while it flowed from the faucet. He entered the bathtub and lathered the rag that hung on the rack. He proceeded to give himself a birdbath, thoroughly scrubbing his genitals, stomach and thighs. His mind worked at a feverish pace as he contemplated ways to get rid of the girls. He did not want to be rude, knowing there may come a time when he would need their services again. He finished the quick wash up, concluding that he would use the ruse of impending sales to escape. He dried himself and walked back to the room naked.

"What are y'all finna do," Slick asked coldly. Turning his back, he garnished himself with a fresh pair of boxers and gym shorts.

"I don't know. We ain't really got nothing to do. We was just gonna chill with you. Why," Ashley inquired.

Slick walked over to the tall dresser and recovered his cellular phone, which had been ringing non-stop. He checked the various numbers to see which ones were customers and relayed the results to the girls.

"I got to slide out and make a couple of moves real quick. But I'll be back later on if y'all wanna stop back through," Slick said, returning a business call on his phone.

"Alright player," Tina said. She took the hint that she and her friend had served their immediate purpose. "We probably going to go and have a few drinks or something. If you are going to be out, you can call me and I'll let you know where we're at." Tina nudged Ashley and both of the females began to get dressed slowly, provoking Slick's sexual ambitions once more. He controlled his eyes and suppressed his desires while a voice answered on the other end of the line.

"Hello… yeah… everything good….yeah, I got that for you….I'll be here when you get here." Slick cut the conversation short and repeated the process for other missed calls. After completing protocol for three more customers, Slick reached in his closet and slid the Carolina blue sweat suit off of the hanger. He slipped the bottoms on, followed by a long john undershirt. He then jumped into the white and blue Nike Huraches before putting on the jacket.

"Daddy, can we have this for the road," Ashley asked. She was holding up the small amount of cocaine that was left on the CD case. Slick noticed the desperation in the girl's eyes while awaiting his reply.

"Sure. Go ahead and knock yourself out," Slick said coolly. He then grabbed his house keys in a ploy to hurry the slow moving females. "My peoples outside waiting for me so y'all got to come on."

"You ready Tina," Ashley said, as both of the girls were putting on their shoes.

"Yeah, we can go to Stooges for a while. I know the bartender there and we can get free drinks," Tina informed. "He must think I want him or something the way he be pouring them Tequila shots."

"You probably want him, with your freaky self," Ashley interjected while Slick escorted the girls out of the room to the front door.

"Both of y'all are terrible," Slick interrupted. "Y'all might need to go to nymphomaniacs anonymous the way y'all be talking." The girls let out a quick laugh. "Nah, it's been real though. I might get at y'all later on if I'm out and about. But you girls stay safe out there."

"We will," the girls said in unison. They gave Slick a hug at the same time before they walked out the door. Slick could not resist squeezing the romps of both girls as they pranced away.

As soon as they closed the apartment building door, Slick did not hesitate to invade his stash spot and retrieve the ounce of cocaine he had left. He got the substance and quickly re-entered his bedroom where the smell of raunchy sex confronted his nasal passage. He hastily treated his nostrils with two swift doses of dope. The drugs took effect as Slick grabbed a much needed cigarette from the half-empty pack. Slick barely took three drags from the square, when the cellular phone rung.

"Yeah….You out there already…Alright, I'll be out there in a minute…Okay!" Slick flipped the phone close and gathered the product, scale and a couple of bags. With his materials ready, Slick went to the parking lot where his customer waited.

Upon entering the car, Slick engaged in the normal pleasantries that preceded transactions. After supplying the drugs, he then prompted the driver, an older black man named Ernie, to take him to three other spots to meet more buyers. The driver complied and they set off on a mission to distribute cocaine.

Before returning to the apartment, Slick instructed Ernie to stop at the Seven-Eleven two blocks from his home. He exited the car and bought another six-pack and more Newports. He returned to the vehicle with the intentions of having an all-night affair with the white powder in his pocket. When they came back to the parking lot Slick bid farewell and walked up the sidewalk to his lonely abode.

Slick went into the apartment and headed for the bedroom without bothering to refrigerate the beer. He sat down on the bed and instinctively cracked open the bag of cocaine. His anxiety peaked the moment that he brought a large scoop of powder to his nose and inhaled. He repeated the process in the opposite nostril and laid the bag beside him.

The drugs attacked his central nervous system vehemently. He could feel his heartbeat racing rapidly, while his throat and head became numb. All of a sudden a strong feeling of despair and loneliness overcame Slick.

Although he had just experienced what many men only fantasized about, there was an empty void that consumed his spirit. He knew he had a few so called friends and clout in the streets, but Slick longed for something more in life. He often times wondered about the lifestyle he lived and the people he dealt with every day. He knew the end result of the game he played, but still felt obligated to the streets and people he supported with the money. He lived a comfortable life it seemed on the outside. However, internally, he was constantly at war, with his conscience and moral values battling his worldly and natural desires. With his mind contemplating his purpose on earth, Slick grabbed the remote and flicked on the television.

"Twelve American and British soldiers were killed today in a fierce gunfight in Baghdad. Officials say that a troop of UN forces were ambushed while conducting a routine search of a compound that authorities believed to be a headquarters for terrorists. This latest attack brings this month's death toll up to sixty-six for American soldiers. The president said in a statement released earlier that this loss will by no means deter our plan to secure the oil fields and bring down this evil Iraqi regime. There will be more news and updates to follow. Back to you Ed…"

Slick considered the commentary on the fighting in the middle-east. His analysis dampened his already low spirits further. He had heard of conflicts in Europe since a child. This was the first time, however, that he had heard of America being an aggressor in that region. He noticed the hypocrisy of the president's statement. Was the goal to bring down Saddam or control the oil of that country?

Slick saw well passed the ruse of bringing democracy to an oppressed country and deciphered the campaign for what it was: an attack on a smaller and less formidable opponent in order to have power over their resources. He figured that if democracy was the ultimate goal, there were far more deprived candidates that needed it more than the Iraqis.

With his political dilemma aside, Slick turned his attention toward God. Why, would a loving Creator allow such calamity in the world? How could He let a few evil factions wield so much power over the righteous majority and use that authority to induce, persuade, and deceive the masses while accomplishing their agenda?
Why did he have two loving parents when many across the globe had none? Why were so many of his black American cohorts so mentally possessed by music and movies that they would live out the songs and lyrics they heard, only to bring death and destruction to their own communities?

The last question that came to mind befuddled Slick something terrible. Why was he unable to quit his abuse of cocaine, despite his numerous late night prayers for help? The answer to the last thought was even further out of sight as Slick picked up the bag to and took two more snorts.

His own problems and those of the world continued to perplex Slick, just as the drug he ingested elevated his alertness. Slick thought he heard a noise outside of his window and peeked out the blinds. His eyes scanned the landscape of trees and bushes lining the premises. He detected nothing unusual but his wide eyes continued to dart between the shadows of darkness. Slick caught himself on the edges of paranoia and closed the blinds before he became entrenched in finding something in the night that wasn't there. He had spent too many nights peeking out the windows only to find the blank stare of daylight returning his glance as the sun rose.

Slick walked back to the bed amidst the buzzing of his cell phone. The word that appeared on the screen brought more misery. Slick allowed the phone to ring until the title MOM vanished from the caller identification.

Even though Slick loved his mother and needed to talk with her, he could not bring himself to answer the phone in his present condition. This negligence towards his family was further evidence that he had a serious problem. He had read several dissertations on addiction and he knew that avoiding and withdrawing from friends and family was a telltale symptom of abuse.

After clearing the missed call moniker from his phone, Slick scrolled down to other calls that he'd missed. His soul grew more desolate when he realized that his oldest sister, Tia, had called. He thought about the close relationship that they shared since he'd moved to Virginia. The two could talk about mostly anything and she had always held his best interest at heart. He was the youngest and only boy of three siblings and Tia tried to give him the best advice concerning any situation he encountered. He had not yet confided with her in reference to his drug use, but he knew that if he did she would not condemn him. Her response would be to pray for him and offer assistance in any way she could. He considered calling and pouring his heart out to his sister at that very instance. The idea disappeared abruptly as Slick decided to find consolation and solace in the very object that caused the pain, cocaine.

The cigarette burned in the ashtray while Slick laid back and allowed the drug to drip into his lungs. His mind automatically reverted back to the episode that he had engaged in with the two girls. The obscenity and the lewdness of his actions caused vomit to rise in his stomach. The portrait of unnatural acts sickened Slick. He remembered the misuse of his sperm and was ashamed that he would waste his seed in that manner, knowing how badly he wanted children. His random and casual sexual encounters may have been the reason that he had been childless thus far. He reasoned that he was being punished for his total disrespect and lackadaisical approach towards an act ordained by God.

He was reminded of a passage in the Bible that he'd read about Onan. Onan was commanded to marry his brother's widow to keep the family bloodline alive. While having sex with his new wife, he did not ejaculate into her, but instead allowed his sperm to hit the ground. The Bible said that the action displeased God and therefore God killed him on sight.

Slick shuddered at the thought of how many times he had deviated from the true purpose meant for his seed. He began to feel more wretched as he tried to calculate the number of women he had been with over his lifetime. Slick determined that there was no hope of redemption for him in God's eyes so why should he even think about changing his life. With that erroneous assumption Slick turned to his god and took a few more snorts.

· ·

Slick pulled the hammer back on the three fifty seven magnum revolver. He held the gun steady as his eye strained to see out of the peephole. His senses told him that there was something or someone who was out to get him. The noises that he heard in the hallway, outside of his window and on the back porch kept the gunman on his toes and ready for action.

Slick eased away from the front door and tipped to the sliding glass back door in the living room. He held the weapon behind his back while he peered through the side of the curtain. Slick's heart jumped when he thought that there was a shadow moving in the distance. He turned his head and was relieved to know that the movement was only the wind blowing leaves of an oak tree. He moved away from the back door and proceeded to the bedroom with caution.

It was already five forty-five in the morning. Slick was delirious due to the massive consumption of alcohol, cigarettes and cocaine over the last twenty four hours. He stepped over the half dozen bottles that littered the floor with the carefulness of a soldier walking through a mine field. Slick made it to the bedroom window with the firearm raised in firing position. He gawked out of the window blinds expecting to find an assailant lurking in the wings of blackness.

After five minutes of staring into the night, Slick was assured of no danger, at least for the moment. The paranoid man sat gently on the bed, not wanting to release his grip on the handgun, but not able to ignore the jones he had for more coke. Slick placed the gun within reach and then satisfied his craving for drugs.

Slick felt like an imbecile. He had stayed up all night sniffing the product that he was supposed to be selling. Not only that, but he had walked around the house all night with a gun peeking out windows in fear. This was not the first time he had underwent this routine but the scenario was getting old for the young man and his body was paying the price.

The twenty five cigarette butts that filled the ashtray testified to the damage Slick was doing to his lungs. Not to mention the twenty-four empty bottles of beer that overlaid the top of the trash can. The unrestrained usage of alcohol was no doubt taking a toll on his liver and kidneys.

Adding fuel to the fire was the fact that Slick had not eaten at all that day, neither had he cared to. He was too busy engulfed in gambling, drugs and sex to have any concern for his health. His tolerance had been defeated, however, as Slick's body's need for rest overcame his unrelenting desire to do more cocaine.

Slick lay down on the bed and became comfortable enough to put the gun under the mattress. The pounding in his chest and the thumping of the veins in his forehead alerted him to the fact that he may have done too much drugs. He started to feel lightheaded and began shaking slightly. Slick got up from the bed and tried to walk the jittery sensation off. His breathing became shorter and more direct as Slick began to worry about what was happening to his body.

After splashing water on his face, Slick returned to the bed and lay down, hoping that the racing of his heart would slow down. He didn't consider that during the course of the day he had snorted almost a quarter ounce of cocaine. The reminder of that amount alone almost sent him into cardiac arrest.

Slick turned to the only source of defense he knew would prevail in this circumstance. Unable to get on his knees, Slick began to say a silent prayer on his back. Slick started his petition to God, but it seemed there was a blockage to the pathways of heaven. His words didn't formulate correctly and he felt like he was going to pass out. Sitting up once more he decided to stop praying. The only words that he was able to say were "The blood of Jesus, The blood of Jesus."

Slick kept repeating the phrase he'd learned as a child. This mantra was apparently the most effective weapon against any force or spirit that would attack the Christian believer. He had heard of miraculous instances where people were saved from certain death or adverse circumstances just by pleading the blood of Jesus.

Evidently, the reports were merited. Slick began to feel immediate comfort and relief as he spoke the plea over and over. He still needed help. Slick could feel the muscles of his chest constricting in an abnormal manner and he thought he was on the verge of a stroke. He then decided to call his father, knowing that he would be up early, preparing for Sunday service.

"God Bless you! May I help you," a voice responded on the other end of the line.

"Da," Slick answered. "What are you doing?"

"Well, just reading a little bit, getting my message together for today. Are you alright?"

"No. I need you to pray with me real quick. Just pray for me." Slick's father could hear the nervousness in his voice.

"Alright, son, that's no problem." Slick could hear his father repositioning himself through the phone. Then, without further ado, the pastor began praying. "Our Father who art in heaven, we come to you in the mighty name of Jesus Christ our Lord and Savior. We acknowledge you as our Creator, our Strength, and our Comforter. Lord we know that you are the Beginning and the End, the Alpha and Omega and the Giver and Preserver of all life. We thank you for sending your Son as payment for our sins on the cross. We praise you for the power that we have through the blood that was shed. We know through that blood we have all authority and dominion against any force of the enemy and any effects of sin. Lord, we confess our sins to you this day and ask for divine forgiveness in Jesus name. God we accept Jesus as Lord and Ruler over our souls and we commit our spirit into your hands. We thank you for hearing us and accepting us into your kingdom.

Father I come to you on behalf of my son. Lord I bind the hand of the enemy that has come upon him to destroy him. Father I plead the blood of Jesus over his life and I rebuke Satan on every hand. I command you right now Satan to take your hands off of him and flee. Lord I commit his life into your hands and pray that your will be done in and through his life. Whatever the situation is we speak victory and deliverance in the name of Jesus and we proclaim it and count it done. Lord I ask that your heavenly angels will come down and fight every battle that he is engaged in right now. Lord we pray these things, believing that whatsoever we ask in Jesus name it will be done. Lord we thank you, we praise you and we give you all the glory, in Jesus name, Amen....Amen....and Amen!"

Slick continued to say thank you Jesus as the prayer ended. He had been saying those same three words through the entire prayer. He had learned to do that as a child, praying with his godfather, another minister. Repeating that phrase reinforced whatever was being prayed by the leader.

After his father stated the customary conclusion to the prayer, Slick repeated Amen three times also. The ancient Hebrew word was spoken to bring whatever was being prayed into existence. The comfort and the power of the prayer had an immediate impact on Slick and an unexplainable peace suddenly overwhelmed him.

"You alright now," his father asked.

"Yeah, I'm good. I appreciate that. Thanks a lot."

"You're certainly welcome son. Take care of yourself okay."

"I will. I'll talk to you later on though."

"Alright, son, I love you."

"I love you too dad," Slick returned. Both men hung up the phone knowing that the problem was solved.

Slick lay back on the bed and experienced a calm months removed. He continued to praise God silently for the answer to the prayer. He considered getting up and going to one of the local churches. It was one in particular, Calvary Revival he loved to attend. The pastor was a fiery, energetic man who spoke the word and pulled no punches. He knew that he needed to be in the presence of God and was motivated to go.

His excitement dwindled, when he thought of the gun under his mattress. He was more dismayed when he remembered the drugs in the hallway, the cash in his closet and his need to keep up his lifestyle by dealing.

How could he go to church and praise God, knowing that when he left there would be many people calling him to engage in all types of sin. Furthermore, he was not even sure that he wanted to give up some of the pleasures he enjoyed for a life of servitude and discipline. He was caught between two worlds. Slick dozed off, not knowing, that the events in the days to come would be one more way that God was calling him from the life that he had chosen.

4
Scarface

Slick awoke feeling much better than he had when he went to sleep. The soothing spiritual words of "Trouble in My Way" added an additional balm to his soul. He always felt downtrodden after a night of intoxication and oftentimes would relieve the hangover with more drug and alcohol abuse. The words to the song gave him an incentive to be sober, at least on Sunday, and he vowed not to do any drugs for the entire day, with the exception of a little weed.

The alarm clock beside his bed read one thirty. He rushed to get dressed, thinking that he was late for the game. Every Sunday, without fail, Slick would go to a sports bar to watch the Indianapolis Colts. His god brother played tight end for the Colts and Slick never missed seeing him in action. If he couldn't watch the game in person he was definitely going to be in front of a screen somewhere cheering his buddy to victory. The urgency subsided when he realized that the Colts were playing an evening game and it would be broadcast on national television that night. He still got up and prepared to hit the shower already feeling like he was behind schedule.

In the shower, Slick thought about the different courses that he and Donnie had taken in life. Both had been raised in the same church, with the same support system. Both were incredibly smart and excelled in academics. The similarities ended with the choices that each had made as a teenager. While Slick had gravitated to the glamour and allure of the streets, Donnie took heed to the guidance and advice of his parents and stayed away from negative influences. At a pivotal point, Donnie answered the call and accepted Christ at the age of eighteen. Slick decided to reject God's voice and continue in sin.

The results were evident four years later as Donnie's obedience led him to the NFL and Slick's waywardness led him to numerous jail cells, hard ache and a life defined by unfulfilled potential. Now Slick's defiance had him drowning in an existence of drugs, violence and misery.

"Sometimes when I'm feeling low…no place to go…Jesus comes along…and He makes me strong…For I know…oh, oh, oh…Jesus is real…"

Slick exited the shower and was met with John P. Kee's gospel song, "Jesus is Real." He blocked out the words to the melody, girding himself in Enyce jeans and a matching shirt. After dressing, Slick checked his cellular phone's call log. The screen alerted him to six missed calls he wanted to ignore. Due to his way of life, however, he was obligated to respond.

Slick returned the most recent and important call first. It was his connection. Far-do was almost forty, but he dressed and acted Slick's age. He always told jokes and was the type to laugh at his own punch lines first. This irritated a lot of people but to Slick it only added to the banter.

Another thing that Slick liked about Far-do was his philosophies. He had a quote or a saying for every conversation under the sun. Some made no sense at all but some did possess the slightest bit of relevancy. One of Slick's favorites was "he who sleeps on the floor, never falls off the bed." Simple in nature, Slick dismissed the axiom for a while until he asked about the meaning.

"You see, when you sleep on the bed, you're comfortable," the elder man explained. "It's like you're on top. You're riding high. But one false move and you can find yourself down, on the floor, in the dumps. But when you're already on the floor, you know that there is no place lower you can go. You're not comfortable, so there's always room for improvement. Nothing can really bring you down because you're already grounded."

The clarification was frighteningly understandable. This enlightenment gave Slick a newfound respect for the adages spoken by Far-do. Slick still held the man at a low esteem in regards to his character because of some of the other vile things that he spoke and the sordid things he was involved in. However, he continued to hold Far-do close, because he did business exceptionally well and he introduced him to many movers and shakers in the area. Slick kept that in mind as he dialed the man's number.

"Yo," said a cool deep voice on the line.

"What's up with you fat boy," Slick jested, referring to the man's slight obesity.

"Yo what's up nigga. You still got Koko over there. Ha, ha, ha. Ha, ha. Tell her I said hi. Ha, ha, ha. Ha, ha, ha!" Far-do joked Slick about his relationship to the girl that he'd introduced him too. Far-do knew her wild nature beforehand, but allowed Slick to become involved with her anyway.

"Yeah, whatever man. You gotta lot of jokes don't you. Knowing you, she probably over your house right now with the rest of them skanks that you fool with," Slick retorted.

"Nah, not today homeboy. But for real, what you doing today?"

"Nothing. Why, what's up?"

"Well, me and the fellas going over to Fat Boy house to watch the games, eat, smoke, drank and all that good stuff. I was calling to see if you wanna ride with me. I'm about to bounce in ten minutes."

Slick considered the invitation to the football party in Norfolk. It was always a wild affair at Fat Boy's, another older hustler who had taken a liking to Slick. Whether strippers, gambling or just plain grinding, he always kept it live. It was at Fat Boy's, that Slick attended his first trick party and was amazed at the caliber of girls who would sell themselves for a few dollars. Despite the sure fun, Slick declined preferring to stay in the Beach, where his customers were used to meeting him.

"Nah, I'm a chill here for a while. I might be through there for the night game though."

"Yeah that's right. Them bum ass Colts on ESPN tonight ain't they? Well, I'll see you later then. Oh yeah, if you want any of them jerseys, you better get it now because I'm not taking none with me and I won't be back this way until tomorrow."

Slick thought for a minute. Fardo's reference to jerseys was their codename for powder. With less than an ounce left, he was running low. He knew that many of his white clients liked to get high and watch the games. He decided that he had better re-up now, while he had the chance.

"Yeah, bring me two of those Lawrence Taylors" Slick ordered.

Far-do understood that Slick wanted four ounces from the number of the player, which was fifty-six. With twenty eight grams in an ounce, two jerseys would equal four ounces. If he wanted nine he would say Steve McNair and so on. They didn't consider themselves hot with the law, but one could never be too careful, especially when handling large amounts of drugs.

"Alright, just give me ten minutes and I'll stop through on the way out. Have everything ready though, 'cause I have to be in and out," Far-do instructed.

"For sure, just call me when you finna pull up and I'll be out there waiting for you."

Slick confirmed the price tag before hanging up the phone. He then went to his closet and grabbed four thousand dollar stacks. He peeled eight hundred dollars from one, leaving thirty-two hundred needed for the buy. He then put the eight with the money already in his pocket. He hadn't counted that money since the dice game but mentally tallied that it was about fifteen hundred give or take. He normally liked to keep a grand on his person. He never knew when he might need a lot of cash fast and didn't want to be caught with his pants down.

This practice may have been to his detriment around the hustlers he associated with because some of them didn't have that much to their name, let alone to walk around with. Slick was never worried about getting stuck, however. Slick used another one of Far-do's maxims to thwart potential robbers. "I can give you more than you can take," is what he told all those who questioned his money habits.

Slick started returning the calls of the customers he'd missed. He chatted with each before determining what they needed. Most just wanted to confirm his availability and to ensure he had product for later in the evening. Slick disliked being prepped in that manner but regarded it as a necessary nuisance. His phone rang again after hanging up with the last client and he discerned that it was Far-do without checking the screen.

"You out there already," Slick asked assumingly.

"I'll be pulling up in fifteen seconds," his supplier replied.

"Alright, homeboy." Slick flipped the phone closed. He then grabbed the thirty two hundred dollars on the bed and headed for the door.

Slick opened the apartment building's door to be greeted by the sight of Fardo's purple Lexus pulling a parking space. Slick approached the shiny vehicle with specks of gold glitter embedded in the paint job. Slick laughed to himself thinking that the sparkly dots gave the whip a feminine vibe. He wondered why this felonious drug man would be driving an automobile that was fit for a stripper. Nevertheless, he kept his bewilderment private as he sat on the passenger side.

"Just to let you know, I told Koko you'll be over the way later on. So she'll be expecting you when you get there. Ha, ha, ha, ha, ha, ha, ha, ha." Far-do made another crude joke that was funny to no one but himself. He lifted the console and handed Slick the drugs.

Slick examined the package needlessly, as he knew that the cocaine Far-do supplied was always of pristine quality. "Here you go," he said, handing over the cash. "Oh yeah, tell your girl that I said y'all can have her for today."

Slick responded to the earlier insult with one of his own. He then got out of the car, shutting the door lightly.

"You know it's all good, baby. You know what they say. It ain't no fun, if the homeys can't have none," Far-do yelled out the window while driving away. Slick held up the peace sign without looking back and kept walking until he reached the building.

Before entering his crib, Slick made the detour to the stash spot and hid the coke in the usual position. He would not keep more than an ounce inside the apartment for fear of a trafficking charge. He could deal with a simple possession, but he could not allow himself to be apprehended with amounts that could send him away for a multitude of years.

Slick entered the house and was confused about what to do next. He wanted to relax but his mind was constantly churning. He knew he had to make up for the loss he suffered in the dice game. He also thought about the impending warrant and ways that he could dodge the arrest. Ultimately, he decided he could not rest and he returned the call from Flash, whose name was on the missed call log three times.

"What's up little bra," Slick asked when Flash answered.

"Where you at," Flash inquired in his normally aggressive manner.

"I'm at the crib. Why, what's the problem?"

"Ain't nothing. You got your eyes on you?" Flash asked if Slick had his digital scales in the slang that they used to avoid speaking recklessly on cell phones.

"Yeah, they right here."

"Alright, I'm right around the corner. I'll be there in a minute. You got some Backwoods."

"Nah, but stop and get me a pack too. Call Black and tell him to bring some smoke."

"That's what's up," Flash agreed before he clicked off the line.

Slick was aware that his day had officially begun. Flash was the ringleader and wherever he went the rest of the gang was sure to follow. Slick was prepared to host the day's activities once again. No sooner than Flash would arrive, there would be members of his clique calling and requesting to know his whereabouts. Once they heard the location, it would be déjà vu all over again.

Slick primed his residence for company. He organized the front room and made sure his bedroom was secure. He then took the three fifty seven from beneath the mattress and transported it outside to the storage area. He didn't need protection from the boys and didn't want the police coming in with the warrant and discovering the firearm. Virginia gave a hefty five year sentence for an unregistered handgun so there was no telling what they would dish out for possession of an illegal gun by a convicted felon. Slick took a lot of chances but tried to cut down the percentages of incarceration whenever possible. He switched the gun in place of the scales and returned inside.

Within minutes, Slick was alerted to the presence of visitors by a knock on the door. Not bothering to ask the guests to announce themselves, Slick opened the door and welcomed Flash into the living room.

"What up cuz," Slick said while closing the door and twisting the lock.

"Hold up Slick. Don't lock it. Face is right behind me." Slick unlocked the door and stuck his head out. His eyes met the frame of the five foot four older hustler, known to the boys as Scarface.

"What's going on with you homeboy," Slick said, as he stuck his hand out.

"I can't call no shots," Face responded in a northern accent. The man gave the host a half-hearted hand shake as he entered the house. Slick closed and locked the door while Face and Flash made small talk in the living room.

Slick was surprised to see the two men together, however, because they were just involved in a disagreement over dice a couple of days ago. Slick disregarded the small beef as an afterthought. Besides, he'd come to blows with the boys in a game before and it was always forgotten within a couple of days.

"You got those eyes, Slick," Flash asked like he was in a hurry.

"Yeah, hold up. Let me go get them."

Slick disappeared from the midst of the two men to the confines of his room. He thought about the mystifying persona of the man who was in his house. He had seen Face a few times before. Actually, the man was in his house briefly during a dice game the previous week. Slick noticed his peculiar betting and his watchful demeanor. He had won a few hundred on a couple of large bets and left abruptly.

The boys knew him from back in the day. He was older than everyone else, probably in his early to mid-thirties. Slick had heard the crew talk about his tendency to rob friends and foes. Slick dismissed the accusations as folklore and judged the man on the way he presented himself currently. He had even purchased a few throwbacks from the man after a winning day on the dice. As a matter of fact, Slick had yet to wear the Joe Namath or Ozzie Newsome shirts that he'd bought. Therefore Slick held no reservations about dealing with Face on any level and was certainly not worried about the man holding him up.

Slick reappeared to the men and beckoned them into the kitchen, the customary place for business. "Here you go, blood," Slick said to Flash, offering him the scale.

"Appreciate it big cuz." Flash then turned to Face. "Show me what that work look like again," he said to in a serious tone.

Scarface reached deep into the pockets of his Evisu jeans and produced a large bag of cocaine. "Man I got this from the city," he explained. "This ain't nothing but that fire. That's all that's going around up there." Scarface held the bag in the air. Slick calculated that it was probably a big eight, street slang for a hundred and twenty five grams or an eighth of a kilo.

"Let Slick see it," Flash said, turning his attention to the cocaine expert. "What you think about that. I know you know what it is as much as you put up your nose."

Slick emitted a slight laugh at the cheap shot Flash threw at him. He didn't hide his habit from anyone and did not care who knew. He would pull his bag of dope out anywhere, in front of anyone and satisfy his desire when the time called for it. There were so many people in his circle, past and present, who got their noses dirty, that it was second nature to him not to seclude his usage. However, too some people like Flash, who didn't indulge the use of the substance was considered taboo. Therefore, Flash always rode him hard.

"Let me see it Face," Slick interceded, not bothering to respond to Flash. He examined the mounds of rocked up cocaine in the bag and noted the shine of the product. He also discerned the flaky texture of the coke. All the characteristics, led Slick to believe that the dope was indeed the best of the best, uncut fish scale. "She look like that thang to me," Slick said before giving the coke one more test. He unzipped the bag, dipped his nose deep inside and took a huge breath. The potency was evident as the smell tempted Slick to renege on his earlier promise to himself. "Oh yeah, she official! No doubt about it."

"How much you want for all of it," Flash asked catching the man off guard with his straightforwardness. Slick watched Face's body language as he tried to think of a price.

"Whew! Like I said, everything is high right now. I mean, it ain't really that much work floating around. To tell you the truth, I need twelve an ounce right now."

Slick looked sideways at Face, after hearing the rate.

"You trying to go half with me Slick," Flash asked. "What's that, about twenty four apiece?"

"Nah, I'm good right now. I just got right from my peoples. But you go 'head and do your thing though," Slick said leaving the room. He left the men to their own devices, not wanting to express his disapproval.

The price was entirely too high, Slick thought as he sat down on the couch and opened the Backwoods. Twelve hundred an ounce was a price that was acceptable only in a drought. He would never pay that much because he sold his coke wholesale. Sometimes, twelve hundred would be what he charged per ounce.

Flash on the other hand did not sale the cocaine pure. He would cook the raw coke into crack and produce up to an ounce and a half in additional weight by adding baking soda. That's the reason that it may have been a good buy for Flash, but a horrible move for Slick.

"A yo Slick, You got some bags in here," Face yelled from the kitchen.

Slick finished twisting the last blunt that he had from a quarter he'd purchased the previous day. He rose from his seat and strolled into the kitchen. He reached above the counter where the two were standing and opened the cabinet.

"How many do y'all need?"

"Just give me two," Flash answered. He had a look on his face like he had just bought some magic beans or something. He opened the bag and dropped the mass of white rocks that covered the scale into the sack. Slick knew from experience that the quantity of drugs on the scale was two ounces. His estimation proved correct as he watched Face count the twenty four hundred dollars on the counter.

With business completed and everyone satisfied the men got ready to leave. Slick cleaned the scale and wiped the counter down to negate the buildup of any illegal substance on the surfaces. After sanitizing the area, Slick proceeded to the front room to let the dealers out.

"Shoot something," Flash said before walking out the door. Flash was ready to gamble every day and knew that all he had to do was mention dice and Slick would be game.

"Oh, it's whatever nigga," Slick replied, showing no signs of weakness. "Call the boys! You know where I'm at."

"That's what's up. Let me put this work up and I'll be back in a few."

"Y'all gonna be shooting right here," asked Scarface.

"Yeah, you trying to get some too." Slick gave Face an indirect invitation to the game.

"Yeah, let me go handle something and I'll be back through," Face replied.

"Alright, that's what it is." Slick closed the door and immediately fired up the blunt he'd rolled. After inhaling a few totes, he felt the strong desire for a beer. He headed to the icebox and was surprised to find two Heinekens left. He cracked the top to one with a lighter and went back to the living room to recline on the couch.

He flicked on the television to find Mike Vick and the Falcons battling Donovan McNabb and the Eagles. Slick pulled on the reefer hard as he drifted deep into thought. The weed always gave him insight on things he otherwise had no interest in. He took in the commentator's dialogue.

"We are witnessing two of the greatest running quarterbacks that have ever played the game."

A running quarterback, why couldn't black quarterbacks be a quarterback that had the ability to run? It seemed like the announcers always labeled the black player and tried to make his asset a liability. There were many white players who had the same skill set and he'd never heard that title bestowed upon them. Steve Young, Archie Manning and Fran Tarketon were never labeled in that manner.

It seemed the announcers were also good at magnifying black's mistakes and minimizing their accomplishments. Slick noticed how people talked about how great Montana was, but failed to acknowledge that he was throwing to three or four great black targets that would make amends for errant throws. Joe would throw a seven yard pass and the receiver would run for eighty three yards and the quarterback would get credit for a ninety yard pass.

Vick could throw a seventy yard pass in the air to one of his bum receivers and it would be called a fantastic catch by the broadcaster. Such hypocrisy had been around for a long time and Slick was certain that it would continue. This was just one of the many topics that befuddled Slick concerning the world as he kept sucking on the blunt. He got higher and higher as the cigarette got shorter and shorter and time began to stand still in his head.

■ ■

"What up," Slick said answering his phone.

"Yo Slick, where Flash at?" Slick detected the distinct sound of Boss's voice on the other end.

"He left about thirty minutes ago. He said he was coming back though. Why, what's the deal?"

"Damn, that nigga said he was gonna be here when I got here. I brought the smoke he asked for and everything. That's right. You did say you wanted some too, didn't you?"

"Yeah, where you at though?"

"I'm right outside. Me, Akbar and Spray finna come in there."

"Yeah." Slick gave his one word synonym for goodbye and hung up the phone.

Two minutes passed before there was a hard knock on his door. Slick opened the door to find the three expected guest. The group filed into the living room and took places in the usual spots. Boss pulled his inventory of weed from his underwear and produced a large amount of different sized bags.

"I got some dubs, quails, and dimes. I'll let you get two dubs for thirty," Boss proposed.

"Nigga, they don't weigh but two point five each. I'm still getting shorted if I buy two. I used to sell quarters for twenty five and you going to sell me two grams less for thirty."

"Look man, this is Virginia. You can take them prices back to North Carolina, Goldsberg or wherever it is you from. That's why you ain't make no money in the first place," Boss countered.

"Man please, just give me one of them slack dubs, and be happy that I'm spending money with you anyway. Don't make me call Watts." Slick threatened to call a more affluent and generous weed man, who also shot dice with them.

Boss handed over the small bag and accepted the twenty from Slick without reply. Slick pitied the misguided hustler because of his lack of wisdom. He would break his weed down to smaller amounts and charge outlandish rates in an attempt to make maximum profit. It would take him longer to finish and many customers would go elsewhere to get a better deal. When Slick sold his weed, he would sell large amounts for cheap prices, therefore ensuring a quick return of profits and a higher rate of repeat business. This practice made his business much more lucrative at the end of the day.

"Call Watts anyway for me Boss. Let him know that we about to shoot. Call K J and them too." Slick expressed his desire to get the game started and he knew that Boss was too eager to see him lose money.

Boss dialed the numbers and confirmed that Watts was on his way with his brother Capone. Watts and Capone were relatives of a famous music producer who originated from Virginia Beach. They were also aspiring rappers themselves, so they were always promoting their latest mix tape or project. They went to New York and California on several occasions and always returned with details of star laden parties they had attended. They even allowed Slick and the boys into the studio at times to watch them at work and even let some of the crew lay down their own tracks.

Although Slick had no musical aspirations of his own, he admired the brothers for their work ethic and persistence. They always held true to the faith that their uncle would somehow provide a conduit for them to make it in the music industry. With that notion firmly implanted in their heads, the two worked feverishly to produce projects and promote new artists in their quest for stardom.

Slick saw the situation for what it was. Watts kept some fire weed and Capone always knew where the ecstasy pills were. Other than that, they were just the average everyday hustlers that made their living in the Beach. They were good people to know, however because they knew a few high profile cats in the area, and they had developed somewhat of a small cult following among people in their age bracket.

"Roll that up," Spray said to Boss as there was a knock on the door.

"Throw in on something then Spray. You can't keep smoking for free."

"All my tree you blazed up yesterday, nigga you better roll up!" Spray got excited and was about to start stuttering when Boss started laughing.

"Alright, nigga, chill out, I got you."

Slick answered the door to find Flash, standing with Capone and Watts. He welcomed them in and they greeted the players already in the room with customary hand slaps and fist bumps. Slick retreated to his bedroom and counted three hundred dollars from the top of the knot in his pocket. He then put the extra cash in the inside of a suit jacket pocket in his closet. With that gesture, he had defined his limit for gambling that day, win or lose.

After stashing his cash, Slick reentered the front room where his guests were smoking and watching the football game. Slick interrupted the revelry with his insistence on starting the dice game promptly.

"This ain't no rest haven for hoes. Y'all niggas know what you came to do. The dice right there in the kitchen like yesterday. Don't nothing move but the money."

Slick's brief statement was met with assertions of a competitive nature. Everyone insinuated that they were ready to roll. Slick retrieved the dice from the kitchen drawer and threw them on the floor in the midst of the men.

"Pee wee for the bank then. I'll go first," Flash said grabbing one die. He threw it nonchalantly and watched as the cubed object yielded a three. "That's good enough right there."

Next, Akbar and Spray scooped the other two available dice and rolled simultaneously. "Yeah, can't nobody beat the fever," Spray exclaimed after rolling a five. Akbar's die stopped abruptly on a four and he stood up in silence knowing he had no chance to hold the bank.

"Boss, Watts, what y'all gonna do." Slick persuaded the men to take their chances before he rolled, but the two declined. Both men knew how easy it was for the bank holder to lose a bundle in a hurry and neither of them wanted to put themselves in that predicament.

"Don't worry about it then, I'll go 'head and beat the five since nobody don't want no money today." Slick picked up the die and enclosed it in his fist. He blew into the small opening and let his fingers open slowly as he swept his arm forward. "Six," he ordered, while the die was still in motion. The onlookers let out gasps of frustration as the die obeyed the command. "Just like they had ears," Slick teased.

"This nigga here always get the bank first," said Akbar with a detestable expression upon his face.

Slick made a few more sideways comments as the men moved the couches around in order to create more space in the living room. Slick had just barked out his rules when there was a knock at the door.

"Who is it," Spray yelled, being closest to the door. A faint voice spoke from the outside and Spray glanced through the peephole to confirm that it was Scarface. Spray let him in and closed the door. All the players gave him a quick assessment then returned to their focus on the game.

"Just in time Face," Slick informed, addressing the newest gambler. "I got three hundred in the bank, twenty dollar bets or better, push you pay and trips double. Money got to be down to be good. Anything off the rug is no good."

"I got it stuck," Face said without blinking.

The room grew silent as the bet was made. By sticking the bank, Face had wagered the entire three hundred in one roll. Slick looked on stoically while Face dropped fifteen twenties on the ground solidifying the bet. He looked around the room and noticed the skepticism on the boy's faces.

"Don't get scared now Slick. You always be talking that big money shit. You got somebody on your level now," Boss said. Slick could feel the man's burning desire for him to lose.

"How your man say on the song? I ain't never scared. Let's do it."

Slick grabbed the dice and took a deep breath. He shook the dice hard in his right hand. He stooped down and let the dice roll gently out of his hand. He could not believe the results. He had already pictured himself handing Face the three hundred dollars in his mind, when he saw the three, three, two that showed on the tops of the dice.

"Deuce," Face exclaimed with glee. From his conduct, one would have thought he had already beaten the point before he rolled. Slick glanced around the room and noticed the looks of dismay that covered faces. Most did not want Slick to win, but if he did, they would at least have a shot at winning some of the pot. With Face, however, one never could tell. Unlike Slick, he would quit at the drop of a hat if he had won enough.

Everyone watched in silence as Face picked up the dice. He kneeled down to one knee and rolled the dice in a motion that resembled an old man trying to start a lawn mower. The dice yielded a four, five and a two on that try. Slick breathed a sigh of relief.

When the man moved to regain control of the dice, Slick noticed the imprint of a small pistol in the man's right back pocket. Slick felt no uneasiness about the twenty- two revolver however, because Face had it on him every other time he'd seen him. Slick had even seen it a few hours earlier when he and Flash conducted business. So it was nothing new to him.

Slick braced himself for the inescapable defeat as Scarface threw the dice once more. He almost let out a yell when he saw that Face had rolled an ace.

"One, two, three," Slick called out the numbers of the dice. Slick picked up the money in front of Face, along with the dice. He shook the dice gently in his hand and awaited Face's next move.

"I got the six stuck," Face said without missing a beat.

The tension in the room was thicker than November fog. Slick glanced around amid the astounded looks on everyone's face as he prepared to roll. He waited for Face to count the bet and could tell by the size of the stack that the bank was covered. The buzzing sound of his cellular phone went completely unheeded while Slick focused on his next roll.

"Three, two, five," Slick called out after rolling. He felt a release of pressure when he didn't ace.

"Real close to an ace. You got to ace out now." Scarface rooted for Slick's demise.

Slick gathered the dice and swished them around in his open palm. Without closing his fist, he stood straight up and finessed the dice so that they came out in a straight line from his hand. Slick watched the small cubes spin and contort until they came to rest on two ones and a three.

"Tracy," Slick called the point, soliciting everyone's attention. "Let me hit the blunt, Flash."

Slick stuck his hand out nervously, knowing that three was an easy number to beat with six hundred dollars on the line. Flash handed his partner the weed while Face gathered the dice. Slick pulled the blunt hard three times and passed it back.

"Alright, come on baby. I need you to bang Tracy from the back for me!" Face continued to coerce fate in his favor before letting the dice fly. "Right now!"

Slick could hardly bear to watch. He glanced at the action on the television before bringing his eyes back to the rotating dice. He could not believe the results.

"Deuce, that's what I'm talking about. Let's get money." Slick uncharacteristically showed unbridled emotion. He could not help showing gratitude for the nine hundred dollars in winnings. The regular gamers were equally proud of his victory and gave nods of approval.

While Slick collected and recounted the money, he saw that Face was digging in his pocket and counting a large sum of money himself. Before Slick could arrange his currency, Face made his presence felt with another compulsive gesture.

"Bet the twelve," he said, indicating that it was all or nothing.

The spectators began to stand up and gather around to get a closer glimpse. Slick felt a sense of calm and comfort, knowing that the heat was off of him. He could only lose three hundred but stood to win a sum of over two thousand in three rounds of dice. Slick shook his head in amazement before commencing to roll the dice again.

"Is that twelve right there," Slick asked, referring to the large wad of green Scarface had dropped on the floor.

"It's all there. Shoot the dice, Slick."

The host detected animosity in Face's voice. The envious look on his face testified to the anger Face held from losing so much so fast. Some guys, such as Slick, could lose money with a smile on their face. He knew that the deficits could always be made up for in the long run and the cash came so easy in the first place that he rarely placed any value on it. He held close to the reasoning that it could all blow up in smoke in an instant anyway, so why get so uptight about it.

Face on the other hand was a different breed. He had entered the game with a mindset that if I win, I win, but if I don't, I'll get it back, one way or the other. By any means necessary. Slick had no idea how soon he would learn of the man's true character.

"Man, these boy's crazy," Boss commented from the comfort of the sidelines.

"They just getting money, that's all. You know Slick gonna bet it all. That nigga there don't care." Spray answered Boss in the comical voice that he was prone to use when things got edgy.

Slick blotted out the excess noise and began to shake the dice. The few puffs of smoke he inhaled began to take effect and he was calmer than before. Without a care if he won or lost, he rolled the dice onto the carpet in a carefree manner. Slicked watched the dice come to a stop and wasn't even anxious to see the outcome. There was no point achieved so he rolled again in the same manner. The dice stopped on two fives and a four.

"Box car, beat the four. It's on you playboy." Slick spoke with a little more confidence in reference to his present point. He knew that Face's confidence was low due to his inability to beat a two and a three. Slick was so comfortable with his point that he retreated back by the couch and lit a cigarette.

Face, on the contrary, showed his nervousness when he grabbed the dice. He stumbled against the end table and dropped one of the dice from his hand. He repossessed the mishandled die and shook all three in a violent manner. The violence spilled over to his facial expression as his eyes squinted and his mouth curled in determination. He spun the dice with low arc, literally rolling them on the floor.

"Damn, ah man, what in the world is going on. I can't even beat the four!" Face's disappointment peaked as the dice read four, four, and three.

Slick picked up the huge stack of cash, while he comprehended the pattern of the dice. Every point that he had rolled, Face had lost to it by one number. Slick considered it to be his lucky day and accepted the winnings. Face would not give up, however and continued to throw money on the floor. "Forget it. Bet it all!"

Slick looked at the pile of bills that were scattered about in front of Face. His intuition told him that the amount was nowhere near the twenty-four hundred in the bank. Slick started to shoot without confirming the amount, but relented when he thought of the potential problems that could occur.

"How much is that right there," Slick asked, trying to be as polite and gregarious as possible. When a person has lost two grand in a matter of five minutes, you do want to show them the utmost respect. At the moment, there was certainly no need for any loud or egregious statements, especially with the level of tension in the atmosphere.

"I don't know. Whatever it is, shoot it." Face answered the legitimate question with an aura of irritation. He seemed agitated and in a hurry to get the roll over with. This impatience raised red flags in Slick's mind and he was determined to know the amount.

"I got to know how much it is. I can't roll without the bet being clear," Slick explained.

"Well, count it yourself then," Face interjected.

Slick looked around the room in his own bit of aggravation. He kneeled down slowly and separated the different denominations of currency. He moved slowly, taking his time to let his opponent know that he was just as serious about his change than anyone else.

After getting through the bulk of money, he judged it to be only a little over five hundred and fifty dollars, five sixty one to be exact. He figured that this was the man's last bet and losing would send him out the door. Even though Face had given the impression that the bet was more than it actually was, Slick decided to do him a favor, all in good sportsmanship.

"Six-hundred, that's what it is. It's really five-something, but we'll shoot like it's six. Same rules push pay, trips doubles." Slick restated the rules so there would be no confusion.

"Shoot it," Face said, with a stern countenance.

Slick scooped the dice and looked around at the boy's with a slight smile on his face. He knew that this would be the roll to end all doubt and relieve the anxiety that stirred inside him. Something deep within, had already told him that he would be victorious, but for some odd reason he still felt like he was in danger of losing something. Far be it from him to understand that the something would be his life.

"Six...three...one," Slick called out, as the dice stopped one at a time. He picked the dice up and rolled again. "Five...two...four, nothing!" Slick announced the points when the dice came to a complete stop. "This is the one right here," he said, almost silently. "I can feel it!" With the last statement, Slick cuffed the dice in a half closed palm and tossed them with a lackluster technique. "Six...six...five! Fever in the funk house. It's on you to beat the five, Face!"

Slick handed the opponent his ill-fated destiny in the form of three dice. He then stepped back to spectate with the contentment of a john in an all-night brothel.

Scarface asked everyone in the room to step back. He insinuated that the reason he couldn't when was that too many people were crowding the game. Slick agreed and asked those who were too close to retreat. Some of the boy's left the room altogether, not wanting to be the cause of anyone's malcontent. Slick knew, however, that the reason for Face's anger was losing huge amounts of money to points he could have and should have defeated.

"Alright girls, don't leave me out in the cold. I need you right now. Come and get that money back for daddy." Face prayed to the dice gods with the same fervency that Slick had prayed earlier that day. He shook, blew and kissed the dice, along with numerous other rituals. "Okay, six now I say!"

Scarface pleaded for the one and only point that could beat the five. His prayers were unheard as the dice landed a four, two and a one. Undeterred, he repeated the same routine, adding other séances to the act but still failed to point. He picked up the dice and this time skipped the antics, preferring to just shake and roll. This action pleased Slick the most when he observed the numbers on the first two dice five and three. The other dice came to rest on a three which meant that Face had tied the point.

Slick was elated because just like in blackjack, a tie goes to the house, in this case the bank. Slick bent down and salvaged the cash keeping his mouth closed and his eyes on the loser.

"Y'all gonna be right here," Face asked walking towards the door.

"Yeah, we ain't going nowhere. We gonna be right here shooting," Slick informed.

"Alright then, I'll be back. For real Slick, don't go nowhere. I'll be back!" With that last statement, Face turned solemnly and exited the apartment.

Slick closed and locked the door behind the dejected victim. He felt liberated from the shackles of expensive betting. He proceeded into the kitchen to arrange his winnings. He separated the original three hundred along with the twenty-one hundred and folded them together. He then wrapped a rubber band around the cash and stuck it into his back pocket.

Slick stuck the other portion of the dough in his right pocket while he headed back to his room. Closing his door, Slick stashed the majority of money in a different suit pocket than he did before. He kept only the nearly six hundred dollars on his person to gamble with. He returned to the front room where the commotion was loud as ever.

"Let me hold something, Slick!" Spray jokingly asked the winner for a few dollars. Slick would probably have given it to him, considering the mood he was in. Unfortunately, Spray asked in front of too many people.

"I ain't got it bra. It ain't nothing popping. You can roll something though." Slick reached in his left pocket and threw the teenager the sack of weed, knowing that the gesture would pacify the youngster.

"A yo Slick, I'm gonna tell you something," Flash said. "You know he gon' rob us right! The nigga coming back and he gon' rob us. I hope you got your pistol on you." The seriousness of the remark caused Slick to reply.

"Why you say that?"

"Man, that's Face," Akbar added. "That's what he known for. He tried to rob us back when we were kids."

"I'm telling you, Slick. You better watch that nigga when he get back," Boss included.

"Matter of fact, call Grim or Banger," Flash instructed to nobody in particular. The command gave clarity to his reputation as a boss. He was the only one in the room who was aware that none of his childhood gang was packing. If it did go down, he realized that he would be up the creek without a paddle. "Banger supposed to be on his way anyway. Call him Spray and tell him to hurry up."

Banger was Flash's older brother. He was rowdier than his younger sibling but had managed to stay out the game. His main aspiration was becoming a rapper, therefore he and Watts were real close. They had made a few songs and had chemistry together.

Aside from music and basketball, he was very avid with gunplay. He had been the suspect in numerous shootings, but instilled so much fear in the neighborhoods that no one ever came forward to identify him. Even though he was not licensed to carry a firearm as Grim was, his nine millimeter pistol was like his American Express card. He never left home without it.

Slick saw no need to take up arms. He figured if Face came back for a stickup, he would just give him the money in his pocket. Losing that five fifty was nothing compared to the two thousand he'd already put away. Actually, if he had to give it all back, it would be far more tolerable that losing his life.

Slick reasoned that if he had a pistol in the midst of the holdup, it would only increase the chances of gunfire being exchanged. Either he'd be dead or worse, he'd have a body on his hands. There were only a few matters in which Slick felt justified in killing a person. Illegal drug money was not one of them, neither were women. Family and dear friends, on the other hand, were a different subject altogether.

Boss made the phone calls. Both shooters said they would be there within an hour. Slick answered a few calls from various customers, between marijuana totes. Tina informed him that she was in the area and wanted some weed. Slick told her to come over while Boss was there and get whatever she wanted. He always provided the boys with business that was out of his arena.

"Y'all think he really coming back," Capone asked.

"What you worried about it for nigga," Watts said to his brother. "You don't got nothing to do with it."

"Oh, he coming back! I already told you that. And he going to rob us," Flash reminded the men, this time more vehemently. He then walked outside to meet his baby momma and came back in with his two year old daughter.

If he was so sure of the imminent robbery, Slick wondered, why subject his own daughter to the danger. Slick considered the move as another casualty of sanity in the warped world of drug laden decisions.

Slick opened the door when he heard Tina knock softly. Tina walked in the room to find it filled with smoke and hustlers for the second day straight. Slick directed her to Boss who served her a dime sack and offered his number. She refused politely and sat on the arm of the chair beside Slick.

Everyone in the room small talked while passing weed amongst each other. Tina then extended farewells to everyone in the room. They responded with a few vulgarities and sexual advances. She laughed them off as she and Slick approached the exit. There was a knock at the door.

"Who is it," Slick asked, inches from the door. After an inaudible response, Slick placed his eye to the peephole and noticed Scarface standing sideways accompanied by a large man that he had never seen before. From looks, he had to be at least six foot five and weigh around four hundred pounds. The knotty dreads and the circumference of his eyes let Slick know that the man was definitely a drug addict of some sort. Every ounce of Slick's intellect urged him not to allow them in. But once again his mindset of invincibility overruled his common sense and he opened the door.

"I'll be right back," Slick said to the men, permitting them to enter as he and Tina walked out. The door slammed behind the men and Slick and his female homey walked to her car.

"You should give me some of that money you won," Tina suggested. She got into her car while Slick shut the door for her. "I want to go to the mall."

"Come back when it gets dark and I got something for you," Slick said. He then gave her a kiss on the cheek and walked away.

He felt the vibration of his cell phone before his feet hit the sidewalk. It was Koko. She asked Slick if she and her daughter could spend the night. Slick liked her nerve, considering the pending warrant he had because of her. She could be sweet at times, however, and Slick held a soft spot in his heart for her daughter. He also for some reason was attracted to her standoffish nature and he liked her regardless of how much trouble she caused. Slick agreed to her request and she said that she would be there later.

The large man was standing by the doorway when Slick walked into the apartment. Slick found Face sitting in the midst of the players on the edge of the couch. It seemed like everyone was waiting for Slick. Flash's daughter, Nya, ran around the room playfully, ignoring her dad's many commands to sit down. There was a mixture of laxity and uneasiness in the room. Some smoked and some looked at each other nervously.

Most suspicions were directed towards the stranger who stood by the door like a sentry guarding a palace. His position should have alarmed Slick to what was about to transpire, but Slick was preoccupied thinking of how much more he could win from the Face.

"Y'all ready," said Face, when Slick penetrated the circle. "Let's get it on then!"

"Ready when you are," Slick said.

Slick stood about five feet from Face by the back door. He watched as Face bent down and picked up the dice, which still held the failed point of his last roll. The man straightened up, at the same time throwing the dice in the air towards host. Slick stooped to pick up the dice when he heard a small click by his head.

"Don't move!"

The two words resonated in his mind with the force of a wrecking ball smashing into a dilapidated building. Through previous experiences, Slick did not have to look up to know that a gun was pointed at his thick cranium. He straightened his body and glared at the small silver twenty two aimed six inches from his face. He lifted both of his hands in full view.

"You got it cuz," Slick said, trying to keep the gunman calm. He knew that robbers normally only shot you when you were uncooperative or they were afraid. Slick did not want to induce either of those scenarios, especially when there was a toddler in the room.

"I need it all, from everybody. Drop all the money on the floor," Face said to the whole group. "Slick, where's the trey- pound. I know you got the three-fifty-seven, where it's at? I'm telling you, let me get that gun." Face moved closer to Slick, while keeping a wondering eye on everyone else.

"I ain't got it on me. I don't keep it here yo," Slick said sincerely.

"I know you got it man. Don't play with me. Let me get it now."

"I'm telling you Face. I don't got it. It ain't here man." Slick wondered how he knew about his gun anyway. Then he remembered how the boy's joked and talked about gunplay and what they would do to one another during dice games. No doubt that Face had heard one of the idle comments that one of the crew made concerning Slick's weaponry.

"Let me get the money then. All of y'all Flash, Boss, Spray! Everything, drop it all on the floor!" Face waved the gun around the room to emphasize his point.

Slick was the first to drop the fat stack of money onto the floor beside him. Face evidently thought it was the full amount that he lost. He picked the money up without a second look. He then moved to Boss and Watts, who had already laid their money on the floor.

"Oh my God, come on Face. Don't kill us man! Oh Lord!" Capone paced back and forth in front of the gunman frantically. "You can have it. Take it all," he said, throwing bags of weed in the air. He kept the charade up for a few minutes until his brother calmed him down. Capone would later attest that it was a ploy to distract the gunman, but Slick dismissed it as a frightened reaction.

Face moved to Akbar and Spray. The blank stare of both indicated that they were going to be trouble for the stickman. He moved the gun towards them, demanding their cooperation. They returned his commands with the same solemn looks as before. They made not the slightest motion to their pockets and sat on the couch in silent defiance.

"I'm telling y'all. Give me what's in your pockets. I'm not playing!" Face seemed to get impatient.

"Here you go Face," said Flash. He handed him the five hundred dollars that was in his pocket, sensing the robber's irritation. "Man, just chill. You see my daughter right here. Don't do nothing stupid!"

"Y'all too, I hate to do it but I need that," Face informed, turning his attention back to the resistors.

Finally Akbar reached slowly into his pocket and dropped his paper on the floor. Spray reluctantly followed suit, mumbling a few words under his breath. Slick gazed at the large man guarding the door and notice he still had his hand in his pocket. That let Slick know that he did not have a weapon and was only there to watch the Face's back. If he did have a gun it would have been out and trained on the victims too.

Slick's idea to disarm the perpetrator disappeared when he analyzed the facts. He had not lost anything and was still up two thousand. It would be foolish to initiate a scuffle when he did not know who would assist him. His brainstorm was prematurely interrupted.

"Slick, where the three-fifty-seven at. I know you got it in here somewhere." Face made one last ditch attempt at confiscating Slick's method of retaliation.

Slick held firm in his concealment and the robber gave up. He pointed the gun at Slick, while he back peddled to the door. His co-conspirator opened the door sensing it was time to leave. Face followed the bodyguard through the door and pulled the door carefully behind him. Before the door closed, Face reappeared suddenly and pointed the gun back into the crowd that was set to pursue him. Everyone froze in mid stride.

"And if anybody got a problem with it we can handle it now," Face challenged. He then pointed the pistol towards the top of the back door and fired a round.

Everybody in the room ducked for cover. Slick heard the bullet bounce off the door frame and ricochet into the dining area. The warning shot kept the men from going after Face immediately.

"Is everybody alright," Watts asked the group.

Each one confirmed their well-being, amongst a chorus of expletives and threats. Cellular phones flipped open and voices were raised as the victims plotted revenge. Everybody announced their losses to one another.

Boss had submitted nine hundred, which was a fortune for him. Akbar forked over four hundred and fifty, Flash five hundred, Spray three and Watts six hundred. All total, the robber escaped with roughly what he had entered the contest with. It would have been better for him and everyone involved if he had not played.

"Where you at," Flash yelled into his phone to his brother. "That nigga Face just robbed us! Come on!"

"You got the ratchet on you," Spray inquired of Grim through the phone. "Yeah, we in here now!"

Grim and Banger arrived at the door a few minutes later. They had been riding together. "We just past that nigga on Bonney road," Grim exclaimed. The two regretted not knowing beforehand. They would have handled the situation then if they had known sooner.

The mad men filed out of the house. Slick went to the storage room to get his pistol. Boss, Akbar, and Banger piled into the car with Watts and Capone. Slick, Spray, and Flash, hopped in the car with Grim to embark on a violent search and recover mission. A quick detour was made to drop Nya off at Flash's aunt's house. The men then sped toward the interstate in route to Norfolk, Face's city of residence.

The twenty minute ride seemed like an hour to Slick. The boy's made several calls in an attempt to locate the man's whereabouts, while Slick sat silently in thought. What would he do if they did find him? He glanced down at his hand, which was wrapped around the handle of the silver magnum. He himself felt no ill will to Face, who did what he had to do. Slick understood that his own actions had put his life in danger and these happenings were just a part of the lifestyle.

His feelings aside, he considered the other side of the coin. In the streets, you can't let anything slide. If so, one would be labeled as weak and would be susceptible to all sorts of violations. It was times and circumstances like these where transgressors had to be dealt with violently. Statements had to be made and examples had to be set. It was the latter theory that Slick used to verify his presence in the vehicle. He was further persuaded by hypnotizing lyrics of the song that blasted through Grim's speakers. Fifty Cent's lyrics provided fuel to the fire already boiling in each member of the car.

"Murder...I don't believe you...Murder...fuck around and leave you...Murder...I don't believe you....Murder, murder, your life on the line..."

■■■

They had searched for hours. The posse that had gotten up to five cars and eight guns had dwindled down to one lone Mitsubishi and two pistols. The cry for blood had been reduced as the time moved past nine o'clock. Slick sat in the backseat anguishing over missed sales and the fact that he had the girl, Koko, waiting inside his house.

They had gained entrance by a spare key, but he still was not comfortable with her being in the house alone. She had been grimy before and took a few items. Slick knew that she was capable of snooping and didn't want her to come across any of the stashes and get missing.

On the exit ramp leading to the apartment, Slick still had to listen to promises of revenge and regrets over what had transpired. The event had lingered in his mind for an hour or so, but after the extensive searching Slick had accepted the event and moved on. All he could think about was breaking his vow of sobriety by filling his nose with cocaine. After that he planned to have rough sex with Koko and then get high some more. He knew that neither of these actions would solve his ultimate problem, but they would provide a temporary outlet for his tensions.

He got out of the car to find Koko on the apartment complex lawn smoking a cigarette in the dark. When he approached her, he examined her eyes to see if her pupils were dilated. She had a sober demeanor so Slick deemed that she had not helped herself to any of his product

"Where in the world you been," Koko asked confrontationally. "I know you saw me calling you. You a nothing ass nigga, had me waiting in here like that!"

"I love you too," Slick replied grabbing her by the waste. "Come and give me a hug, baby!" He slid his hand down to her backside and gave it a squeeze. She pushed him off of her.

"I ain't giving you shit. Get your damn hands off of me!"

"Give me some head then," Slick added. He let out a burst of laughter at his quick comeback. Apparently, it wasn't funny to Koko. She punched him in the back as he walked by. He ignored the attack, making her angrier. He endured an assortment of curses and insults as both of them entered the house.

Slick walked in and automatically began to straighten the living area. The room was in such disarray from the earlier chaos that had occurred. He vacuumed the carpet, emptied ashtrays, wiped the tables and rearranged furniture in an effort to erase the memory of the ill-fated dice game. Koko offered no help at all. She just came in periodically to harass the janitor.

"Give me some powder," she asked, just as Slick completed his custodial tasks.

"Wait a minute trick." The harsh response would have incurred the wrath of the average woman. However, Koko was not the run of the mill broad.

As with many of the girls Slick came into contact with, she preferred to be disrespected rather than adored. Years of verbal, mental, and physical abuse had her confused about the correct way she should be treated. She had once related that she didn't think a man loved her if he didn't hit her. Her preference, as she told Slick, was to be beaten up and then made loved to. She would often times provoke Slick to violence and then seduce him into a sexual episode. This was not healthy for either of the two, but Slick naively fell into her twisted web of manipulation on several occasions.

"Hurry up babe. I want to get high." Koko yelled from the bedroom with little concern for her daughter.

Slick entered the room and gave the girl a stare. He took the revolver from his waistline and placed it on the top shelf of the closet. He removed the half ounce of dope from his briefs and opened it up. "Here you go," he said reaching in the bag and handing her a rock that weighed about two grams. "Crush that up for me and don't ask for no more."

The girl readily accepted the coke and put it in a dollar bill. She folded the Hamilton and brought a lighter from her tight Roc-a-Wear jeans. She beat the lighter against the money, opening and closing it between assaults, to ensure that it was fine enough to sniff.

After preparation, she took two large scoops of the drug into each nostril. She sneezed three times, as the initial contact was prone to induce. Lighting a cigarette, she regained her composure and handed the bill to Slick.

The man looked at the dope in the dollar, trying to muster the courage to resist. He victoriously laid the drug on the bed and walked away. Five steps away from the bed, he about faced. He took a business card off the nightstand and slid it through the fine powder. The coke stuck to the paper and he lifted it to his nose and tilted his head back, the beginning of the end. There was no turning back now and he knew it. He ingested three large toots and gave it back to the girl. He walked around the room as the dopamine was released in his brain.

Koko kept sniffing the cocaine while Slick left the room. He flipped on the television and turned to BET. Nelly's explicit video, "Tip Drill", was in mid view. The video aroused Slick instantly, as fat round bottoms in thongs paraded across the screen. The girls bounced, shook, jiggled and enticed, causing Slick to need instant gratification. He called Koko's name.

"What," she replied snappily. Like most cokeheads, she hated to be disturbed while getting high.

"Come here!" Slick spoke in a tone whereas she knew he was serious.

Seconds later she appeared in the foyer a few feet from the couch. Slick grabbed her aggressively and unbuttoned her pants. Her minor protests went unheeded as he threw her on the loveseat face down. He then pulled her up on her knees by her waist and began to strip her of the tight jeans. She looked back at him, slightly resisting. When the jeans got to her knees, Koko voiced her opposition, but still lifted her legs one at a time so that the garments could be more easily shed.

"What you doing Slick? Stop it!"

"Shut up and take your drawers off!"

Slick could tell by her voice that Koko liked the domination. She poked her rear to make the descent of her thong less problematic. Slick stuck his finger into the open space and was energized to find her already moist. He removed his pants and underwear speedily and wasted no time inserting his self into her.

Noises of resistance and struggle soon became sounds of bliss and pleasure. Slick drilled the conquered women maliciously for forty minutes straight. He exerted authority by pulling her hair, smacking her tail and hurling all sorts of demeaning insults. He turned, twisted and flipped her every way possible for the entire duration.

She displayed her satisfaction with the rape by gyrating and pumping her pelvis in between moans and groans of approval. Feeling his climax approaching, he took as many strokes as he could before ejecting from the lady and spewing his potential kids all over her. His goal being accomplished, he left the girl face down on the sofa breathing heavily and headed for the showers.

■■

Slick exited the shower to find Koko on the bed still unclothed. Her nose was too far into the pile of cocaine to notice his arrival. She no doubt wanted to continue the adventure but Slick had no further interest for her tonight. He looked at the girl while slipping on gym shorts and a t-shirt and pondered the reason he still dealt with her. She had caused him much headache and worry, not to mention the current warrant for his arrest. He dismissed the memory as he felt anger beginning to rise.

"Let me hit that," Slick asked.

"Here you go," Koko complied submissively.

The two users sat on the bed and passed the cocaine back and forth religiously. For hours they talked and sniffed and sniffed and talked. Slick had informed her of the happenings earlier that afternoon and she had conversed about her troublesome childhood. After consuming too much, Slick drifted into his normal state of paranoia.

All of a sudden, he had the feeling that Face or some other robber was about to invade his home at any moment. He grabbed the revolver from the top shelf and went to the window. He peered out of the blinds, feeling the night air from the hole that Koko had poked two weeks ago. He kept cocking the gun and releasing the hammer, an action which terrified Koko.

She tried to console him but it was too late. He bounced from room to room, checking doors, locks and windows. When he was not snorting, he was straining his eyes to the limits, searching for shadows in the darkness.

"Babe, it's four o'clock. Ain't nobody out there. Won't you come to bed with me?" Koko tried unsuccessfully to coerce him into relaxing with sex and conversation but he was too far gone. The only thing that would slow him down was the massive headache forming in his brain from sniffing too much. He sat down on the bed and put the revolver under his mattress.

He lay down on the bed and tried to slow down his thoughts. He looked at the woman and her three year old child, intruding upon his comfort. He theorized on the reason they were there. He knew that she was no good for him. One, because of her attitude and two because she had the same habit he did. He always felt guilty about having sex with her and doing cocaine. So why then did he continue in such a state? The dilemma baffled him until a scripture surfaced in his mind from his youth.

He thought about the verse he'd learned from Romans the first chapter. "And just as they did not see fit to acknowledge God any longer, God gave them over to a depraved mind to do those things which are not proper." Another verse in the same chapter also came to mind concerning the subject. "For this reason God gave them over to degrading passions, for their women exchanged the natural function of their bodies for that which is unnatural."

Those two passages explained both of his problems. He had rejected and disobeyed God for so long that he'd become powerless to resist things that were pleasurable, but unhealthy. He had been given over to drug use, sexual impurity and greed. His mind had become totally ruined due to his own desire to continue in wrong.

It was the same with the girls he dealt with. The reason they would do so many perverse acts, is that they had been given over to those things. Their minds were warped into thinking that lesbianism and promiscuity were natural instead of unnatural. Slick's mind was corrupted into thinking that group sex and multiple partners would replace his need for God. Now that he realized those things would not fulfill him, the only way out was to turn back to God and ask for His help.

The problem with the solution however, was that he had to live completely for God, being one hundred percent obedient and abstaining from those pleasures. Slick was not sure that he was ready to make that commitment. He found himself in a catch twenty two.

His degenerate mind told him that he could either keep sinning and be miserable or live for God and be miserable. He did not see the upside of giving up those pleasures, nor did he see the detriment of continuing in his lifestyle. Slick decided momentarily to defer his decision. He closed his eyes and tried to go to sleep. He could not, however so he attempted his late night ritual of praying.

He began to cry out to God in silence to deliver him from the drug usage. He prayed with all the fervor and words that he thought made prayer successful. Being as though he didn't have every intention of doing completely right by God, his prayers were in vain.

He should have known from his upbringing that God knew the deepest desires of his heart and even though he was praying with his lips, his heart was still focused and content with the lifestyle he lived. He completed the futile prayer, once again feeling better. He drifted off into a light sleep, not knowing what the near future held for him

5
Locked

Slick was awakened by a knock at the door. It seemed he'd only been sleep for minutes. He looked over to Koko and her daughter, both of whom had not budged. He automatically assumed that it was the police and started to clean the room of any potential criminal charges.

First, he flushed all of the materials he used for inhaling cocaine. Then he emptied the ashtrays that were filled with blunt roaches. Next he removed the handgun from beneath the mattress and hid it between blankets and bath towels in the hall closet. Finally, he secluded the bag of coke from the night before in an air vent above the stove that he had loosened for that purpose.

"Maintenance," a harsh smoker's voice bellowed between knocks. "Maintenance, is anybody in there?" Slick remained quiet while scanning the front room ensuring no paraphernalia was in sight.

Afterwards, Slick moved towards the door to look out of the peephole. Before he reached the door, he saw the deadbolt lock turn to the right. He checked the chain and found it securely in place. When the door opened, the chain blocked the intruder from entering. The super continued his attempt to enter by proclaiming his presence.

"Maintenance, I'm here to fix the window before the storm comes today."

Slick thought about the existing hurricane warning declared for the Tidewater region. Hurricane Isabel was scheduled to touch down between six and eight o'clock p.m. and it was expected to be a level five. Newscasters advised all Virginia Beach residents to remain indoors during that time. Emergency alerts had flooded several programs the night before, so Slick knew the visit was not a hoax.

"Yes sir," Slick said to the man through the opening. Paul, the elderly white man who patrolled the grounds as a handyman, was actually a regular customer to a lot of the boys who sold crack in the neighborhood. "Can I help you?"

"Yeah," the man said nervously. "We have to fix your window that's busted out. There's a storm coming today, so we wanted to get to it early. It'll only take a few minutes."

Slick consented and allowed the man to enter. He closed the door and unhooked the chain. When he opened the door again, the maintenance man did not make a move to come in. Instead, four Virginia Beach police officers appeared from around the corner and walked in the door.

"Are you Taylor Richardson," a short Greek looking officer inquired.

"No, he's not here. Is there a problem officer?"

The fat lawman that flanked the leader produced a photograph and showed it to the others. The lone African American officer shook his head in confirmation. "Yeah, that's him."

"Mr. Richardson, could you put your hands behind your back please," the lead man asked more in the form of a command than a request.

Slick pleaded for an explanation. "What are you talking about? What are you doing?"

"Sir, put your hands behind your back," the head officer instructed again. He put his hand on Slick's shoulder and moved in behind him. "We have a warrant for your arrest."

"For what, I haven't done anything. What's this about?" Slick knew better to resist four policemen physically. He had more than his fair share of assaults from overzealous beat cops with chips on their shoulder. He would, however, give them a verbal run for their money. "What's the warrant for?"

One of the back- up officers read the contents of the pink paper he held in his hand. "Domestic assault on a family member," he relayed.

"A family member, what are you talking about? Don't nobody stay here but me. You got the wrong one!"

"Do you know a Candace Braswell? She says she stays here and you assaulted her."

Slick knew about the assault charge, but the family member business was a shocker. He could not believe the girl told the magistrate that she resided with him. He was furious.

"Koko, Koko, come here! The police out here! Come tell them everything is alright." Slick beckoned the girl from the room and she came promptly. When she saw the police, she stopped at the threshold of the room in a stunned silence. "See, there she is! She is right here! Everything is good. Tell them Koko!"

Slick went back and forth between the law and the plaintiff, bidding both to rectify the situation on site rather than in front of a magistrate at the court house.

"Yeah, I mean everything is fine. I mean, I don't want him to go to jail. We mean we….we already worked it out."

Koko stumbled over the words nervously. Slick couldn't discern whether she was more afraid of the police or the repercussions that would come from him. Slick did sympathize a little with her, knowing the damage had already been done. It was out of her hands. That, in no way stopped him from trying to persuade his captors to release him.

"See! I told you. Everything is fine," Slick addressed the officers in vain.

"I'm sorry Mr. Richardson, the warrant has been signed and we have to execute it. I'll walk you back to your room so you can put on pants and a shirt," the leader offered.

He and Slick passed Koko in the hallway. Her eyes met his and she knew there would be hell to pay. He slid on the same outfit and shoes he'd wore the day before. When Slick was fully dressed the cop cuffed him and led him to the front door. Slick made his final plea.

"Well look. At least make her get out. This is my apartment and she doesn't stay here."

"We have this address for her on the warrant, unfortunately sir. Does she have any clothes here," the enforcer asked.

"Man, I'm telling you! The broad don't stay here," Slick said, steaming hotter with every word.

"Well, I apologize, Mr. Richardson, but we can't make her leave. Her address is listed as 4109 Wales drive, Virginia Beach. She has clothes and a child here. There's nothing we can do."

Slick was flabbergasted. He could not believe it. First the girl he slept with on a regular basis had him charged, knowing full well what he did for a living. Then, she had the audacity to come and make up with him a week later. Now, he was being taken into custody, while his accuser was allowed to reside in his place as if it were her own. He shook his head in abhorrence to the girl, the law and the whole situation as he was escorted from his home.

The lawmen led him to the awaiting patrol car. Slick put his right foot on the floor of the car before bending over and sticking his backside into vehicle. He then twisted his body to face the front of the car, while bringing his left foot inside. This was a routine Slick had performed several times in the past, so he needed no help from the rookie cop who tried to assist. The door slammed shut and Slick braced himself for the silent ride down to the precinct. His heart burned with contempt for the officers and the handcuffs shackling his wrists.

His anxiety fled when he contemplated the charges. Jail was by no means a new frontier for the career criminal. He had been locked up in jail all across North Carolina. Wayne, Wake, Durham and Guilford were just a few of the counties whose facilities Slick had visited. In his eyes, the charge was so minute there was no reason to worry.

A simple assault in his hometown yielded only a five hundred dollar secured bond. Slick thought that he would receive no more than a thousand dollar surety, locate a bondsman, pay the hundred dollars and be on his way. Slick laid his head back on the top of the cushion and planned his activities upon his release. Unbeknownst to him, however, was that the commonwealth handled matters differently than he was accustomed and it would be a much longer time than he anticipated before he would see the light of day again.

■■

"Mr. Richardson," the overweight Puerto Rican deputy called. "The magistrate will see you now."

Slick stretched his legs, eliminating numbness that accumulated during his long wait on the cement bench. He had waited hours for the magistrate. Several others had gone before him only to return disappointed. Slick endured the proclamations of innocence and explanations of crimes by his fellow detainees. He was relieved to escape the dialogue and sauntered gingerly over to the deputy, as the blood started to flow properly through his limbs.

"Have a seat right here please, sir." Slick heeded the deputy's instructions and sat on the metal stool in front of the magistrate's window.

The young Caucasian woman ignored the presence of the black man who sat before her. With her head bowed, the full brunt of her attention was geared towards the small stack of papers on her desk. She scribbled an unrecognizable signature on a few documents and placed them in a gray tray behind her. The official then shuffled a few other papers aimlessly in a clear attempt to delay the process. Slick scanned the contents of her desk and noticed her name plate. The brown and white label spelled out the title, Ms. J. L. Schollotti.

Slick tried to get a handle on the young woman's credentials. In his opinion, she was no more than twenty-eight years of age. Slick recognized the origin of her name as Italian and deduced that her blond hair was a disguise. The tribal tattoo around her wrist gave Slick the impression that she too was a party girl. Slick wondered how many lines of coke she had done over the weekend on her off time. He also pondered how many people had her mafia relatives killed before she had been appointed to pass judgment on lesser offenders.

Slick had always detested the system of having people, who were just as prone to commit crimes, policing their fellow citizens. He had known several public officials and servants who were equally or more deeply involved in criminality than he was. Crooked policeman, judges, district attorneys, and lawmakers had all crossed his path at one point in time. This hypocritical front was a main catalyst for Slick's rebellion. His stare met the woman's perpetual avoidance of eye contact.

"Mr. Richardson."

"Yes ma'am," Slick replied. He was taken aback by the gentle voice coming from the hardened exterior.

"Sir, you have been charged with domestic assault on a family member. You have the right to remain silent and anything you say can be used against you. You also have the right to an attorney to represent you. If you cannot hire your own you can apply for a court appointed attorney. Your first appearance will be tomorrow morning at nine o'clock, where you can exercise these options then."

Slick absorbed the words of the magistrate. He could have recited the Miranda warning in reverse as he'd heard it so many times. He waited while the woman focused on the computer screen and punched several characters on the keypad. Slick figured she was now obtaining information on his criminal background in order to set a bond. Slick hoped that his North Carolina record would not be visible in Virginia's database. If it wasn't, his record would be spotless. She asked the inevitable question.

"Mr. Richardson, have you ever been convicted of a crime of any sort."

"Yes," Slick reluctantly responded.

"What were they?"

"Resisting arrest, and disorderly conduct," Slick said, giving two of the lesser offenses in his long history.

"What is your birthday," the lady asked firmly.

"Two, twenty-six, seventy-eight."

"Social security number?"

"Two, three, eight, five, six, three, four, four, nine." Slick rambled off the numbers in a monotone voice. He knew those nine characters contained mounds of data pertaining to his checkered past. His high hopes dropped as the young authority pounded the top of her keyboard. He waited in suspense for the next words.

"Have you ever lived in North Carolina?"

"Yes," Slick answered innocently.

"How long have you lived in Virginia?"

"Since the end of two thousand and one."

"Wow!" The magistrate shook her head as she scrolled down the screen. "Let's see. You only mentioned two charges. If this is correct, it seems you may have left a few out." She hit a few more buttons and continued to dig into the records. "Hit and run..., assault on police officer..., possession of stolen firearm..., DWI..., possession of marijuana..., gambling."

She continued to narrate the file as she searched. "There's communicating threats..., assault on female..., driving while licensed revoked..., DWI again..., armed robbery..., common law robbery..., destruction of property..., another DWI..., more possessions of marijuana...larceny."

Slick rested his head in his palms while the magistrate continued her presentation. His heart sank deeper into his stomach the more she read. Her voice drifted off as Slick thought about the relevancy of the charges to the present situation. Most of them had occurred before he reached the age of twenty-one. He felt that they should have no bearing on the amount of his bond. After all, he had already paid his debt to society for those actions so why should he have to suffer again. This view was not held by the woman.

"Mr. Richardson, you have over fifty charges that have been filed against you and more than thirty convictions. This shows a pattern of total disregard for the law and disdain for authority. Also, you have not resided in Virginia for more than two years, which makes you a flight risk. I am persuaded in lieu of these factors to give you no bond. You may hire a lawyer to conduct a bond hearing on your behalf. Until then, you are remanded into the custody of the Virginia Beach Sherriff's department."

This was unthinkable. Slick never fathomed not being released for a misdemeanor. He had heard of Virginia's strict laws, but never expected to be treated in this manner. If he was innocent until proven guilty, Slick wondered, why was he incarcerated as if he'd already been convicted? He dismissed the assertion as just another one of many inequalities in the justice system. Slick expressed his objection.

"Madam Magistrate, I have gainful employment and am a productive member of my community. Most of those charges occurred years ago and I haven't been in trouble since I migrated to this state. It is imperative that I have a reasonable bond so as to not be in jeopardy of being dismissed from my job."

Slick made his plea in his most educated and eloquent disposition. He figured if he showed his vocabulary, the woman would perceive his intelligence and formulate a different view, regardless of his adverse history.

"I'm sorry Mr. Richardson. I understand your concern for your employment, but I cannot ignore the fact that you have repeatedly found yourself on the wrong side of the law. My decision on the matter has been rendered. As I said earlier, you can retain the services of an attorney and set up a bond hearing. The judges in court are usually more lenient and you should receive a bond then."

Slick endorsed the papers she handed him through the small opening. He already knew the content of the material so there was no need to read it. He stood up and sarcastically thanked the woman, internally accepting his fate. The Latin deputy escorted Slick back to the holding area, this time locking him in a cell to be processed and admitted. His request to use the phone was denied.

He adjusted to the lonely four by six foot room not knowing how long he would be a castaway. Holding his face to the small window, he observed the deputy walking away to pursue other obligations. He scanned the administration area and pitied all of the servants who milled around aimlessly. Those whose orders they obeyed were the same people who deserved to be behind bars themselves. Their same superiors would be the exact persons who would lock them away if their unknown crimes and acts were exposed.

Slick sat on the metal bench that was as equally uncomfortable as before. He thought of the girl occupying his house and wondered if she had cleaned him out or held him down. His mind ran rampant with scenarios of what he would do. He had no qualms about seriously hurting the woman at this point, even though it contradicted everything he stood for.

Slick allowed himself to relax, forgetting Koko and focusing on getting out. He knew that he could call a few people and direct them to hire an efficient lawyer. His only worry was how soon the attorney would be able to schedule the hearing. He had the need for a bond reduction hearing once, and from his recollection that process took two weeks. Slick didn't want to remain in custody for that long, but the situation was beyond his control. He conceded to the fact that he would at least be in jail for the night.

With his fate determined, Slick lay back on the hard bench and laid his head on his arms. The sleep that he'd deprived himself from the previous week suddenly came back to stake its claim. His incarceration was a moot point as the weary young man dozed into a much needed sleep.

Slick was awakened by the turning of a key against the lock. He lifted his head only to be stricken with discomfort. His neck singed with pain due to the awkward position he was in for the last three hours. He stood up and rotated his neck while doing a few other calisthenics to loosen the stiffness. The door opened to reveal a gorgeous black female deputy, who reminded Slick of Stacey Dash. He attempted to straighten his disheveled appearance before the guard fully entered the room.

"Mr. Richardson," she asked in a voice equal to her beauty. Slick confirmed his identity with a simple nod. He did not acknowledge the guard by name even though he read the word Jackson firmly planted upon her chest. "We have your paperwork finished and you are ready for processing. Come with me please."

Slick followed the turnkey out of the small cell, past the administration area and down a long corridor. Slick could not keep his eyes from below the woman's waistline. Her enticing lower body became even more appealing when she walked. Her hips swayed from side to side, while her bottom jiggled with every movement of her thick thighs. Slick tried to suppress his fascination with the woman by engaging in small talk as they walked. The jailer was all business however and didn't entertain his chatter the least bit. Upon reaching the end of the hall, she allowed him to take the lead and instructed him in which direction to go.

"Turn left at the hallway and continue straight back until you reach that door ahead of you." The sternness of the command let Slick know further that there was no point in fraternizing with her. The rigors of being a jailer had obviously hardened the once gentle specimen and Slick perceived that there was no penetrating her tough defenses.

Slick reached the door and waited for the deputy's next order. She walked up beside him and pushed a button on the right side of the door frame. A buzz and an opening followed her gesture and the two entered another space which resembled the first administration area. His overseer guided him to a bench in front of a fingerprinting room. He took a seat at her suggestion and waited patiently.

"Rogers, I have one out here for prints and photo!" The authority announced her presence to an invisible person beyond their eyesight. She peeked into the room when she did not receive an immediate response. "Rogers," she spoke again, this time going in the room. "I have a guy out here, but I need to go back over to admissions. Will you be alright with him?"

"Yeah, Jackson, I'll be fine. As a matter of fact, you can take this one back with you. I'm just finishing him up."

The black stallion emerged from the room flanked by on overweight white deputy with a thick mustache and a thin white inmate with long blond hair. Slick examined the contrast between the two. One was obviously on drugs of some kind, probably methamphetamine or heroin. The other should have been on drugs to curb his excessive appetite. The only non-eyesore was Jackson; and she had just exchanged him for a hippie and left him in the possession of the John Candy look a- like.

"I have two more to bring over so I should be back in about ten minutes," Jackson said, walking away.

"Ten-four," the fat man replied. He turned his attention to Slick and motioned for him to enter the room behind him.

Slick followed the man and was led to a counter with a computer on top. Embedded inside the surface of the desk was a smaller screen, resembling a scanner. Surprisingly, there were no inkpads, rollers or fingerprint cards in sight. The room was also void of the numerous file cabinets and stacks of folders that he was accustomed to seeing. The deputy began entering information into the computer as Slick marveled at the high tech system. Slick continued to examine the technological advancements of the judicial system until he was given instructions by the deputy.

"Mr. Richardson, I'm going to take your left hand first and print each finger individually. Then I'll do the four fingers simultaneously, before doing your palm. Then I'll repeat the process with the right hand. Just relax and hold your hand limp, so that we can get this over with as quick as possible."

"I understand," Slick replied. "This is new to me though, Rogers. I'm used to having my hand smeared with ink and pressing down on those index cards."

"Nope, not here," Rogers interjected. "They made it a little easier with the implementation of these computers. I like it because it cuts down the paperwork."

Slick did not reply. He preferred to keep the conversation to a minimum with the overweight man, who had already begun to process his prints. The images appeared on the monitor as soon as Rogers rotated each finger. The deputy clicked the mouse on the desk and saved each photo into the records, ensuring the ability to identify Slick if he ever committed another infraction.

"Alright sir, next, I want you to step over to the blue line and face the camera." The guard spoke with his eyes glued to the screen, not looking at his prisoner. "Okay, look straight into the lens." The jailer clicked the mouse once before giving his next command. "Turn to the left now please."

Slick followed each order and the ordeal was complete. He walked back over to the guard and viewed his profile. It seemed that every time he took a jailhouse photo, he was displeased with the results. He thought the pictures always made him look rough and unkempt. He wondered if it was the lighting they used, to give the public a bad opinion of the person in the mug shot.

The guard instructed Slick to sit down and wait for transportation back to the admissions area. Ten minutes later, Deputy Jackson appeared to retrieve the prisoner and complete the booking process.

"Stand up and follow me Mr. Richardson."

Slick gave immediate compliance to the command and was led to the property room. The deputy at the window was involved in a heated conversation with a cohort.

"You're outta your friggin, mind to think Peyton can even stand next to Tom's jock strap. The guy's a complete bum without Harrison, Wayne and James."

"We're gonna see who's who and what's what when Manning sees the Pats this year. He's way too smart to keep losing to Belichek." The deputy outside defended his favorite while turning to acknowledge his new visitors.

"O'Malley, Roberts....this is Taylor Richardson. He's to be dressed out and he is going to cellblock C2b," Jackson instructed her coworkers. Then she turned abruptly and left Slick in the custody of the men as they continued their discussion, performing their duties simultaneously.

Slick was made to undress and underwent visual searches of his mouth, scrotum and underarm area. A further act of degradation was imposed when he had to spread his butt cheeks, bend over and cough. Slick complied quietly as he had endured this humiliating process many times before.

After the search, Slick was provided the customary orange jumpsuit and shower shoes. Then, the deputy tossed him a bag that had a blanket, sheets, towel, rag and other necessities needed for his stay.

Upon girding himself, Slick signed a paper acknowledging the reception of his personal items by the jail. The only property he admitted was the twelve hundred and thirty-two dollars that was spread out in various pockets of his jeans. The amount and displacement of the money incurred several accusations from the deputies regarding Slick's occupation. He ignored the men while his confident silence confirmed their speculation.

Slick was led by O'Malley to a set of elevators that opened as soon as they approached. Slick entered and turned to face the front doors.

"Face the rear of the elevator," the Irish guard said in a forceful tone.

Slick stared at the man defiantly for a few seconds before following the order. His mind fumed at the thought of obeying another man who wielded complete power and control over his body. The tension continued to mount in Slick's innards as he considered the many other deputies that he would encounter who loved and abused their state given power.

The elevator came to a stop and Slick exited through the doors followed by the jailer. The noise and commotion that came from the various cages were comparable to a small sports arena. Inaudible screams exuded from prisoners who had somehow adapted to the state of chaos.

Slick walked the narrow corridor and noticed several acquaintances and cohorts from the streets. Slight head nods and one word greetings were the only form of acknowledgement however, as he didn't want to associate himself with anyone until he knew their status.

Cellblock C2b was a large open room with sixty beds; fifteen bunk beds on each side of the room. The rest of the space was taken up with a few tables for eating, two toilet stalls and two showers. There was also a television that rested high on the front wall right below the ceiling. Slick entered the room and passed inquisitive stares while walking to his assigned bunk. He found his resting place and started to establish his temporary living quarters.

He began by throwing the mat on the top bunk. He then attempted to cover the mattress with the extra small sheet that was given him. After a few tries Slick finally succeeded in positioning the cloth over the majority of the mat. He then placed the blanket on top and discarded the remaining items from the bag on the bed. The state soap, toothpaste, toothbrush, deodorant and jail handbook was placed in a corner of the bunk. The cup, spoon and toilet tissue was placed in the adjacent corner. Slick folded the extra sheet, towel and rag in the form of a pillow and hopped on the rack to rest his head and gather his thoughts.

No sooner than he got comfortable, his solitude was interrupted by a familiar voice.

"Slick….Slick…! What up my man?"

Slick raised his head, and encountered the forlorn face of a teenage consumer of cocaine and weed. He slightly remembered providing the youth and his friends with drugs but couldn't quite recall his name.

"What's going on home boy," Slick replied in an uninterested tone.

"You remember me? It's Rick, from Thalia Trace. I used to come through and cop mad tree and stuff with little Leslie and them."

Slick recognized the boy with the mentioning of Leslie, a young Latina girl who brought him repeat business. "Okay…yeah! I know who you is."

"Yeah man, I been in here for about three months. They got me on a B & E and grand larceny. It's my third, so they ain't give me no bond or nothing. My P D said I'm looking at about two years but I ain't sweatin' it. But look at you. What happened? They ain't get you with no soft or nothing did they?"

Slick looked around the room to see if anyone was paying attention to the conversation. Then he refocused on the young white teen with contempt. Nosiness and talkativeness were prime reasons for getting stomped out in places like this. Evidently, Rick was unaware of protocol or used to getting beat up, but there were no way you were supposed to discuss why a man was in jail unless you knew him or he volunteered the information.

"Nah, ain't nothing like that," Slick said still surveying the room. "Just a misunderstanding, I'll be out before you knew I was here."

Slick closed his eyes in an attempt to express his desire for solitude. The user finally realized this and decided to leave the elder man alone.

"Okay, if you need me I'm right over here on the end bunk," Rick stated as he walked off slowly expecting a response. Slick ignored the remark and opened his eyes slightly to scan the room for anyone else he knew. When he saw there was none, he relaxed and began to drift deep in thought.

His mind reverted back to the days of his youth. He never envisioned himself being enclosed in a jail cell at age twenty three. All of his instructors throughout adolescence would have placed him in graduate school at this point. Even his own mind could have never predicted him being in his present state. Slick began to wallow in anguish, wondering how his situation became so dire.

His spirits were lifted, however, when he considered the more serious condition of his closest childhood friend. William, or Cisco as he was called, was serving a twenty year sentence for a murder seven years earlier. Slick kept in regular contact with his friend and was regularly advised by him to stay out of situations that would lead to incarceration. Slick thought of the disappointment it often caused Cisco when he learned of Slick's charges.

Even though Cisco had a large amount of time, he would often be more of an encouragement and an inspiration to Slick, than Slick was to him. This often led Slick to ponder how Cisco allowed himself to be induced into such an act. With the scene fresh in his mind, Slick began to relive the times and events that led up to the fateful decision that would affect several lives for many years to come.

6
Murder

1992-1996
Goldsboro, NC

Goldsboro, North Carolina was a small town with a population of around 50,000 people. The majority of the residents were hardworking, middle class citizens who instilled the same values in their children. With the community being so small, most citizens knew one another and families were connected through church, school, recreational, neighborhood and community affiliations. It is in this social structure that Cisco and Slick became close friends.

Slick grew up on Taylor St, in a middle class area on the south side of the city. Both of his parents had government jobs, his father for the postal service and his mother for a federal prison. This gave him the label among his peers as a "rich kid" and was the source of much ridicule in his teenage circles.

Little did his friends know that both his parents were born, bred and raised in the projects and had struggled to improve life for their family buy the sweat of their brow. The fact that Slick and his two sisters had both parents in the home was an abnormality for most. Also, Slick's parents were deeply involved in a local church that limited members from being involved various social activities that were considered normal for others.

This church, Tabernacle of Prayer for All People, evolved into a second family for Slick and most of his close childhood friends came from this congregation. There was Boogie, the pastor's son. Brake, Wood, and Donnie were three brothers who were all Slick's age and claimed him as their own. Another close family was the Johnsons, who had two sons and three daughters. There were many other families in the church, but it was these three that would have the most profound influence on Slick's life.

Coming up in the church, a young man endured certain rites of passage. Besides chasing the innocent girls, one rite was being granted a chance to play the drums. At ten or eleven, most capable boys would venture into the profession of drumming. With Boogie being the head drummer, he enjoyed the most prestige. As Slick, Brake and June, the Johnson's eldest son, began playing, they increased their skill level and were allowed to play more. However, Brake and June continued to excel while Slick didn't possess the desired ear for music and his aspirations soon subsided.

Besides activities in church, most of the boys were deeply involved in athletics at the local boys club and recreational centers. Mostly all of them were exceptional basketball and football players and earned many trophies and M.V.P awards. They engaged in fierce competitive battles which usually ended with punches being thrown and balls hurled over fences. This desire to win was deeply embedded in them all and would continue to influence their life.

As the kids got older however, they began to find out there was life outside of the church. This was mostly due to older friends and family who did not attend church and were involved in what the members would call "worldly activities." These acts included selling drugs, drinking, sex, gambling and other vices that seemed exciting to the youngsters. As Tia, Slick's older sister, Boogie and Brake began to be influenced by persons outside the church, the trickle-down effect materialized in the younger members.

During this time of the early nineties, Cisco and his two brothers moved into Slick's neighborhood. Slick had known him from school, but had never really hung out with him otherwise. One summer day in 1992, Slick chose to accompany Brake to Cisco's house instead of going to the boys club, which was his normal routine.

Brake and Brain, Cisco's older brother, were good friends. They had already begun to dabble in the street life of smoking weed, selling crack and having sex. With Brake serving the role as Slick's big brother, naturally Slick wanted to follow in his footsteps. He had already smoked a few blunts and gotten drunk with Brake and was eager to engage in making fast money on the streets. This was the one reason Slick chose Cisco's house instead of the boy's club.

That day, Slick and Brake arrived to find several teens standing in the yard of the three bedroom house in Berry Downs. The boys were gathered into two groups according to age. The sixteen and up group were enclosed in a circle passing blunts, drinking beers and discussing exploits. The boys who were Slick's age were passing a football and bouncing a basketball while telling jokes about each other's mother. Slick walked over and joined his group while Brake mingled with the older cats.

Slick knew all of the younger boys. Blaze was a tall dark skinned kid who was an only child and stayed fresh. Dooky was a chubby light skinned livewire who always stayed in some sort of mischief. Shon was a smooth pretty boy type who switched girlfriends almost daily.

Douglass was Cisco's twin brother. The two were like day and night, as Cisco wanted to be a gangster and Douglass was content eating cookies and watching television all day. Marcus, a heavyset boy a year older than Slick, was also around. Slick liked Marcus because he stayed out of trouble and had a good perspective on life for such a young age.

The older boys were led by Bad Boy. The son of an infamous local gangster, he had a head start on the life and had shown many the ropes. He also was the boyfriend of Slick's sister Tia, so Slick had a mythical perception of him from her. Slick had spoken with him on many occasions and liked his New York persona.

Big Sal was one of Brake's closest friends. He was very hyper and did basically whatever he wanted. G was a tall deep voiced cat who considered himself a player. Seymour was Cisco and Brain's cousin and was already involved substantially in the drug game. Bill Skins was a very dark ball head kid who just liked to smoke and be around the action. Then there was Boogie and a few other heads that were just beginning their life of crime.

Somehow during the reverie, Cisco managed to secure one of the blunts in circulation among the older boys. He brought it around to the younger crew and enticed them with it.

"Here you go Blaze. Hit this right here mama's boy," Cisco said, taking a long hard pull off the brown cigarette.

"Hell nah," the tall kid said. "I ain't smoking that stuff. I'm drug free. Plus I can't get to the NBA like that."

"You know your mama gonna beat that tail if she find out that's all. You just a punk, scared of your mama," Cisco teased.

He then moved to Shon, who instantly waved him away with a shake of his head.

"I should've known better than that. Here you go then Marc. I know you can handle it."

"You better go head man. You know I don't mess with that. I need my brain cells." Marcus gave Cisco a strong two handed shove, as the smoker blew rings of smoke in his face. Cisco laughed menacingly as the THC took effect on his brain.

"Here you go. Let me see it," said Slick, reaching his hand out and taking the joint.

"Uh oh, Lips Manlis, it ain't gonna be none left after them soup coolers finish sucking on it." Cisco ridiculed Slick about the large size of his lips. Slick was used to the jokes by now and was ready with a comeback of his own.

"I don't know how you got the smoke passed them big beaver teeth o' yours," Slick said inhaling the toxic fumes. "I'm surprised you didn't bite the blunt in half with that woodchuck mouth."

Cisco laughed and came right back. "I know you better not go home high like that or your daddy gonna pull out that holy water and make you confess. You gonna have to wear that white collar for thirty days straight."

Everybody bust out laughing. They knew about the strictness of Slick's parents and their dedication to church. Slick had to come back hard and decided to go real low.

"Your daddy would've still had his collar but they caught him smoking, butt naked in the back of the church." Slick alluded to a rumor about Cisco's father, a preacher who supposedly had done some unholy things. Everybody always joked about it but this time Cisco didn't take kindly to it. Plus, all the boys laughed which didn't make it any better.

"What you say about my daddy punk," Cisco said. He handed the blunt to Dooky, who took it immediately in the midst of a fit of laughter.

Cisco charged at Slick, who stumbled backwards. When he got his footing he turned and tried to run, but Cisco stuck out his foot and tripped him. Caught off guard, Slick lost his balance and hit the dirt, sliding a few feet as his momentum carried him forward. Everyone laughed and embarrassment overtook the dirtied victim.

Slick got up and ran towards Cisco, who had a running head start. Slick felt a pain in his leg and realized that he wasn't going to catch him. He scanned the yard and found a steel pole. He grabbed the weapon and hurled it after the fleeing teen.

His aim was dead on. The beam struck Cisco in the back and the impact sent him flailing to the pavement in pain. All the younger kids went to his aid and Slick felt immediate remorse, not knowing the damage he'd inflicted.

Cisco was helped to his feet and then refused to be helped any further. Slick stood in the distance and wondered what would happen next. The answer came when Cisco came at him with his fist raised. Slick did the same and prepared himself for battle.

Then a voice came from the crowd of older thugs. It exuded authority and commanded respect.

"A, yo, y'all break that up. Y'all bugging. Y'all little niggas ain't gonna hurt nothing anyway. Brake, Brain y'all make them squash that shit!" Bad Boy gave the orders in his New York accent and everybody took heed.

Brake and Brain took their two protégés and induced them to shake hands and make up. Reluctantly the two obeyed and all the other young boys gathered around. Dooky and Blaze broke the ice by making lighthearted jokes about what had just transpired.

"Y'all wanna go play basketball at my house," Marcus suggested.

At once everyone agreed and walked the two blocks to the host's house. Teams were picked and the boys played basketball like nothing happened. From this point on, Cisco and Slick would become the best of friends and be together almost every day.

Time moved on and the youths advanced in maturity and mischief. By the age of seventeen, Cisco had dropped out of school. Slick had traded his love of books and sports for fast cash and excitement of the streets. Dooky was still in school, but was already a convicted felon. Blaze had begun running with hustlers and thugs of all kinds. The allure of the streets had seduced each, and would continue to plague them for years to come.

The crew's headquarters was Cisco's mother's house. With three boys and no male figure, Trixie, as she was called by the boys, was more lenient than most moms. She was very open and allowed all of the young men to talk with her freely about anything. She was always very nice and extremely attractive for a woman of her age.

"Y'all boys don't go out there and shoot nobody today," she would say. Or, "I know y'all had them fast tail girls in here last night!"

"Well, what you want us to do momma," Cisco would answer. "We men….and real men do real things."

"Well, all I know is that no bodies or babies better not turn up around here."

While liberal in her discipline, Trixie was well aware of the number of guns they had, the amount of girls they caroused and the large bags of weed they constantly blew. By now, her sons and most of their friends were pushing large amounts of drugs and she witnessed the money that was being generated. Slick reasoned she would have rather known than not know, so she allowed things to transpire close to home.

Slick loved Trixie because of her relationship with her boys. He could never imagine doing and saying some of the things that he saw and heard in front of his mother. Therefore, he spent the majority of his time at Cisco's, when he wasn't gambling, hustling, or chasing girls. The latter was somewhat new to him because he had recently lost his virginity.

At seventeen, Slick had transferred to a different school because of his disinterest. His exposure to the streets garnered more attention than "The Canterbury Tales" and Old English plays. Therefore, he didn't do the work and barely attended class. The new school was in a rural area and was considered "country."

Although he was popular, handsome, and half-street, Slick had yet to accomplish every teenage boy's goal: to get some. Snatch, coochie, draws, skins, or trim, the boys called the female sex organ by many names. Slick played the role as if he had reached that pinnacle, but in reality it was just a façade.

It wasn't the fact that he couldn't talk to girls. Slick kept a steady rotation of girlfriends. He also had been in numerous situations where the opportunity was presented.

Slick would get halfway or almost there and then invent an excuse to stop. In actuality, the youth was simply scared. No girl had made him feel comfortable enough to try it with. That is, until he met Teresa.

Teresa was a fifteen year old, light-skinned sophomore, who attended the new school, Eastern Wayne High. With big pink lips, round eyes, thick thighs and fat butt, she was attractive but not ideally Slick's type. She was not a high class, popular girl. Instead, she was sort of low profile, which probably attracted him to her when they bumped into each other in the lunchroom doorway.

"My fault shorty, you aight," Slick said in a mellow voice, slowed by the blunt he had smoked on break. He took a look at the girl, holding her books close to her large chest. The red birthmark on her left cheek captivated Slick for a second.

"I'm okay," the young girl replied. She then gave Slick an innocent stare, while she chewed a piece of bubble gum.

Slick sensed an opportunity and spoke again. "Let me get a piece of that gum?"

"I got one piece left but you can have it though."

Teresa dug into the pockets of her tight, cutoff shorts and gave him the gum. Slick knew he had her by the tone of her voice, but decided it to play it cool. He really didn't want to talk to any girl in particular because they all were so new.

"I 'preciate that yo. And I'm a talk to you later when I see you again, alright?" Slick brushed up against her firm breasts as he moved through the doorway.

"Okay then. We'll see."

The next day, Slick was approached by a girl he knew from church. Angie was a year younger than he and was fast. She tried to give Slick some on many occasions, but he declined. She was cute and cool but Slick knew her since they were toddlers. Even though she had blossomed, Slick held too many unpleasant images of her from childhood. He still flirted with her whenever he saw her, however.

"What up Slick…your big head, big lipped self!

"Watch your mouth shorty, before I choke you up," Slick retorted.

He then grabbed Angie by her waist and pulled her close to him. His hand routinely moved down to her buttock. Slick squeezed the soft flesh as if he were a farmer at a fruit stand. The girl leaped away, feigning indifference.

"Ayeee! Boy, get your hands out my crack!" She swung a fist and hit him in the shoulder. "You can't do that no more. My girl said she like you."

"Who's your girl?"

"My friend Teresa, you know her. She said she talk to you yesterday."

"Man, I don't know no Teresa," Slick insisted. He was high as usual and had already forgotten about the previous day.

"Light-skinned, thick, with the birthmark on her face." Angie stood with her hands on her small hips. "She gave you some gum. Don't try and front like you don't know who I'm talking about"

"Oooooh, you talking about her. Oh, yeah, I ain't know her name though. She alright, though. I'll holler at her," Slick uttered, playing it smooth while hiding his excitement.

"Well, here you go," Angie muttered. She handed him a small piece of paper. "This is her number and she said call her. Don't never say I ain't look out for you."

Slick slid the paper in his pocket and extended his arms inviting a hug. Angie accepted and entered his arms for the embrace. Slick held her tight and close.

"You know I got you sis. I'll always love you. Anything you need just let me know."

Slick rubbed her back, shoulders and down the side of the girls arms. Then, he grabbed her waist, placed both palms on her butt and yanked her to him.

"Anything," Slick repeated.

"Boy you are crazy!"

She pried her way free and walked across the yard. Slick watched as she walked away, switching her hips. Her intent was to look sexy but the result was just the opposite. Slick thought that the way she moved and gyrated made her look stank.

Over the next week or so Slick and Teresa got acquainted through late night phone conversations. It wasn't long before Slick was making the twenty minute drive to go see his new friend in the neighboring town. He had even brought her to his house and allowed her to be around his parents, something he never did.

One evening, while his peoples were at church, Slick brought his newfound girlfriend to his house with the intention of having sex. They began the normal routine of kissing and feeling and Slick started to get nervous. Teresa, being more experienced, began to undress Slick and stroke his manhood.

Slick was not comfortable because he didn't know what to do next. He didn't want to expose his inexperience to the younger girl but his fear paralyzed his ability to perform. As usual, he thought of an idea to back out.

"I gotta use the bathroom," he lied.

"Okay. Go ahead."

Slick pulled his gym shorts up and went to the bathroom. While peeing, he racked his brain for a solution. He concluded that he would tell her a lie. He returned to the room in a fake panic.

"Hey yo, we gotta go! Get your clothes on. I forgot my momma and them coming home early tonight. Come on."

"Dang, what time they coming," Teresa inquired. She grabbed her clothes and hurriedly dressed as Slick did the same.

"Man, it's almost nine o'clock. On Thursdays they get out at about eight-thirty so we gotta bounce."

"Oh baby," Teresa sighed, as she pulled him to her lips.

Slick was now comfortable that he was free so he grabbed her and began to kiss her passionately, furiously rubbing her breast and tail.

"I know baby. We'll have plenty of time for that though. Now let's go before I get in trouble."

Slick took her home and called her later that night. They talked as usual but Slick sensed that something was wrong. His suspicion was confirmed when Teresa confronted him.

"Can I asked you a question," she asked.

"Yeah, what's up?"

"Why come when we was in your room and we was about to do it....why your thang wasn't hard?"

Slick was caught completely off guard. He didn't know whether to lie or tell the truth. But the matter of fact way in which she asked, Slick decided to keep it honest with her.

"If you want me to be real, I'll tell you." He hesitated for a moment to gather courage, and then spoke. "To tell you the truth, I ain't ever done it before."

There. He had said it. The burden was lifted. The relief was temporary however as he thought of the consequences of his forthrightness. How would she look at me now? His worries were quelled by her response.

"Oh! Okay! Don't worry about it baby." Then she paused. "Do they go to church tomorrow?"

"Yeah, why?"

"I said don't worry about it. I got you. We'll do it tomorrow."

And that was that. The next day Slick picked her up, brought her home and took her in the same room. They repeated the foreplay of kissing and groping until Teresa carefully guided the virgin penis into her womb. His honesty afforded him to relax. He settled into a groove after the joy of actually "getting some" subsided. Teresa was patient and Slick enjoyed seven or eight ejaculations as he did not want to stop.

From that point on there was never a problem. Slick continued to advance his skills in the bed. He and Teresa would have sex daily for the next two months. This new frontier had Slick feeling like he was finally a man and his actions began to show it. He felt that there wasn't anything else to learn. I'm making money, smoking and drinking, and knocking boots. I got guns, I gamble and I'm in the streets. This is the life.

Slick wasn't the only one who was feeling himself at this time. His road dog Cisco had money, a baby on the way and had just copped a new whip. With a fascination for arms, he bought every gun he saw: mac elevens, trey-pounds, nines and forty-four revolvers. This ready for war persona kept the possibility of gunfire prevalent in the lives of Cisco and his cohorts. It also proved detrimental on many occasions.

One instance, Cisco was in a beef over a minor drug sale. A fiend had chosen Cisco's crack over another local hustler. Disappointed and broke, the man walked over to Cisco's car and punched him in the face. When Cisco opened the door to react, the man ran. Being a little overweight, he knew he could not catch the runner. Cisco hopped in the car and sped home, knowing that he had something in the hall closet that would catch Randy Moss with a fifty yard head start.

"Blaze, I need you to drive me somewhere," Cisco said walking in the house. He went straight to the closet andpulled out the mac.

"What's up," Seymour asked noticing the gun in his younger cousin hand. Brain, Slick, and Seymour were gathered around the kitchen table all rolling blunts.

"Nothing, I'll tell you about it later. Come on Blaze and bring the nina!"

Cisco walked outside and Blaze complied with the request, always ready for action. The other three continued their cipher, while discussing possible reasons for Cisco's actions.

"You know that boy 'bout shell. He got the mac and the nina. He crazy," Seymour contemplated. "Blaze aint got no L's and can't drive. Both of them niggas finna going to jail."

"I don't know what the hell wrong with that young nigga," Cisco's brother added. "He already been running around talking 'bout he Tony Montana for years."

"My boy straight. He talk that gunplay, but y'all know he ain't gone kill nothin' and shole ain't gone let nothin' die."

Slick knew his man wasn't soft but he didn't consider him a head buster either. They had their minor scraps, but most often it was Cisco who was the voice of reason to keep someone from doing something drastic. On this day, however, his cool head didn't prevail.

After searching for and spotting his attacker in a nearby project, Cisco instructed Blaze to drive while he unloaded the fully automatic machine gun at the target. The man saw the vehicle first and took off running. Undeterred, Cisco lifted the weapon and fired a multitude of bullets at the fleeing prey.

Frustrated by his errant shots, Cisco ordered Blaze to circle the block so they can find him. They rode around without any regard for the public or the surely placed phone calls to police. Finally abandoning the assault, they sped out of the projects and down a main street where they were apprehended by the police. Evidently, the man had called the police from his cell phone as soon as the shooting started.

By this time, Slick had left the crib to go collect money from a few customers. While riding down the street he noticed the gray sports car of his friend pulled over with several police cars around it. He pulled over to see his two friends face down on the ground and the weapons on top of the car. Slick shook his head helplessly and went to inform Brain about the situation. Luckily, Cisco was given a small bond and Blaze was released without charge. A few hours later, Cisco was home, smoking, drinking and laughing about the whole matter.

While Slick and Cisco were wilding, Dooky was getting money and engaging in his own street warfare. He had chosen to move weed as his product of choice and enjoyed a connect that kept him stacked with pounds. Because of his flashy nature and reputation with the girls, a lot of other street factions labeled him soft and tried him on numerous occasions. He proved able to hold his own with his hands and he was even more reckless with a gun in his hand.

Once, Dooky had got in an altercation with an older hustler, Freeze, who was known to be a livewire himself. Dooky was smoking with friends before school when they were approached by Freeze and his boys. With Dooky being the most flamboyant, he was the logical victim to target. Arguments ensued and Dooky was severely beaten by the older boys while his friends ran.

"Damn homeboy," Cisco exclaimed, as Dooky walked into his house later that day. "What in the hell happened to you boy?"

Slick examined his friend. His left eye was black and swollen shut. His bright yellow face was covered with red scrapes and bruises. His top lip was puffy and he had a hole in his mouth where two of his teeth should have been.

"Shit nigga, say something," Slick stated.

Dooky stayed silent with a stoic look on his face. It seemed to Slick that he was in another world. Dooky refused to say what happened. He stayed quiet until the moment his brother came to pick him up.

Reports came through the grapevine to Slick and Cisco. It was established that the beef wasn't even with Dooky, but with AZ, the grandson of a prominent businessman who'd also succumbed to the life of hustling. Dooky, as would become his trademark, took the challenge to his friend personally. He stepped up and took the beating but no one expected what occurred next.

The same night Dooky convinced his older brother to help get revenge. They drove to Freeze's project and spotted him standing on the side of a building. With fury and anger, Dooky leaned out the window and sprayed his father's .45 caliber pistol erratically until it was empty.

When the smoke cleared, three people were hit, all of them innocent bystanders. No one was injured seriously and Freeze got away unscathed. Despite his reputation, the older teen later came to ask for a peaceful end to the situation. A truce was made but tensions would remain for years between the two.

Dooky was arrested the next day and charged with several counts of assault with a deadly weapon inflicting injury. Because of his age, the system treated him leniently and placed him on house arrest before trial. When the case was disposed, Dooky ended up with no jail time and intensive probation. Even though this was his first involvement with guns, beefs and the courts, it would definitely not be his last.

Blaze had the ability to drift from strip to strip because he was familiar with all the hustlers. He wasn't too heavy in his hustle yet. It appeared to Slick that Blaze was just hanging around to learn the ins and outs of the game. Evidently, he soaked up many aspects. He was patient, made seemingly wise choices and stayed out of trouble for the most part. He frequented Cisco's house and began to stay around more often, practically living there.

While the younger boys were coming unto their own, several older associates were emerging as major players. Slick's god brother Brake, had teamed up with Big Sal and a New Jersey born hoodlum named Crazy Stan. The trio stumbled upon major connects who saw their passion for money and kept them stocked with pounds of cocaine. In turn, they kept the streets of the small town flooded with crack and gained a reputation for serious business in the game.

Brain and Seymour were also doing well for themselves respectively. The two had an inside track with Brake, Sal and Stan. This relationship allowed them to stockpile ounces of drugs for distribution. This had a trickle down affect as Slick, Cisco, and a newcomer named Stubbs reaped the benefits of a constant supply.

Stubbs was a fourteen-year old who stayed across the street from Cisco. He had witnessed the action from a distance and one day got the courage to invite himself over. Cisco took a liking to the chubby, dark-skinned kid and began smoking and kicking it with him. Before anyone realized, Stubbs was officially part of the family and proved valuable in many situations.

It was under these conditions that Slick and Cisco existed in the summer of 1996. Slick had graduated high school and was moving large amounts of crack around the city. Cisco and Blaze would post up at one of the many crack houses and set their shop up. Money was flowing continuously and everybody was enjoying the fruits of their labor.

Cisco liked to smoke expensive weed while chilling with his newborn daughter, Mya. Seymour liked to smoke weed, shop and chase a bunch of women. Brain was a gun fanatic, always coming home with a new tool. Slick didn't like to spend much of his money but he did develop a gambling habit.

Slick also had a steady flow of different girls. With the money he was making, it seemed that every girl he met was game. He didn't even have to talk much most of the time. He just made suggestions and they were complied with. He did have a couple that he dealt with on a regular basis, but his unrealistic standards would not let him become seriously involved with any. Little did anyone know that a female, would be at the heart of a matter that soon turned deadly.

Despite the outer appearance of luxury and comfort, the game was about to reveal its true form to the young players. Although Seymour and Brain were getting money, too much is never enough. One simple act of greed would serve as the catalyst that would destroy a band of thieves and turn close friends into strangers.

Seymour was dating the girlfriend of another prominent hustler in town, Powerful who was then locked up. Before he went in, however, Powerful left a large amount of dope that he hadn't moved with the girl. She, not knowing what to do with the drugs, gave them to Seymour.

A few months later, Seymour, Cisco and his mom were in the mall when they were approached by Powerful. He had just been released and was well aware of who had been given his work. He had already declared that it was the dope, money or warfare.

"Hey yo homeboy," he growled, walking within inches of Seymour's face. "Don't you got something that belong to me. Don't you owe me something?"

Seymour, who had already spent the extra money, was on mute. He didn't want any trouble and sidestepped the aggressor, attempting to walk away.

"Hey nigga, I know you hear me talking to you," Powerful persisted. "I need mines or I'm a do something to you. And that's for real."

Seymour and Cisco tried to play it cool and ignore the man. Powerful was intent on trouble and walked behind the men hurling insults. Then he gave Seymour a strong shove in the back that sent him springing forward.

"Man, y'all some faggot ass punks. I'll kill you, him and his mama," Powerful expressed including Cisco in the matter.

"Man you better go 'head with that," Cisco retorted. "That's my mom you talking about dude!"

Nigga, fuck you and your mama," Powerful snapped back. "What you gonna do cocksucker?"

Then, without warning, Powerful hocked and spit on the back and shoulders of both men. Cisco instantly started to retaliate but his mother's voice prevented it.

"William! William," Trixie screamed. "Come on boy. Don't you get into trouble out here over this mess! Come on!"

Cisco relented amidst a barrage of threats and curses. In the confusion, Seymour had removed himself a safe distance away from the affray. Eventually, the ruckus subsided and both parties departed.

"I'm a kill him," Cisco vowed later that night. "You watch! I got to. That nigga spit on me and said he was gonna kill my mama. Nah, I'm talking 'bout murder now." He pulled vigorously on a blunt of hydro between rants. Seymour and Brain stood close by awaiting their turn.

"Yeah, that nigga got to go," Seymour said in a low tone.

Seymour was tagged soft by many in the streets. He'd been the target of several robberies and failed to retaliate on any occasion. Consequently, he was glad to let his counterpart Cisco assume the lead.

"I ain't worried about that clown," Brain interjected. "I keep the nine in the console and the chopper in the trunk. One false move and I'm a blast him to oblivion."

The conversation was ongoing when Slick entered the barn in the backyard. He wasn't surprised to hear of the incident with Powerful. The twenty-one year old dealer was known for starting beef and finishing it. Slick had a few brushes with the menace himself. He always avoided altercations by minimizing contact and dealings with the hustler.

Two weeks after the incident, Slick was laid up in the Hampton Inn with Tika, a young chocolate beauty he had dealt with in high school. He had bumped into her buying a blunt in the Arab store. He hadn't slept with her yet and didn't want to let the opportunity slip by.

"You ain't gotta smoke none of that garbage," Slick said as she walked through the door. "You know I keep some of that exotic to blow on."

"For real, it's like that nigga," she replied. "I know you still got my number so call me after nine o'clock. I'll come chill."

Slick called and picked her up around ten. He made a few runs, grabbed some food and headed straight for the suite. The girl got comfortable as the potent weed and strong liquor performed their magic. Before Slick knew it he was knee deep inside the girl. He would keep her there all night, going round for round, until both were exhausted.

While Slick was handling his man business, Cisco and Blaze were riding around town smoking and making sales. Even if there was no money out or nothing to do, Cisco still preferred to drive around and get twisted while zoning to Pac, Nas or the Wu.

"It was my only wish to rise...above these jealous coward niggas I despise...when it's time to ride...I was the first off this side...Give me that nine...I'm hard to kill..."

On this night Pac's "Ambitionz Az a Ridah" played in the stereo as Cisco and Blaze were coming from making a sale. It was two a.m. in the morning and the streets were desolate, void of people and cars. Cisco decided to slide through various drug areas to glean for any late night fiends. Turning on a downtown avenue, the riders saw a figure cross the street. As they passed, Blaze casually alerted the driver to the identity of the walker.

"A Cisco," Blaze murmured. "You know who that was back there right."

"Who...where," Cisco answered. He wore glasses and sometimes had problems seeing.

"Back there on the sidewalk. That was Powerful."

"Nigga you lying," Cisco exclaimed, slamming on the brakes. "I know that nigga ain't out here like everything gravy."

"I'm telling you man. That's him. I looked the man dead in his face," Blaze persisted.

Cisco checked the rearview mirror in an attempt to prove Blaze wrong. He squinted for better focus, but still couldn't discern the figure. Finally, he reversed the car far enough as to where he could see the man.

"Hell, yeah, that is him," Cisco confirmed. "You got your .25 on you right?"

Blaze reluctantly shook his head yes.

"This what we gone do. I'm a drive around the block and then we gone switch positions. Drive back around and drop me off at the corner he was heading to."

Blaze complied with the plan and switched to the driver's side. Heading back to Powerful, Cisco removed his own .25 from his front pocket and secured it in his waistband. When they rounded the corner, they spotted Powerful on the sidewalk about fifteen yards away.

"Stop the car," Cisco said, already grabbing the door handle. "Ride around the block again and come back."

Blaze slowed the car and Cisco leaped out. He stepped behind the car as it eased away. Then he crossed the street approaching where his adversary had stopped and stood as if waiting for someone. Cisco solicited his attention.

"A yo man! Let me holler at you for a minute!"

Powerful turned and looked at Cisco with disgust. "What you want? Matter of fact, what are you even doing out here. This my strip right here," he continued. "You better take your ass back on the other side of town before something happen to you."

"See! That's what I'm saying right there," Cisco responded. "Why you think you so hard all the time? You ain't gotta act like that."

"Nigga, I do what I do because I'm me! I'm P! You can't do nothing to me! I'm Powerful! You just a nobody ass nigga!"

"Oh yeah, you Powerful huh," Cisco responded, reaching in his beltline. He pulled the silver weapon, raised it to the man's face and instantly pulled the trigger.

Nothing happened.

"You thought you was gone, didn't you" Cisco joked, lowering the gun.

"Nigga, you ain't crazy! You ain't real enough to shoot me. I'm Powerful! You can't do nothing to me. You wait 'til I see you next time. You better have something bigger than that twenty-five you got right now."

Cisco's negligence in releasing the safety had spared Powerful's life momentarily. Realizing his error, he half-turned his body to release the safety on the gun. Cisco then faced the victim, raised the gun and squeezed the trigger all in one motion.

BLAAAAWH!!

The lone shot resonated through the empty night air. The bullet struck the victim in the lip and travelled upwards exiting the bottom of Power's brain. The ill-fated man fell to the ground with his eyes closed and blood pouring from his head. Cisco surveyed the scene and determined Powerful was dead. He then walked towards the street as Blaze rounded the corner.

Miraculously, Powerful got up from the ground and started to run. Cisco, terrified by the resurrection, froze for a few seconds before giving chase. He raised the gun again and fired a shot that struck Powerful in the lower back. Undaunted, the prey continued to sprint as if he had not been hit. He reached a nearby apartment complex and began banging on the nearest door.

"Help, help me! This nigga trying to kill me," Powerful pleaded, hoping someone would come to his rescue.

His pleas went unanswered and Cisco finally caught up. He dragged the mortally wounded man around the side of the building into a patch of bushes. Powerful, aware of his fate, stopped yelling for help and began taunting his killer.

"Nigga, you can't kill me! I'm Powerful. Hahaha…hahahaha! You wait! I'm a see you again."

"Be quiet," Cisco demanded, worried about attracting attention. He bent down and placed both hands over Powerful's mouth to quell the noise. He then maneuvered them around the man's neck and began to strangle him. He choked with ferocity, but the more he squeezed, the more his victim laughed.

"Aahaha…hahaha! You can't kill me! I'm Powerful. I'm coming back for your ass. Hahahaha….hahaha! You watch, faggot!"

Cisco was surprised at the resiliency of his opponent. After a few minutes however, the loss of blood and asphyxiation proved too much to overcome. With several clots of blood in his throat, Powerful uttered a few more curses and gasped for breath. It never came.

Cisco wiped the blood from his hands on his jeans and picked up the .25. He surveyed the scene before exiting the brush and spotted Blaze parked ahead on the main street. He sprinted in a low crouch to the car and dived in. Blaze saw all the blood and knew they were in deep. Barely saying a word, he sped the car down the block headed for Cisco's house.

When they arrived, Cisco exited the car and immediately began to vomit. The reality of what he'd done and the images of all the blood triggered an already weak stomach. He hurled for two minutes before regaining control and making it into the house.

Inside, the two began the cleanup process. Cisco showered and changed while Blaze burned the soiled clothes in the backyard. Then they drove to the Neuse River and dumped the murder weapon. After returning, the two spent the rest of the night corroborating alibis and discussing the possible ramifications of what had just occurred.

At seven a.m. the next morning Slick was awakened by a 911 page. It was Iris, a local crack addict that provided Slick with early morning business. Because he spent so much time on the block gambling, he was one of the first she would call. He looked over at the girl lying next to him. Holding true to the "money over broads" mantra, he reached over Tika and grabbed the phone. Iris answered on the first ring.

"I need two fifties baby. I know it's early but this money is rolling!" Hurry up too," she added in an excited tone.

"Aight, I'll be there," Slick replied.

He eased out of the bed, slid on his clothes and crept out of the room. Entering the car he reached straight for the blunt in the ashtray and lit it up. After a long inhale, he cranked the car and turned up the Pac full blast. Slick also had developed a habit of having to smoke and listen to thug music while handling business.

When he approached the block, he noticed yellow tape, EMS, and several police cars on a side street he passed. After making the sale, he doubled back to see what the commotion was about. He parked several yards from the scene, got out and walked. He ran into Slim, one of Powerful's homeboys standing on the corner.

"What up Slim," Slick inquired. "What's going on out here? What happened?"

"They killed him man! They killed Powerful," Slim said sorrowfully.

"For real, who?"

"I don't know, but that's my nigga over there. I saw him with my own eyes. I can't believe my nigga dead, man."

Slick instantly felt a pain in his heart. Even though they'd had a few run-ins, Slick didn't wish death on anyone. He scanned the crowd and saw many familiar faces milling around. His curiosity cured, Slick returned to his car. Contemplating what to do next, he decided to go wake the boys up and deliver the news.

Upon his arrival, Slick was surprised to hear music and loud voices coming from the backyard. It was barely eight a.m. Slick ventured around to the back and saw that the barn door was open. He entered and found Seymour, Brain, Cisco, and Blaze engulfed in a whirlwind of weed smoke, liquor, beer and loud rap music.

"Hey y'all, guess what? I just rode through the strip and saw the law, ambulance and everybody standing out there. They just found Powerful dead in the parking lot."

"We already know," Brain stated with a devilish grin on his face.

Slick surveyed the whole room, studying the body language of each occupant. Blaze stood off to the side with a look of deep regret and worry. Brain, was lively and exuberant; bobbing his head to the music and drinking like he had won the World Series. Seymour exhibited a concerned aura and it seemed to Slick that he was thinking hard about something. Cisco was smoking and guzzling Hennessy straight from the bottle, something he rarely did. Slick knew then from the atmosphere that someone in his presence had committed the murder.

Slick first assumed it was Brain. He was astounded when Cisco took him aside later and revealed the details. Slick handled the revelation with mixed emotions. He knew his friend had just committed an act that would have detrimental consequences for all parties involved, including him.

A short while later, a car horn sounded loudly. The edgy criminals hurried out front, expecting to see all white detective cars. Instead, it was a green jeep with Florida tags, occupied by a man and a woman.

Slick recognized the people as Blaze's mother and uncle. This was confirmed when she partially exited the vehicle and summoned Blaze to the car. Without saying a word, he strolled to the car and entered. The car reversed out of the drive way and disappeared out of sight. None of them knew that it would be quite some time before they would see Blaze again. His absence would be the cause of later speculations as to his part in the crime.

Over the next few days, the town of Goldsboro was ill-at ease. The police had no leads and were arresting anybody with a record. Powerful had so many sworn enemies, the investigation was like grasping for straws. There were several factions around who weren't unhappy about his demise.

For the first week, no heat came towards Cisco. However, rumors were starting to circulate that it may have been somebody from their crew. In a town that small, word of mouth quickly become fact and spread like wildfire. Soon, they began receiving calls from various people saying things like, "I heard it was y'all," and "everybody knows y'all did it". The pressure of keeping the secret was too much and the boys started talking too loosely around the wrong people. A few days later, the police came knocking.

The detectives assigned to the case already knew Cisco from previous gun charges. He was the first person they came for. They informed him that they had a witness that placed him at the scene and asked if he would take a polygraph. Under pressure from the savvy, veteran detectives and naïve to the damage his willingness to cooperate would do, Cisco agreed. Hours later he came back with a somber look on his face.

"They said I failed miserably," he stated.

"That don't mean nothing," Slick advised. "You know them joints ain't admissible in court."

"I know," Cisco informed. "But they talking about they got a witness and all that. He said tomorrow, they gon' take what they got to the district attorney and secure a warrant for first degree murder if I didn't cooperate."

"You ain't say nothing," Seymour asked concerned.

"Nah, I ain't say nothing. For real, they ain't got shit," Cisco declared. "It won't no witness out there. It was a ghost town at three in the morning."

"You shouldn't have went at all," Brain interjected. "I wouldn't have went nowhere. If they aint got no warrant, I ain't got nothing to talk about"

Brain was right. Cisco wasn't obligated to talk to the police. That trip into their territory allowed the detectives to use their professional skills to probe for any signs of guilt. They were trained to ask questions and read body language to detect any weakness in their subjects. Evidently, something in Cisco's demeanor was suspect. The next day, they returned and Cisco was charged with first-degree murder.

Within hours of being processed, Cisco was released. Trixie worked for the courthouse for years and still had clout downtown. There was no problem for her to satisfy the $100,000 dollar bail. Even without her connections, she could have posted the full amount herself. She was very successful in the insurance business, along with many other investments and ventures.

When word reached the streets of Cisco's arrest, utter chaos began. The same day of his release, the house was flooded with calls; some friendly and some not so friendly. Many threats were made by Powerful's associates over the phone and through third party methods. Knowing the loyalty and reputation of Powerful's people, Cisco braced himself and prepared for war.

"I don't give a damn," Cisco spit, holding the AK-47. "They know where I'm at! We ain't hiding either. We can bang it out whenever, wherever! Tell them niggas to bring it."

And that is exactly what they did.

About a week after the arrest, Brain was leaving the house with his girlfriend Pop. As he turned the corner, she saw three tall figures standing in the wooded area beside the street. When Brain passed the men, they emerged from their cover, each firing high powered handguns at the car.

Brain, super high off weed, was oblivious to the danger. The loud gunfire was drowned out by the volume of Pac's "All Eyes on Me" blasting through the speakers. Luckily, his girl was alert and heard the shots.

"Baby, somebody shooting at us," she said calmly.

Brain glanced in the rearview mirror and slammed on brakes. He could see the three shooters retreating back to the woods. He turned the next block and circled around. He removed the mac-10 from under his seat and loaded the chamber. With the gun in hand, he searched the neighborhood without success. From the profile of the men, however, Brain knew exactly who they were.

"Them niggas was just busting at me," Bang told Slick and Seymour when he returned. "They came out the woods on me and Pop and started spraying!"

Brain continued to relate the incident. Slick knew the identity of the attackers from Brain's description. GK, Slim and Stone were three of Powerful's closest friends, which made them the most likely candidates to retaliate.

This presented a dilemma for Slick because he associated with all three men. He had balled with GK, went to school with Slim, and forged a bond with Stone from his early days on the block. He still conducted business and mingled amongst all three.

Slick was mainly about money, rather than trouble. The reason he was able to go on any strip in town was that he maintained positive relationships with everyone he encountered. Even with the cats who didn't particularly like him, he somehow managed to be civil in matters of money. Slick also knew that the money would always be there. The trick was to stay out of the beef, drama, and other pitfalls.

So essentially, Slick had no issue with the men. However, his allegiance to his friends made him a potential adversary to all three. He had studied the "The Art of War" and knew that the enemy of his friend was also his enemy. Slick would realize the validity of that statement in a matter of time.

A few days later, Slick was standing on the corner of Slocumb and Spruce Streets finishing the last of his pack. GK rode through and noticed Slick. He pulled his car to the side and leaped out, with a tech nine in his hand. Slick looked the man in the eye as he approached.

"What up," Slick said.

"What up man," GK replied. "What's up with you and them punk niggas? You rolling with them niggas like that or what?"

"Look man, you know them my niggas. And if it's going down, I'm a ride with them. But you know we go back, so I ain't got no problem with you. I mean, it's whatever."

"Yeah man," GK replied. "I know we cool but the only reason I got the joint out 'cause I ain't no how you was gone carry it. If it was like that, I just would've just rode up blasting."

"Nah, it ain't no problem. I'm just trying to get this money and stay out of it," Slick stated.

"All I'm saying is be careful," GK advised. "Cause when I see any one of your boys it ain't no talking."

Slick and GK momentarily agreed to let their ties from childhood trump their loyalty to the streets. Slick saw the big picture and just wanted to stay out of trouble. He had seen and heard of too many lives lost over money and women, both of which could be replaced. GK, however, had just lost a friend. Blinded by fury, he was bent on revenge. This desire for vengeance would place multiple lives in danger days later.

The next week, Slick, Seymour, and Cisco were riding around smoking and making runs. Even with the current tumult, fiends still wanted to get high. The three continued business as usual, except for the ever present need for firearms. Slick drove with a .380 tucked in his waist. Cisco rode shotgun with a .357 magnum on his lap and Seymour played the back seat with a nine on the seat next to him.

Their precautionary measures proved merited as Slick rounded the corner leaving a drug spot and saw Brain standing in the middle of street beside his car. The driver side door was open and Brain had the AK-47 aimed down a side street firing rounds. Slick rode up on Brain as he stopped shooting.

"That nigga GK just rode by and let off with a tech." Brain exclaimed. "I couldn't get a clear shot 'cause that old lady right their drove right in the way."

"There he go right there," Cisco screamed, looking in the direction his brother was pointing. "Come on Slick! What the fuck you doing? Let's go!"

Slick wasn't enthused about pursuing the shooter. However, the swaying power of the moment and the loyalty to his friend was too much to resist. There was no way that he could abandon his friends in a dangerous situation. He cocked his weapon and circled around to chase GK, who had made a right turn a few blocks ahead.

Slick reached the corner on which his GK had turned. He rounded the curb and found GK standing in the middle of the street. The military style gun that he wielded was unfamiliar to Slick but the bullets that rapidly exited the gun were not. Slick slammed on brakes. All three men opened their doors and sought cover from the relentless barrage of shells.

Cisco was the first to react. He knelt behind his opened door and returned fire through the rolled down window. Slick, who was closest to the line of fire, ducked behind the car. He spotted the safety of a brick porch and fired erratically back at the shooter, while running for cover. The whiz of rounds passing his ear and the sounds of them ricocheting off the bricks let Slick know to stay low.

Seymour had also retreated from the line of fire. He fired a few sporadic shots as he ran down the street away from the attack. Cisco was still positioned by his door taking police style shots at his mark. He had only one round left in the revolver and suddenly realized that their handguns were no match for GK's high powered weapon.

The assault finally ended with GK apparently running out of bullets and returning to his car. When Slick saw the vehicle move, he rose up and fired the remaining bullets in his gun. The shots were errant and the GK disappeared down the street. When the smoke cleared no one was injured. The only damage sustained was Cisco's whip, littered with a few holes.

The trio went back to the house to regroup. No sooner than they arrived the police were also pulling up. The detectives interrogated the usual suspects about their involvement. Cisco handled the men with charisma and led them to believe that he was the victim.

The police finally left and the boys immediately began to smoke and drink. Brain had returned and all four laughed and joked about what had just occurred. It seemed as if the young men were numb to the danger involved, in a state of euphoria, caused by the street dreams they were living.

The next few weeks continued in the same vein. Throughout the town, several different beefs had escalated, so there was a shooting almost every day. The police mistakenly linked all the action to the Powerful killing. Therefore, every time something occurred the law would implicate or question Slick and his boys.

Two weeks after the GK shootout, Seymour was shot in the back at the Studio, a local nightclub. He and Brain were sitting in the parking lot when an unknown gunman opened fire on the car.

The surprise attack left Brain unable to retaliate even though the he had a nine in the console beside him. He did gather himself eventually and returned a few rounds. The shooter escaped unscathed however, and Brain screeched out of the parking lot en route to the hospital.

The next week, the identity of the shooter was revealed as Boo, a career goon and stick-up artist. Cisco was the first to initiate revenge. He gathered Slick and Seymour, fresh out of the hospital, and the three embarked on the quest to find Boo. While searching through various drug spots one day, they spotted him standing in the yard of a crack house on the west side. Thinking that Boo hadn't seen them, Cisco instructed Slick to circle the block to give Seymour a direct shot at his attacker. Slick complied and Seymour readied the mack-10 from the back seat.

Boo must have seen the car. By the time Slick returned to the street, the potential victim was standing by the road, looking vulnerable and unaware. Slick approached as Seymour lifted the gun and aimed out the window.

Slick got closer, expecting to hear the clatter of the machine gun. Instead, the only shots would come from Boo, as he unveiled a .40 caliber pistol from a towel and opened fire. Slick instinctively threw the car in reverse and backed down the street. When they were out of harm's way, Slick snapped on Seymour.

"What the hell are you doing back there? You trying to get us killed or what? Why you ain't shoot?"

Seymour gave a sigh of exasperation. "The joint was on safety."

"What," Cisco interceded. "Man, you trippin'. You know you supposed to be ready to bust at all times!"

The three would not know how much Seymour's miscue came to getting them all killed until they reached home. Inspecting the car, Slick found two bullet holes less than an inch from the gas tank. Slick was infuriated as he envisioned the explosion that would have left him incinerated.

Several other incidents of violence erupted throughout the remaining weeks of that summer. Slick had come under fire one night from an unknown passerby on a moped. Seymour and Brain continued to accumulate riffs with various peoples around town. Even Dooky was involved in a war of his own that would eventually warrant the help of his childhood friends. Other groups around town were also at odds. These multiple skirmishes created volatile situations everywhere and transformed the normally quiet town into a virtual war zone.

As the year progressed, the turbulence subsided. Cisco began preparing for trial, while Slick was loathingly preparing for college. Meanwhile, no one had heard a word from Blaze. Rumors began to surface that he had delivered a statement to the prosecution, implicating Cisco. The allegation could never be confirmed, but the mere possibility of it had everyone on edge.

"We got to kill him," Cisco suggested one afternoon. "No way, I can't let him live and testify against me. After all I did for that dude and he going out like that!"

"Nah, ain't no way in hell Blaze turned state," Slick defended. "That's just something they saying to get you to take a plea."

"So why we ain't heard nothing from him then," Brain added. "The least he could do is holler at niggas and let us know what's up. It just seemed suspect for him to bounce like that."

"Y'all know how that nigga is," Slick included. "He just probably scared to death. Don't jump to conclusions. Let's just see how everything plays out."

Everybody had their own opinions. Cisco's suspicions were seemingly confirmed when Blaze returned only a few weeks before the trial like nothing happened. Cisco, true to form, welcomed him back with open arms. He recanted his initial thoughts of betrayal and allowed Blaze back into the circle, even letting him reside in the house again. Slick, however, was still somewhat skeptical because of the timing of his arrival.

On the first day of trial, Slick, Blaze and others accompanied Cisco to the courthouse. Cisco was confident that he would beat the case, believing that they had no legitimate witnesses. So when the district attorney offered a manslaughter plea of seven to ten years, it was rejected. Cisco's reasoning was if the plea was that low, the state must have a weak case. He would go to trial.

The next day, however, the prosecution informed the judge that they had a witness ready to testify on the state's behalf. Amongst pressure from his lawyers, Cisco agreed to accept a plea for second degree murder and avoid a possible life sentence. Because he rejected the original plea, the judge imposed a stiffer sentence of 16-20 years. This was done as an apparent punishment for wasting one day of the court's time.

There were mixed reactions when the judgment was announced. Ace, Cisco's girlfriend burst into tears. Trixie held her head in her hands and shook vigorously. The victim's family shook their heads in agreement and consoled each other with hugs.

Apparently, Cisco was unfazed. He glanced back at his supporters with a smile on his face and threw up the peace sign, as the bailiff took him into custody. This ability to handle adverse situations without emotion was a characteristic that testified to the man's inner strength. This strength would help maintain his sanity for a decade and a half under the dehumanizing conditions of the penal system.

Slick was devastated, losing his best friend all of a sudden. He'd been tight with Cisco since the ninth grade. Even though he had other friends, none were closer than Cisco. He felt betrayed by the world and sunk into a deep state of anger and bitterness. His actions reflected his mind state and he began to drift along aimlessly and get into more and more trouble.

This state of despair would last for Slick's first few months in college as he stayed mostly drunk and high. His spirits were lifted surprisingly by Cisco. Through letters and calls, Cisco encouraged Slick to use his predicament as motivation to succeed in life and not make the same mistake. Cisco realized early that he had made a terrible decision. This wisdom would continue to aid Slick through the years at times when he was at his lowest points. Those letters were no better needed than at a time like this, as Slick reflected on his past from the Virginia Beach jail cell.

Slick considered his friend's advice as he lay on his bunk. He was disappointed that he hadn't made good on his promise to Cisco two years ago of making something of his self. He vowed internally to get his act together and do something productive. He knew he could not sell drugs forever and decided right then to find a way out. This decision of righteousness would be tested severely in the near future as Slick's ties to the underworld would grow deeper and stronger.

7
Back on the Grind

September, 2003
Virginia Beach, VA

"Alright, gentlemen," the tall African-American jailer said to the prisoners. "Stay to the right of the hall. When you reach the holding cell, you'll be called individually for your court appearance."

Slick followed the instructions along with the other twenty inmates he was chained to. He was excited, however, because he had been granted a bond hearing. His lawyer, Tom Kenner, who was also a customer, assured him that he would receive bail.

He'd been there nearly a month. The hurricane that struck Virginia Beach the day after Slick's arrest was a category five and had rendered the city, along with the courts closed. He waited two weeks for the courts to reopen, only to be denied bail at his first appearance.

After the rejection, Slick called Wood, who alerted his lawyer to the situation. He also contacted the victim, Koko, and she agreed to show up for the hearing as an advocate for his release. Even though she caused the ordeal, Slick was nevertheless grateful for the gesture.

The proceedings went according to plan. Slick's lawyer spoke positively on his client's behalf. Koko was also questioned and expressed no objections to his release. The judge then interrogated Slick briefly and granted him a $10,000 bond. He thought the amount was excessive for a misdemeanor assault, but was nonetheless thankful. Slick knew that once he talked to his bail bondsman, who was also a customer, he'd be rescued. He dialed the number from memory when he returned to the cellblock.

"Joe Slack's bail bonding, this is Joe speaking."

"Joe! This is Slick. They finally gave me a bond. You gotta come get me a. s. a. p.!"

"Slick, it's about time. Everybody's been going crazy with all this garbage out here. Don't worry though. I'll be there as soon as I get back from Suffolk."

"Alright, I ain't going nowhere until you get here," Slick joked and hung up the phone.

Slick went to his bunk and gathered the things he'd accumulated during his stay. The large bag of canteen was a result of the daily gambling the inmates did. They played poker, tonk, spades and chess for the snacks, which were the only form of currency. Slick's reason for gambling was not to gain the items; but rather to satisfy his passion for games of chance.

Slick spent the next few hours listening to jailhouse war stories. He also distributed the canteen to those who really needed it. When the guard finally called his name, he gave a few pounds to his fellow inmates and then left the cell.

After the lengthy release process, Slick was let out through the back door of the jail. The first face he saw was Joe's, standing beside his bright yellow Hummer2. Slick embraced the muscular white man, as if they were brothers, and then hopped in the truck.

During the ride to his apartment, Slick and Joe discussed some of the happenings on the street. In the midst of the small talk, Slick's mind was churning. He did not want to pay Joe the full ten percent bond fee of $1000 dollars. Always the negotiator, Slick made a proposal of $500 cash and an equal amount in cocaine. Joe agreed. He made the same offer a few days later to his lawyer, who also consented.

The first thing Slick did upon entering his apartment was take an alcohol bath. After getting dressed, he went to check his stash spot for the cocaine. Even though he had vowed to stay clean, the urge that surfaced when he saw the drugs was insurmountable. Against every instinct in his mind, Slick reached into the bag and took four nostril-sized toots.

The drugs took effect at the same time that his cell phone rang. Slick read the name Pool on the caller identification. He was happy to receive the call from one of his most loyal customers. "Yo, what up P," Slick answered.

"Hey man, damn! What's going on? Where you been at."

"Nowhere, I just had a little situation I had to handle, nothing major," Slick responded coolly. "What can I do for you?"

"Oh, okay. Well, I need an ounce. Uh...it's not for me though. It's for my boss," Pool stammered nervously.

Slick was taken aback by the order. Pool had never purchased more than an eighth of an ounce. The fact that he'd just left jail coupled with the cocaine high made Slick leery of making the sale. However, he needed the money and was sure that Pool would never do anything to jeopardize his freedom.

"Okay. I'm gonna need thirteen hundred though. And I'm not meeting anybody new, so you gonna have to come buy yourself. Where you at," Slick asked authoritatively.

"I'm right around the corner. I'll get him to park a ways off and then walk. See you in a minute."

Slick made the sale and several others that night. His phone rang excessively once his customers knew he was home. Over the next few weeks, Slick made thousands of dollars and once again became entrenched in the lifestyle of drug use, promiscuity, and destruction, despite his intentions to do otherwise.

He'd been in this position before. When he moved to Virginia two years back, he had vowed to keep his hands and nose clean. He even went so far as to go to church and get saved. In hindsight, it seemed that once he made that decision, everything he ever wanted was presented to him on a silver platter. Girls, drug connects and money all appeared like magic. Though these things provided temporary pleasure, Slick was growing to see these things for what they really were; a ploy by an evil spiritual force intent on destroying his life.

Nevertheless, Slick continued to grind. He was making more money, moving more drugs and screwing more women than at any time in his life. This success began to incur the wrath and envy of some of his associates. Slick began to notice a change in demeanor of some of the boys he shot dice with.

"You already making too much money out here as it is," Boss said one day. "What's so bad about it is that you ain't even from here."

"Hell yeah," Ski added. "You got all the wops. We gon' mess around and get the young boys to rob you."

"Nigga, I can give you more than you can take," Slick responded with arrogant indifference. "Y'all niggas just gotta get your hustle game up. It's all out here for the taking. I'm just one man. You can get it too!"

Slick was immune to the off-hand threats and comments by now. He wasn't worried, despite barely knowing anyone he was dealing with. His outlook on things would soon change as events around him began to spiral out of control, leading him to question the motives of everyone around him.

A much needed hiatus was provided in December. Slick flew to New Orleans to watch Donnie and the Colts play the Saints. These trips were a warm solace as the camaraderie shared between the friends had remained the same since childhood. Slick reveled in the success of Donnie, who handled it extremely well. He never judged or condemned Slick for his actions, but certainly didn't condone them. Slick made it a point to attend as many games as he could to support his friend and enjoyed himself tremendously each time.

This time was no different. Slick and Wood, Donnie's brother, arrived in New Orleans meeting Donnie at the hotel. After checking in, they joined Donnie amongst the other players and their guests. Slick was used to the company of multi-millionaires after the initial surprise of how down to earth they were. Slick ate, mingled and chatted with various players until it was time for Donnie to report for meetings and other pre-game formalities. The three exchanged pleasantries and Donnie left with the rest of the team.

"What's the business," Wood asked Slick back in the room.

"Well, you know," Slick said excitedly. "We in New Orleans baby! I'm tryin' to hit Bourbon Street, the French Quarter, and all that good stuff. Oh yeah, and you know I got to crash the casino!"

"It is what it is," Wood replied. "Let's get it!" The two men showered, dressed and got prepared for a wild night.

The first few hours were cool. The men enjoyed the bars, clubs and action that embodied downtown New Orleans. It was everything Slick imagined and more. He talked to, drank with, and groped and grinded on women from all nationalities. Later, the two somehow got separated. Slick drunkenly found his way to Harrah's casino, in which he was ousted from a short while later.

While shooting craps, Slick refused to hold the dice over the table. Used to shooting c-lo in the streets, he wanted to hold the dice up by his head and shake them. After repeated warnings from the house, Slick became belligerent and laced the house man with several obscenities.

In his plastered state, Slick failed to notice the six security officers surrounding the table. When he was tapped on the shoulder, Slick knew it was automatically time to leave. He cashed out his winnings at the window and left without further incident.

After leaving, Slick went to more bars and continued to drink. The next morning he woke up in the room of a Hispanic looking black girl. He remembered meeting her, but had no idea how they got there or what had occurred. He left the room quietly without awakening her. He returned to his own hotel and found Wood, equally disheveled with a similar story. Both men laughed about their exploits as they prepared for the game.

The game surpassed the excitement of the previous night. The energy in the stadium was electric. Both high powered offenses took turns scoring touchdowns. The Colts finally won in overtime on a long pass from Manning to Harrison. Donnie had an outstanding performance with seven catches and a touchdown. He always seemed to excel when his family and friends were present. After the game, the three met briefly before departing in route to their respective flights home.

Returning from the trip, Slick was greeted with a travesty. When he attempted to unlock his door, the progress was impeded by the chain. Stunned, he walked to his back door and saw that it had been kicked in. He entered and found his apartment ransacked. Drawers were searched, beds and couches flipped and clothes were missing or displaced. It was obvious that someone had spent an ample amount of time searching. The culprits were disappointed as no drugs were in the house. Slick had just transported a large amount of money to North Carolina, where it would be accessible in case of emergency. Slick still felt violated and tried to think of who had the audacity to violate his space.

His first thought was of the many dice players he'd had over. One or two of them always knew his whereabouts and they were familiar with the area. Secondly, he thought of the random females he'd entertained at his home. He noted many of them that he'd spoken with while gone were aware of his absence. Last, but certainly not least he considered the customers he'd told that he was out of town when they called. Slick knew could not pinpoint any one in particular and accepted the matter as a warning to watch those around him.

Slick faced another dilemma because of the break in as well. The rental office had called the police because of the property damage. The next step was filing a report. This meant that the occupant had to be questioned. Slick was sure that they would question his ability to afford such a lavish place with no employment. Not to mention the nature of the crime, considered to be a tell-tale sign of illegal activity.

In addition, reports had previously been made to management about the constant flow of traffic coming to and from the residence. Other neighbors griped about the ever present odor of marijuana in the hall way. Along with the fact that Slick's name wasn't on the lease, this last incident was a clear indication that his jig was up in this neighborhood. Slick reacted with precision and formulated a plan.

"Yo Pool," Slick said to his client and friend one day.

"Hey! What up Slick," answered the twenty-year old white man. "What's goin' on?"

"I need a favor real quick," Slick explained. "I got to move from my spot but my credit ain't good. I'm a need you to do the application for me and I'm a look out for you real nice like."

"Okay, sure," Poole agreed. "Not a problem. Just let me know when and I'll handle it."

"Alright, then, I'll call you and let you know when," Slick closed, happy to have solved the matter.

In early January, Slick and Brad were scrounging the Virginia Beach Oceanfront for a suitable place. After browsing a while, Slick noticed a sleek set of studio loft apartments on Cypress Avenue, four blocks from the beachfront. The area appealed to him and Slick concluded this was the place. He gave Brad the money for the application fee and waited while he entered the rental office. A short while later, Brad came out with a lease agreement and a set of keys. Slick thanked him and compensated the favor with a sixteenth of cocaine.

Slick moved in a few weeks later. He adjusted to his new environment rather quickly People who lived closer to the water tended to be more laid back, which suited Slick's personality just fine. He began to interact with his new neighbors and visit various clubs on the strip nightly. His charm and verbal skills enabled him to woo his way into the scene with relative ease.

Meanwhile, Slick's business continued to thrive. Being in a more affluent area of the city, he attracted more upscale clientele. Bank managers, club owners, brokers and other businesspersons became not only his customers but his friends also. He was exposed to a different level of society; people with real money, old money.

They were just as impressed with Slick's intellect and business acumen and considered him more than just an average everyday drug dealer. These new associations led Slick to reconsider his lifestyle. One friend, Sanya suggested he get into real estate and Slick liked the idea. However, the money he was making doing nothing, was too much to abandon.

Consequently, Slick started to decrease contact with his dice crew. Though he still shot dice and conducted business with them regularly, this time he did not allow them to know where he stayed. He took the same precaution with the majority of his customers, having them meet him at a nearby bar or convenience store. The only other people he allowed in the apartment were the various women he entertained almost constantly.

Slick delighted in the cache of girls that he could call and would come at his request. Brittany, a twenty year old white girl, lived across the street. He would call her any time of night to fulfill his needs. Jocelyn, Mamie and Kim were three bi-sexual white girls Slick often invited over for wild escapades. Tonyella was a mixed black and white tall beauty from Hampton. She would spend weeks at a time with Slick, obeying his every command. Mi-mi, a straight jump-off from Chesapeake was one of his favorites. She was pretty, thick and best of all low maintenance. These and many other girls would help Slick relish in his life of excess for the next year.

As the year progressed, the girls were not enough entertainment. Slick still felt alone and began to increase his already excessive cocaine use. In turn, he became more reckless and lazy. He began allowing customers to come directly to his house and once again resumed hosting the dice games.

Slick was somewhat re-energized by the company of the hustlers. Spray, Kwan, and Flash were now getting large amounts of money in the streets. K J, Boss and Grim had also made leaps in the game and were living comfortably. Fredo, another one of the boys from the Oaks, had returned from school and picked up where he left off. The men began to frequent numerous nightclubs together. They dressed like stars spent money like it was fake, and pulled young women like Hefner at the Playboy Mansion.

They also had their share of altercations. With youthful exuberance, the men always seemed to find trouble while out. Many clubs were shut down because of the wily crew. Soon, several owners started to refuse entrance by implementing dress codes. They knew that the group wearing all white T's would not conform. Their caution was warranted as several complexes, cars and people were sprayed at or up by the trigger happy members of the group. Slick once again found himself embroiled in dangerous situations because of the company he kept.

There were also several riffs emerging within the circle, of which Slick was unaware. Before leaving for school, Fredo had turned his clientele over to K J, apparently his closest confidant. Upon returning, he requested his phone and business back. When K J refused, Fredo went and found a major connect and started generating three times the business he'd had before.

Also, someone within the group had stolen a large amount of work from K J. Somehow, the dope ended up in the hands of Flash, who then tried to sell it to Slick who refused. By the time K J heard who had the missing drugs, they were already sold. It was later revealed that his little sister had stumbled across the package and gave it to some young boy she knew. He, not knowing what to do, gave it to Flash. This incident, along with normal jealousy and money issues began to cause conflict regularly. Soon, it would be nearly every man for himself.

Slick sensed the tension and started to implement his exit strategy. He took the advice of Sanya. She thought his personality and people skills would be perfect for real estate brokerage. Slick enrolled in a night class and breezed through the course. He also passed the state examination on the first attempt but was denied licensing because of his lengthy record. Slick was able to appeal the decision and tried to maintain a level of normalcy while he awaited the results.

In the interim, though, he was still partying. One night, in the fall of 2004 he allowed a few girls and a few of the boys over. The women outnumbered the men two to one. All the women were indulging in coke and ecstasy. Slick had also popped one of the aphrodisiac pills. Before the night was over, Slick and his friends had participated in a drug fueled episode of sexual debauchery. The next afternoon, Slick had still not been to sleep. Just as he was about to lay down, he was disturbed by his telephone.

"Shoot something, nigga!" It was K J, begging for a dice game. Even though Slick was disoriented from the ecstasy and in need of sleep, he never neglected a challenge when it came to gambling.

"Bring your fat ass on," Slick responded in a delusional tone.

"Okay. I'm a call the boys and we coming straight there."

The boys came and the dice game began. Slick was totally out of it, but continued to make outlandish bets against K J who had an unusually hot hand. Even the bystanders and shooters that came and went noticed the large amounts of money Slick was squandering in his hypnotized state. By the end of the night, Slick had lost nearly seven thousand dollars. Most of it was won by K J, who eventually quit. Slick watched a small fortune walk out the door as the winner laughed and joked. Slick was left with the impossible task of recouping his losses from the remaining players.

The next day, he was greeted by a loud horn in the parking lot. Slick went outside and saw K J in the driver's side of a new Lexus 300. Flash, Grim, and Akbar accompanied the driver, who yelled out the window to Slick.

"Yeah nigga, you see what you bought me yesterday. I would tell you to shoot something but you probably aint got nothing left!"

Slick caught the bait as it was tossed. In a display of masculine bravado, Slick pulled out the four grand in his back pocket and held it in the air. "Man, I got cake for days," he stated. "I'm still playing with my 96 money. You ain't even close clown!"

Flash let out a laugh. Not wanting to be outdone, he chimed in on the debate. "You always talking 'bout some 96 money. You ain't got no dough!" He hopped out of the car with a large wad of cash in each hand. "I got ten grand in the bank! Now who want some?"

The men filed out of the car and entered behind Slick. More players came and the game once again became intense. They shot late into the night and Slick managed to recoup nearly two thousand dollars from the previous day.

The next week Slick decided he would spend some of his money himself. Since he'd practically bought K J a car, there was no reason he shouldn't buy himself one as well. He called Pool and requested to use his credentials again. Pool consented and later that day Slick drove off the car lot with a pearl white Lincoln Executive Town Car. Slick drove home on cloud nine. The style, body and smell of the new car made Slick look and feel like the legitimate business man he so desperately longed to become.

A few days later Slick was summoned to a dice game at Fredo's. He made the twenty minute drive to the downtown Virginia Beach area. The game lasted nearly an hour until Slick and Worm got into an argument over a disputed point. Fredo joined in and sided with Worm. A brief scuffle ensued between the three and was quickly broken up.

Slick left the game undisturbed as quarrels were common among the shooters. He had squabbled with nearly everyone in the group at one time or another. He returned to his home and was greeted by the familiar sound of a chain blocking his entrance. His heart sank as he walked to the back expecting the worst.

The method of operation was different this time. The sliding glass door that led to his bedroom was pried open. He squeezed through the opening and was shocked to find nothing disturbed. He immediately checked his closet where the numerous stashes of money were kept. He noticed an open pocket on a pair of slacks. He knew then that the five thousand dollars in hundred dollar bills had been taken.

Slick proceeded to check the various other hiding spots where money was held. They were all secure. Fortunately, the robber was satisfied with the take. If he would have searched extensively, tens of thousands of dollars in illegal currency would have gone missing. Slick racked his brain wondering who would know exactly where to search. Once again the prospects were many as he had become extremely lax in his dealings.

Someone close to Slick was scrutinizing his every move and plotting on any opening to obtain his fortunes. Evidently, his lavish spending and frivolous money habits had brought out the wolves like blood to sharks. Somebody was hungry and saw Slick and his possessions as a full course meal.

Slick now knew that moving was again inevitable. The same issues had emerged as from the last residence and Slick did not want to live under those conditions. He would not go far, however, as he had gotten accustomed to the area. Also, most of his business was centered at the oceanfront and he had a comfortable routine for moving his product.

When the report was made, Slick was intensely questioned by the police. "Do you know why anyone would want to break in your place," the forensics officer asked. "And nothing was taken. This seems strange to me. What do you do for a living?"

Slick ignored the questioned and feigned ignorance. "I have no idea who did it or why. Like I said, I wasn't here so I don't know."

The property manager also approached Slick with accusations. "Sir you are not even on the lease," the elderly blond woman stated. "Furthermore, we have not seen Mr. Brady since he rented the apartment. We know you have been staying here and the maintenance personnel already told me about the traffic that comes to your door. We're gonna investigate this just to let you know."

There was no way Slick was going to remain in the apartment another night. Avoiding the heat, he decided to visit his friend Amber for a few days. Amber was a white girl who acted black. Her fat tail and attitude gave proof to her having been adopted by a black family. She stayed across the water in Newport News, a forty-five minute drive away from Slick's crumbling palace.

Slick spent the next two days drinking, smoking, eating and screwing with Amber. He loved his playmate's energy, not to mention her freaky ways. She was another damsel who would do anything Slick ordered.

As a gift to her friend, Amber invited her foster sister over for their last night together. Slick enjoyed another episode of two on one as both of the voluptuous young girls took turns pleasuring him.

The next morning Slick headed back to the beach. He had been on break for too long and his customers had begun to get restless. He also needed to start his search for a new spot. Before he got to the interstate, however, he noticed blue lights in his rearview mirror. He changed lanes to let the vehicle pass. The driver of the police car also changed lanes and sounded the siren. Slick reluctantly pulled over, trying to think of a reason he was being pulled.

Even though Slick wasn't dirty, he didn't have a license. He was also nervous because of an outstanding warrant in the beach. Somehow he had failed to make the court date for the assault on Koko and a writ was issued. Slick thought of a way to escape incarceration as the officer approached.

"What's the problem officer," Slick asked politely.

"License and registration please," the large white officer demanded, ignoring the question.

"Honestly, I don't have my wallet on me. I left it at the hotel. I'm just visiting from North Carolina," Slick lied. "I can give you my information though. Did I do something wrong?"

The officer took out a pen and pad, continuing to ignore the driver's question. "Name, address, and social please," he said sternly.

"Ronnie Faison... 01, 10, 1978. My social is 242-55-9189," Slick recited.

"Okay. Turn off the engine. I'll be back in a second."

Slick took a deep breath as the cop walked away. He had memorized the information of his childhood friend years ago. He had never used the data before, but he was sure that his friend was in good standing with the Department of Motor Vehicles. He was in for a rude awakening.

The officer returned with news that his friend's license was also suspended in Virginia. Ronnie had failed to pay a ticket a few years back. Slick was handcuffed and placed in the back of the vehicle. With incarceration certain, he decided to disclose his true identity, since it would inevitably be revealed by fingerprinting. He was transported to the Newport News jail and given a $10,000 dollar bond for driving. An additional hold was placed on him for extradition to Virginia Beach.

He was then assigned to the dungeon, a row of small two man cells reserved for offenders who had pending charges in other towns. This section operated under twenty four hour lockdown, with a shower every other day.

However, the phone did come around daily and Slick immediately made arrangements to get the $1000 dollars to his bondsman. Slick was still not released after the bond was posted. He now had to wait for extradition to Virginia Beach. He was told by jail personnel that the process could be as long as a month.

Slick once again found himself in the confines of an eight by ten cell. He didn't want to inform anyone of his whereabouts, especially his family. The only person he felt comfortable talking to was Wood, who always made sure that Slick's wishes were carried out in times of distress. When contacted, Wood informed Slick that his mother and sisters had been trying to reach him and were worried. Slick knew he would have to call. There was no way that he could be absent for a month and no one be concerned. Resigned to the circumstances, Slick swallowed his pride and dialed the long distance number to North Carolina.

The pain in his mother's voice when she learned of her son's plight nearly brought tears to Slick's eyes. He'd been the cause of much stress for his mother in previous years. Here he was again, at the age of twenty five, in the same predicament he'd been in at eighteen. If he kept living as he did now, Slick knew that the pattern would continue. He felt distraught as he listened to his mother's words of encouragement and concern. Shame overcame him and he vowed to her that he would do something positive with his life. After hanging up the phone, the heartfelt words of his mother resonated in his mind for the rest of the night.

As he lay on his bunk, he entered a deep state of reflection. Incarceration always induced a time of self-examination for Slick. He began to think of the fruitless and unproductive years of his life. His mind transported him back to another period of life when his actions were sporadic and aimless. He thought of the years he spent in Goldsboro after his short stint at college. He became frustrated as he began to analyze those events and tried to discern how it all went wrong.

8
Back to the 'Boro

August, 1997
Goldsboro, NC

Slick's half-hearted attempt at college had been a failure. After the shooting, studying became less of a priority and he stopped attending classes. The days were now spent smoking, drinking and finding new angles to make money. He longed for the time when he made easy money selling crack. His weed business had slowed tremendously and Slick became homesick. He started to miss the friends and girls he'd left behind in Goldsboro.

By the end of the second semester, Slick realized he was finished with school. When his grades arrived in the mail that summer his parents agreed he was wasting his time and their money. Slick returned to Goldsboro from Durham inconspicuously. His plans were vague. The incarceration of his best friend and the recent events in his own life had the mind of the young man stagnant.

Slick found that things had somewhat changed during his yearlong absence. With Cisco in prison, Brain had moved to South Carolina with his father. He was on the run from gun and drug charges and enjoyed a temporary haven from prosecution in the small town. Seymour was also sent to prison on an unrelated drug case. Even after his release, Slick and Seymour's contact would be limited. The older man seemed to distance himself from his one-time apprentice. Slick had his own reasons for cutting ties with his mentor.

Before going to college, Slick had given Seymour money in advance for a package. Seymour used the cash to pay his connection on a previous debt, expecting more consignment. When Seymour was put on hold, however, he had nothing to give Slick. Weeks went by and Slick remained patient, scoring from others. After a few more weeks of broken promises and put-offs, Slick left for college without the dope or being given his money back. Slick never mentioned it again, but never forgot. His former admiration for the man turned to disdain. Whenever he saw Seymour now, words were few and far in between.

Slick also had severed ties with Blaze. He harbored resentment towards his once close friend because of the perceived role of Blaze in Cisco's confinement. His anger culminated when he punched Blaze in the face a few weeks after returning. The two fought as Slick accused his friend of being a snitch. At the end of the scuffle both men departed in separate directions. Later, Slick would regret his premature judgment. The damage was done, however, and it would be years before the two friends would talk cordially again.

Slick wasn't completely alone though. Stubbs, whom he found out was his cousin, had dropped out of school and was earning cash on the streets moving weed. Since Stubbs still stayed close, he and Slick associated more often.

Dooky was also still around. He continued to move pounds of smoke while working as a front at a family convenience store. He also managed to keep incurring dangerous beefs. Slick would see these two and others daily as they gathered on the same strip to push their products.

"Audubon" was a small residential street in the middle of town. Most of the residents had lived on the block for years and everyone knew each other. The neighborhood was quiet and people considered themselves family.

Slick's great aunt lived on a corner house with a few of her kids and seven grandchildren. The oldest two grandchildren, Blow and Quay, were Slick's age. Along with their parents and siblings, they provided action for the area as something was always happening at the residence.

Slick had known both boys since elementary but didn't discover their kinship until high school. It was then that he began to frequent the house in which his cousins sold drugs, drank, and caroused freely. Though his aunt didn't condone their ways, she was often times too busy with other matters to prevent it. Later, when the activity escalated, she would charge the young men a fee for the privilege of hustling in her yard.

A few houses from Slick's cousins lived two brothers, Bash and Bang. Though Bang was the youngest, he progressed from selling nickel bags of weed to being a distributor of pounds around the city. Bash also dabbled in the game and sold minimal amounts of weed and crack in the area. Together, the four childhood friends transformed the once docile dwelling place, into one of the many known havens for drugs in the city.

As the money came, many childhood friends began to claim the area. Breeze, a long-time friend of Blow, Bang and Quay's soon became a fixture on the set. He sold weight in crack and served as somewhat of an enforcer. Smalls, another friend of the group, started appearing regularly to peddle his contraband. A few years older than the rest, he loved to drink and keep things stirred up. AZ, who was now knee deep in the coke trade, also stopped through in his free time between making moves. Because of his name he tried to keep a low profile whenever possible. The presence of these and other hustlers certified Audubon Street as a bona fide spot.

Slick resumed where he left off selling weed and crack. Unlike his cohorts, Slick preferred to move around rather than stay in one spot. He took his product on any set and had no problems at all. He gambled on the block, rolled dice on Slocumb Street, hustled in the projects and chilled on the North side. He considered Goldsboro his city and didn't let anyone tell him where he couldn't get money. Crews from every set knew him and gave him respect for being a stand-up guy. Slick would come to realize, however, that some of his fellow peers were dissatisfied with things and wanted to start trouble just for fun. Just weeks after his return, Slick's life would be placed in jeopardy by a long-time associate.

One day Slick was on Audubon fooling around with a camcorder when he noticed an ex-girlfriend across the street. Kansas and her family had recently moved in the area, but Slick had paid her little attention. Though he didn't mess with Kansas anymore, he was still cool with her and her family. He was actually developing an interest for her cousin, Keisha, whom he noticed getting out of the car.

Accompanied by Blow, Quay, and Breeze, Slick walked across the street to the girls who were standing in the yard with their kids. He began to tease them with the camera. "Y'all ladies got anything worth-while to say to the audience?"

"Hey Slick! Hey Blow! What up fellows," Keisha spoke to the boys. "Here you go. Here's a kiss for the camera!" The girl puckered her lips and leaned into the lens. She then walked away, looking back to make sure Slick was filming her rear as she walked.

What up Kansas," Quay said. "I see y'all got your feet out today. I like that. What's the deal?"

"You know us. We chilling, trying to stay out of this heat and away from these bama's out here," Kansas said. She then gave a half wave to Slick to indicate that the last comment was directed at him.

"Okay, folks," Slick commentated to his false audience. "Look how she's acting. She think she all of this and that huh? I guess that's how they do it where she from!"

Slick continued to joke with the camera. A few minutes later, Corey, Kansas' new boyfriend rode up with his brother and another homeboy. Corey was a livewire and always seemed to look for trouble. He had approached Slick before concerning the girl but Slick insisted that he did not want her. The two had dissolved the issue and began hanging together, hustling and gambling in the same spots.

This time Corey was in no mood to talk. The fury in his eyes burned when he saw Slick standing in his girlfriend's yard. He exited the car, walked over and yelled into the group of people. "Man, what you doing at my girl's house!" He charged at Slick as the bystanders intervened. "Hell, nah nigga! You ain't got no business over here! What he doing all in your face," the angry man asked his girl.

Slick removed the lens from his eye to see Corey enraged. He tried to remain calm as he addressed him. "A look yo, I'm just over here filming them and the kids. That's all. It ain't nothing else going on homey." Slick stepped out to the street in an attempt to diffuse the situation.

Likewise, Kansas stood in front of Corey, trying to curtail the man's anger by agreeing with Slick. "Calm down baby! It ain't nothing. He just walked over here a few minutes before you came. Please....just chill!"

"Hell nah! Move out my way! Me and this nigga finna handle this right now! I'm tired of niggas thinking I'm playing! What y'all think this is?"

Slick still tried to walk away while being berated by Corey. Feeling his manhood being challenged, he grew tired of the insults and became irate himself. He turned around and reproached Corey. "Nigga you ain't said nothing. We can get it on right now. It ain't shit!" Slick sat the camera on the curb and prepared to square up to his opponent.

Corey's brother, Rell, and Slick's cousins interceded and prevented the two men from fighting. In the midst of the confusion, Corey broke away, made his way to the camcorder, and football kicked it into the streets. Slick heard the crackling of the device and was livid. Before he could react, Corey already had been coerced to the vehicle. He yelled numerous threats as the car pulled away.

"I'm coming back! Believe me! Y'all niggas better not be here when I get back! I promise you!"

Slick returned to the yard where family and bystanders gathered to discuss what happened. The camera was beyond repair and Slick was furious. He listened to Breeze's declaration of dislike for Corey. Revenge entered

Slick's heart and he vowed to make Corey pay one way or another.

When everyone thought that the incident was over, Corey reappeared in the same car but without his brother. His only companion was the all black mac-.22 that he clutched when he got out and started firing.

Rat-a-tat tat tat.....tat-a-tat- tat-tat-tat!!

"Hell yeah...I told y'all niggas I was coming back! What now!"

Corey unloaded the weapon in the direction of the crowd. Everyone scattered. Slick veered towards the front porch, dodging the shots until he reached the door. The gunfire continued while Slick made his way through the house towards the back door. He made it out the back to find Corey standing in the backyard still firing. By the time he saw Slick he was out of ammunition. The gunman then hopped back in the car and pulled off real slow as if nothing had occurred.

After the smoke cleared, no one was hit. A few days later Slick ran into Corey when they were both by themselves. In an action that surprised Slick, Corey apologized and offered to pay for the camera. Even more, he then tried to give Slick a nine millimeter pistol. Slick refused the gun but did spend two hours gambling with him afterwards.

Everyone wasn't as lenient as Slick was. A few weeks later, Slick walked up on a conversation between Quay, Breeze, and Dooky. They were standing on Audubon smoking and drinking as usual.

"I don't care," Breeze said. "When I see him I'm going straight to him. Even if he got the strap on him....we can take it there too!" Breeze had shot a couple of cats as teenager like Dooky had. Both still remained trigger happy and apt to shoot, even when it wasn't necessary.

"I got my joint right here on my hip now," Dooky chimed in. He had been shot by Corey a couple of years earlier. The two had been engaged in an ongoing beef ever since then. "So you know what it is when I see him. I'm blasting on sight. That nigga grimy! Ain't gon let him catch me slipping no more!"

"Who y'all talking about," Slick interjected.

"Who else," Quay answered. "That nigga that love to hate. The nigga that run around here hiding in bushes late at night." Quay had his run-ins with Corey too. Though he was the smallest, Quay had the biggest mouth and liked to talk the most junk. He could hold his own, but many times everyone else would come to his defense if he had any problems. Many issues stemmed from incidents involving Quay's mouth.

"Yeah, I seen that nigga the other day. He came up like nothing ain't happen. That nigga must be crazy," Slick added. "But then again I must be too for sitting down to gamble with him!"

"Yeah, you crazy," Quay joked "You'll gamble for peanuts with a retarded monkey if he asked you to."

"Yeah, and all you do is talk. You should be a commentator for ESPN as much as you tell," Slick came back.

The two cousins went back and forth until Breeze interrupted. "I'm for real though Slick. I'm telling you, watch that nigga! He a snake, man! You can't trust a nigga like that!"

"That nigga ain't crazy as he act though," Slick informed. "He got good sense."

As they were talking, Corey appeared about thirty yards away in all army fatigue. Dooky was the first to notice him walking in the middle of the street. Slick was busy rolling a blunt and didn't observe the scene. Dooky whispered to Quay.

"You got your gun on you, yo?"

"Nah, why, what up?"

"Nothing. Just go in the house if you ain't strapped," Dooky instructed reaching in his waistband.

Breeze took a few steps back from the curb as Corey neared ten yards away. Slick stood beside Dooky preoccupied with the blunt. He was alerted to the tension when Corey and Dooky locked eyes.

"What you looking at," Corey challenged.

Dooky said nothing. True to his word, he ripped the .40 caliber from the holster in his waist and fired rapidly at his target. The loud bang in Slick's ear caused him to stagger backwards. Facing the surprise outburst of rounds, Corey ducked under the porch of a neighbor. He pulled his gun but was unable to get off a shot.

"Fuck you, nigga! Yeah nigga! What! Take that, take that," Dooky yelled, shooting fourteen rounds at Corey.

With only three more shots, Dooky kept the gun trained on the man while he got into his car. He backed down the road and sped away. Unhurt, Corey raised from his crouch and ran to the street. He tried to fire at the car but it had already turned the corner. Slick regained his composure just in time to see Corey running down the street. Because of this incident, Slick would not leave home without his .380 for the next month.

Events like these were not uncommon in the small city. With little or nothing constructive to do, minor disputes over money and women often erupted in violence.

Slick's other hang out, "the block", was notorious for violence and drugs. In its heyday, the four block radius of pool halls, clubs, and crack houses was the epicenter for illegal activity. Slick, along with many others, paid dues and learned the ropes from experiences on the strip. When he returned, however, an aggressive campaign by the police department had dismantled the area and most of the buildings were condemned or destroyed.

One pool hall, however, continued to operate. Willie Simmons was the eighty year old owner of the last building standing. He used the old shack for high stakes card games and as a haven for crack addicts to use. Slick and hustlers would still spend time on the block because of the games and drug sales. Along with Audubon, the block became Slick's second home. He spent much time learning on the block with some of his homeboys from school.

One of these was Bro. He and Slick had attended school together until Bro starting getting in trouble. He had several drug and robbery charges before reaching the age of eighteen. Slick never saw his buddy in that negative light so he kept it tight with Bro. Others whom he'd robbed despised or wanted to kill him. Dooky had even had a few altercations with him. As usual, Slick didn't allow their beef to interfere with either relationship.

One week when the two were on the block, Bro pulled out a large sum of money. "You trying to play twenty dollars head up tonk nigga," he asked Slick counting the money.

"Oh lord," Slick replied. "Who you done robbed now, my nigga?"

"Man I hit a big lick last night. Caught a nigga coming through the cut slipping," Bro said with a devilish laugh. "Nah, for real, I just been on the grind hard all this week." Bro pulled out a small brown paper bag filled with what looked like crack and showed it to Slick.

Slick looked at the drugs and didn't doubt the possibility that they were counterfeit. He also wasn't sure about his friend's claim of innocence. "Be straight up for real. Just tell me so I'll know. I don't want nobody to come dumping all crazy when I'm around you."

"Please nigga," Bro said raising the bottom of his shirt. "They run up on this four-five they want too. Somebody gone have a bad day! What's up though? You trying to gamble or what," he said, deliberately changing the subject.

"You know I stay ready. Willie right up there too. We can get it on right now."

The two walked to the dilapidated building and were greeted by the old man sitting at the table. "Hey Johnny," he said when they walked in. Willie didn't see too good and called everybody Johnny. It was only when a person got close did he recognize them. "Y'all come on in. Have a seat. What y'all bring me?"

"Man, we ain't come in here for all that," Bro said. "You know what time it is. Get your old' ass up and deal these cards, talking all crazy."

"This my place son," Willie responded, but sill grabbing the cards. "I can say what I want. You get you a place and you can do what you want to in it," he said sarcastically.

The three men talked trash with each other while playing cards. The game lasted until nighttime as other players came and joined. Slick thought no more about all the cash his friend had.

A few days later, Slick was on the block when he saw Fresh and his girl ride by. Fresh was also a schoolmate of Slick's from the west side of town. He and Slick smoked and gambled during school and maintained association in the streets. Fresh was normally a subdued, laid back type until one crossed him. He looked unusually angry to Slick when he pulled up to the curb.

"Yo, what up Slick," he said. "You seen Bro around here?"

"Last time I seen him, he was over there on Chestnut street with King and them boys. Why, what up with you?"

"It ain't shit my nigga. I'm chillin'," he said starting to pull away. "I'ma holla' at you later though." Slick watched the man and his girl speed off towards Chestnut Street.

Slick thought nothing of the matter. Fresh and Bro were from the same part of town and were known to get money together. That's why he was so surprised to find out an hour later that Bro had been shot five times. Even more disturbing was the fact that his friend Fresh was the perpetrator.

A story circulated that Bro had broken into Fresh's house and stolen a safe full of money. Word got back and Fresh went searching for Bro. He found him on a strip and hopped out of the car with a .357 Magnum in hand. He shot him first in the legs, crippling him. After asking him about the money, he pointed the gun to Bro's head. In his fury, Fresh pulled the trigger. Luckily, Bro grabbed the barrel and absorbed the bullet in his palm. Although he had a golf ball sized hole in his hand, Bro was spared with his life. Fresh, having accomplished his revenge fled the scene, leaving Bro bleeding on the pavement.

Slick visited Bro after he was released from the hospital. He listened to his friend defend himself while lying in the bed unable to walk. "That nigga talking about I took his safe. When I got hit, I didn't have but $300 dollars in my pocket. If I took all that change, where is it at now then?"

Slick thought of a few ideas of what could have happened to the money, but declined to say. "All I'm saying is be careful. I don't know what you doing out there, but whatever it is, be safe."

Bro's predicament had no effect on Slick. He spent the remainder of the year doing the same things: gambling, hustling, smoking and drinking. Before the end of the year, he found himself back in trouble again. This time it was for a gun.

Slick was gambling in the pool hall one night when the police walked in. They didn't normally bother the gamblers but that night Weeks was present. Weeks was an overweight black cop who carried a vendetta against Slick and seized every opportunity to harass him. Upon searching Slick, Weeks found a loaded .357 Magnum on his waist. The gun turned out to be stolen and Slick was booked on felony gun charges.

After posting the $5000 bond, Slick hit the streets like nothing occurred. He returned to the actions that got him incarcerated. He rarely stayed home and his parents were increasingly concerned for him.

Around New Years, however, Slick received a late Christmas gift. In a two day span, he managed to win over $8000 from Willie playing cards. This was nowhere near the amount that he'd lost to Willie over time, but it was nice to get a sum of money that large.

The next week, Slick had a ball. He bought a Buick, went shopping, and blew money at the club. He also bought a few ounces of crack and a pound of weed to sell. He became comfortable again in the game. Since he was not as hungry as before, he centered his operation back on Audubon, where the money was slower but there was less competition.

One day, while walking in the neighborhood, Slick ran into Amp. He had just moved into the neighborhood and was standing with Blow and Bash. Slick was tight with Amp from the block days and the two always joked when they saw each other.

"What up Lips," Amp said laughing.

"It ain't nothing Headdie Murphy," Slick shot back giving the man a light dap. Slick noticed the dollar bill full of coke in his opposite hand.

"What up cousin," Blow said, punching Slick softly in the chest.

"I'm chillin, trying to get this paper," Slick said. "What y'all up too?"

"Oh nigga, you see what we doing," Amp informed, holding out the bill. "You know how I get down so don't even trip." The man took too small toots after his speaking.

"Let me hit that too, before you kill it," Bash interjected.

"Yeah and I got it after you," Blow said with no shame.

Slick was not surprised to see Blow and Bash sniff. He had suspected it for a while and rumors were out but he couldn't tell. Amp, however, had used coke many times around Slick and even offered it to him on occasions. Slick had never wanted any and always refused. Looking at the relative ease in which each man ingested the drug, he decided he'd give it a shot.

"Fuck it! Let me hit some of that blow too Amp," Slick blurted.

"Who, you? You wanna get jacked? You know you good, but I didn't know you got down though."

"This gonna be my first time. I just wanna see what it's like."

Slick joined the rotation and passed the coke back and forth a few times. He felt nothing at first. When the drug first drained down his throat, he felt a heightened sense of awareness. It was a euphoric feeling like he'd never felt before. He had a certain burst of energy and an uncontrollable urge to go somewhere.

"Okay, I'm a get back with y'all later," he said walking away.

"Hold up Slick," Blow said. "Where you going so fast boy?"

"Man, I'm finna ride. I got something to do."

"Alright, wait for me. I'm a roll with you."

The two hopped in the car. Blow told Slick about a party in Mt. Olive, a neighboring town. Feeling the rush, Slick drove recklessly, while Blow rolled weed. The two cousins hung out all night going from spot to spot. In the morning they parted ways. Though they didn't do any more cocaine that night, a bond had been formed. This was the start of many drug fueled nights that the two would share.

Over the next few months, Slick's behavior had changed. He had crossed the threshold and began doing wild things. He, Blow, and Bash were sniffing coke on a daily basis. His alcohol intake and tolerance ballooned as a result. He found himself at the liquor store frequently. Nothing mattered to the young man as his brain stayed clouded with intoxicants. This behavior would once again lead him to jail.

One night later in 1998, Slick was driving, drunk as usual. Stubbs was on the passenger side. Slick travelled the city with the music blasting. He sped through curves and turned corners wildly, sipping Myers rum straight from the bottle. His erratic maneuvers startled his rider who let it be known.

"Slow your rabid ass down," Stubbs yelled over the music. "What you trying to do, kill us both?"

"I got this over here nigga. You just sit over there and roll up or something!"

"I'm telling you man. You better slow down, that's all I'm saying. You know it's hot as fire over here in West Haven."

Slick increased the volume on the radio to drown the voice of reason. He turned the corner wildly into the housing projects and ended up on the wrong side of the road. To further antagonize Stubbs, Slick decided to play chicken with the oncoming vehicle. He floored the gas pedal while Stubbs looked on. The cars got closer and at the last second Slick swerved, narrowly missing the other driver.

The sight that registered in Slick's peripheral vision was sickening. The blue and black writing on the passing car read Goldsboro Police Department, specifically Weeks. The thought had barely sunk in before the officer made a u turn and engaged his lights and sirens.

"Oh shit," Stubbs exclaimed. "That was the law you stupid fool! I told your dumb ass to be easy!"

"We straight nigga," Slick answered calmly. "Long as you ain't dirty, we good."

Slick thought fast to have been so drunk. He killed his headlights and turned the next corner. He then made the next left onto Rockefeller court, which ended in a cul-de-sac. He stopped in the middle of the street and bailed out of the car. Stubbs stayed in his seat since he didn't have any warrants or drugs.

The police rounded the corner just in time to see Slick disappear between the project apartments. He reached the back of the complex and entered a wooded area. Submerged in the trees, Slick hopped over the train tracks and landed into a gigantic hole. His intoxication coupled with his shortness of breath made him stay put. He sat there quietly, while listening to the police coordinate the search. After twenty minutes, the police were still combing the area even using a canine unit for assistance.

After waiting a little longer and not hearing any voices, Slick assumed the coast was clear. He climbed out of the hole and emerged from the woods. A few steps later he was surrounded by four officers who appeared out of the darkness. With their guns drawn, Slick had no other option but to lay face down on the ground as he was commanded.

Slick was charged with DWI in addition to several other charges. He bonded out the next day, but had to forfeit his car. A prior DWI from his college days made him subject to a statute for repeat offenders. Nevertheless, Slick continued to play the streets. He was oblivious to the mountain of trouble he was building for himself. Without goals and ambitions, Slick couldn't perceive the long lasting consequences of his acts.

Without a car, Slick was relegated for the most part to Audubon. However, he hadn't realized that his aunt's house had become a major strip. Hustlers from all over town had begun to make money, while the originators like Quay, Blow, and Bash weren't really profiting. Since his family started the set, Slick took offense to outsiders who infiltrated only to make money. His attitude towards the status quo intensified the more he hung around.

Slick wasn't the only one feeling sour on Audubon. Smalls, a friend of Blow and Bang was also starting to trip. He wasn't making the money he thought he should and he was frustrated.

One day, Smalls and Blow were having a drunken dispute. Disagreements were not uncommon amongst the crooks. This one, however, became physical. After fussing with Blow, Smalls went on a tirade, confronting everyone around indirectly. Then, without warning, he grabbed Blow and slammed him to the ground.

"Yeah, now what! Whoever want it can get it," Smalls yelled addressing no one in particular. "Y'all a bunch of pussy niggas anyway! Ain't nan one o' y'all faggots gon' do nothing anyway!"

Slick watched Blow pick himself off the ground. He also listened to Smalls rant until he could take no more.

"Homeboy! You need to take that foolishness somewhere else," Slick said seriously. "I don't care what you got going on, but all that shit you talking don't mean nothing!"

"Yeah, nigga," Smalls responded. "I'm talking mostly to you anyway nigga! I don't like your ass anyway! What you wanna do?"

Slick, having said his piece, turned his back to the man and walked away. Seizing the moment, Smalls grabbed him from behind, and slammed him to the ground. The impact of his chest hitting the ground infuriated Slick. Even more, the amount of people watching compelled Slick to retaliate.

After getting up, Slick remembered the five shot thirty-eight snub nose he had in his pocket. Without thinking, he pulled the pistol out and aimed it at Small's head. The fear Slick saw as Small's ducked was revenge enough. But since he'd pulled the gun Slick figured he might as well use it.

"No! No Slick, don't do it," a voiced screamed close to his ear.

Kiki, Quay's sister, jumped in the line of fire while Slick tried to get a clean shot. This moment of interference allowed Slick to relent. When Smalls noticed the gun was lowered. He staggered drunkenly to his car and drove away.

The incident subsided within a few days, but tensions were still high. A week later, Slick was riding with Dooky when he saw Small's car parked at the D&C, a local mini mart. After further inspection, Slick saw him standing in the doorway of the store. Slick told Dooky to pull in the parking lot. When Small's noticed that it was Slick in the car, he went to his own vehicle as if he had a weapon.

"Take me to get my joint real quick Dook," Slick inquired.

"Alright, I'm a go get mine too, just in case," Dooky added. "You never know with these crab ass niggas here."

Dooky made the five minute drive and he and Slick returned to the store. Smalls was still at the door when they pulled in. But this time he was on the phone. No sooner than Dooky parked did the police pull up behind them. They were immediately extracted from the car by Officer White. White was a cool policeman who patrolled the projects. He knew many of the criminals from their elementary days and was therefore more lenient. Slick and Dooky held their breath while White searched the car.

"Whose guns are these," he said a few minutes later. He walked towards the men holding the .38 and baby .9 millimeter pistols.

Slick was speechless. He knew the serial numbers had been removed from his weapon. If charged, it would constitute another felony. Dooky, on the contrary, thought fast and replied.

"That's my brother gun right there," he said pointing at the nine.

White looked expectantly to Slick. All the young man could do, is shake his head. Since, he knew the youths and their parents, White had pity on them. He saw the two for what they were: misguided young men who had been influenced by society. He let them go without charging them but also kept the guns. Slick wondered how much the officer would resell the guns for on the black market. He also contemplated Smalls' actions, seeing the man still inside the store grinning. It was no doubt in his mind that Smalls had called the police.

The year progressed and the summer came and went. In the fall, Slick bought a Volkswagon Jetta from a local crackhead. It only cost him $200 dollars and a few rocks. As usual, Slick drove the car around the small town as if he had license.

A week after he bought the car, Slick was riding in the morning looking for some weed to smoke. After exhausting all options, Slick picked up some high school students who were ditching class. They told Slick that they could find some weed at school and they took him there.

After leaving the school, Slick was caught behind an older white man driving slow in a truck. Slick followed closely, as the senior was driving ten miles under the limit. Slick labored behind the man until his patience could take no more.

Slick decided to pass the slow vehicle. In the attempt, he didn't notice the extra decrease in speed. He also failed to see the approaching stop sign until he was passed it and in the middle of oncoming traffic. The woman, who plowed into his side, never had an opportunity to reduce her speed.

The Volkswagon absorbed the impact and spun around in circles. The van the woman drove bounced off and careened into a pole. Slick immediately tried to drive off but the car was totaled. With crack, an open beer and marijuana on his person, his first instinct was to get clean. He left the boys in the car and stashed the contraband in a nearby yard. After returning to the scene and not seeing any police he instructed the boys to remain silent. He then walked away to a friend's house. He concluded that he wouldn't be charged with anything because the car wasn't in his name.

Unfortunately, one of the passengers was the son of a police officer. After pressure from the kid's father, the police obtained Slick's identity and a felony warrant was issued for hit and run.

For a week, Slick ignored the pleas from family and friends to turn himself in. After assurance from officer Bowers that the felony would be reduced, he made arrangements to turn himself in. However, the officer reneged on his promise and charged Slick with the felony along with a variety of extra charges.

Slick once again bonded out without any trouble. The legal system had proved itself a joke to the young man. He had yet to go to court for all of his other charges. At each appearance he would ask for a continuance and it would be granted. Slick would do this for nearly a year until all of his delays were exhausted. Despite these charges, Slick continued to find himself in adverse situations.

A short time later, Slick was playing cards with a guy named Danny. They knew each other from playing in the same circles and lately had been playing one on one. This particular night Slick was drunk and frustrated. He also had a dollar bill full of cocaine and a .380 pistol on his hip. This combination would prove detrimental to both men.

The two played tonk into the wee hours of the morning, going back and forth, until Danny took control. Slick had become impatient, making foolish and risky plays. Soon he was down to his last twenty dollars. He looked at the mound of cash that was in front of his opponent. At that moment he predetermined that he would take all of his money back if he lost the hand. He dealt the cards and waited for the results.

"Twenty-one," Danny said, dropping his cards on the table.

Slick examined his hand and counted twenty five, a loser. "Hold on, man," Slick said. "I just dealt that. You keep cheating me out of my fronts! I been dealing twice all night. Matter of fact, let me get all mines back anyway," Slick reached across the table and snatched the $500 dollars.

"Oh hell nah," Danny exclaimed trying to stop Slick. "It ain't going down like that! Give my shit back!"

It was too late. Slick had the money in his grasp and stood up. Danny came around the table and charged at Slick. He froze in his tracks when Slick unveiled the chrome .380 from his jacket.

"A look, for real homeboy, I don't want no problems," Slick said calmly with the gun trained on his victim. "Just let me go head about my business. All I wanted is my money back.

"Oh," Danny stuttered, raising his hands. "Oh! Okay then. You got it man. You got it."

Slick kept his eyes on the man as he backed out the door. He could here Danny calling for his roommate, Steve, who had been in the back sleep. Slick increased his pace when he remembered that Steve also carried a weapon. He disappeared into the darkness, hitting shortcuts trying to make it home.

Steve and Danny jumped in the car and gave chase. Slick could see them as he ducked through various cuts to avoid detection. When he finally made it home, he noticed two blue and white police cars in front of his house. He made a detour through neighbors' backyards and escaped capture by staying with a friend that night.

Slick stayed away from home for two days. The morning he returned he found is father, who normally worked, still there. Slick had barely gotten comfortable when he heard several car doors slam outside. He looked out the window and saw three unmarked police cars. Before he could react there was an authoritative knock on the door.

Slick's father, unaware of what happened let the police in and informed them of Slick's presence. The police came into Slick's room and arrested him in front of his father. He was handcuffed and led out of the house. His father watched helplessly as his once productive son was carried away.

He was transported to the Wayne County Jail and charged with first degree robbery. He was first given a $100,000 bond. While being questioned by detectives, Slick grew angry. When he would not calm down, they tried to subdue him. Slick retaliated by punching and spitting on both officials.

The beating they inflicted as a result was criminal. He was then placed in a solitary cell until he cooled. He was given an extra $50,000.00 bond for assaulting the officers. Slick knew that he could not afford such a high bail and prepared himself for a lengthy stay in the jail.

He stayed in for two months. He adjusted to the environment by gambling and smoking rolled-up cigarettes.

He knew nearly everyone on his cell block so it was almost like being on the streets. However, after getting into two altercations, he was moved to the cages where more violent offenders were held. He was placed in a block with murderers who were facing life. Slick was humbled to see how the men maintained their sanity under such pressure. One guy, Paul, was facing the death penalty for double murder. One would never have known it by his calm demeanor.

Finally, Charles Worley, Slick's court appointed lawyer managed to get Slick's bond reduced to a manageable $10,000. Within a week Slick was back on the streets. Upon returning home, he discovered that his parents had found his stash of crack and disposed of it. They had also found the gun, but left it untouched. Slick heard it from his mom when he got home.

"I want you to get that gun out of my house," Mrs. Richardson told her son.

"What gun?"

"That silver gun in your room under the chair! That's what gun! Don't play with me. I want it out of here right this minute!"

Slick complied without even mentioning the crack. He knew that it was already gone and didn't want to discuss it. He grabbed the gun and went straight to Audubon. Ironically, Danny's car was the first thing he saw when he turned the corner. Slick approached the man while he was in the middle of a weed transaction.

"A yo nigga, you know that shit was foul. I didn't take no $1000 and a gold chain from you," Slick said of the story that was told to police. "I just took my money back. If you had a problem you should've handled in the streets."

"I know man," Danny responded nervously, still sitting in the car. "I won't thinking. I was just so mad you pulled that pistol. You know I ain't going to court, but you should at least give me something.

Slick pulled out a hundred dollar bill from his pocket and handed it to the man. "You know you gon' have to drop them charges for real though. I can't do that kind of time for nothing."

"I got you man. You know I wouldn't do that too you." The men gave each other a half-hearted shake and Danny drove off.

Slick celebrated his release by getting drunk and high with the boys on Audubon. He also purchased more drugs and began right back hustling. The seriousness of his most recent offense had no apparent effect on the decision to keep risking his freedom.

Within months, Slick was back rolling. Even though he still had no license, he bought an old school Cadillac. He rode around drinking, gambling and hustling like he didn't have a care in the world. He was living for the moment, not knowing that his actions would soon come back to haunt him.

Before the summer of 1999, Slick was on another gambling binge. One night he was entangled in a poker game in which he had already lost three hundred dollars. Chasing his losses Slick sped back home to retrieve more dough. On his way back, he exceeded the 35mph speed limit by forty miles.

A few blocks away from the game, he passed a parked police car on a side street. The officer pulled out and engaged his lights. Too drunk and tired, Slick didn't even bother to flee. He pulled over instantly, knowing that he would be going to jail for a third DWI.

After blowing a .20, Slick was transported to the familiar jail. He was booked and remanded to the custody of the sheriff's department where he remained overnight. Coincidently, he was scheduled for a court appearance the next morning for his earlier DWI. He was taken to court in the orange jumpsuit. Before his name was called, his court appointed lawyer advised him to plea, indicating he would probably receive probation.

Slick appeased the lawyer and entered a guilty plea. He was floored, however, when the judge imposed an active sentence of twelve months in the Department of Corrections. The twenty-one year old returned to his cell stunned. Never in his life had he imagined doing a day in prison. Now he had to serve a year. Tears of sorrow and despair began to well in his eyes as he lay on his bunk. He thought that if he went to sleep and woke up, it would all be a dream.

The next morning reality slapped Slick in the face with beige concrete walls and blue cell bars. The year he had received was real. Slick walked over to the line to receive breakfast with the other inmates. After eating the slop, Slick wondered around the dayroom, trying to keep a peace of mind. He picked up a newspaper and noticed a leaflet inside. He removed the pamphlet and examined it. The contents provided comfort as Slick read the words.

"The Spirit of the Lord is upon me. The Lord has sent me to preach good tidings to the meek, he hath sent me to bind up the broken hearted, to proclaim liberty to the captives, and opening of the prison to them that are bound."

As Slick read more, the better he felt. The article went on to talk about Bible characters that were imprisoned. David, Moses, and Paul had been killers and Joseph and John the Baptist were held captive wrongfully. The book related how they still became great men of God.

Slick kept those thoughts in mind when he was called later to be transported to the prison. Handcuffed with his wrists at his waists and chains on his ankles, he envisioned himself as one of the Bible greats being jailed for a higher purpose. He acknowledged the fact that his actions had led to this fate and was now ready to accept his punishment. Slick then resolved that he would make the best of this unfortunate situation and become a better man when he was released.

9
Warning Signs

October 2004,
Virginia Beach, VA

Slick spent two weeks in the Portsmouth jail before being extradited to Virginia Beach. When he arrived, he was again denied bail. His lawyer initiated a bond hearing two weeks later. Slick was released the same day in lieu of a $10,000 bond.

The eviction notice posted on the door of his apartment was no surprise. He was three weeks late on the rent and management had already filed the injunction. Having only a few days to move out, Slick assessed his resources to see who could help. He scrolled through his contact list and dialed multiple numbers alerting people to his release and his predicament.

Like clockwork, Slick's phone began to ring that same day. People came and went and soon Slick was out of coke. He called his longtime connect Fardo to make a score. His connect graciously brought four ounces of raw cocaine to Slick's oceanfront loft. Slick continued to conduct business throughout that first night. The pressure had him reeling, however. Before the morning came, Slick had snorted more than an eight ball. He sat up all night peeking out the window, worried of how he could find a place.

The next day he received a call from Sanya. She first expressed her concern over Slick's most recent ordeal. He then informed her of his need for a place. Sanya thought for a minute. She then told him of a friend, who was in a dilemma also. A plan was concocted to help them both.

"I have a friend Stacey. She stays over in Ocean Villa Condominiums, right down the street from you," Tonya explained. "She has to go away for a while and she wants me to sell her condo for her."

"How much does she want for it," Slick asked.

"I don't know. It has a market value of $160,000 but it's kind of slow right now. Plus, she has some issues and really needs to sell, so it might go for lower."

"Well look, I need a spot fast. You think I can buy or at least rent it until it sells?"

"I can't see that being a problem," Sanya responded. "I'll have to talk to Stacey about it but I'm sure we can work something out."

"Alright. Just let me know as soon as you can. Call me tomorrow and tell me what's up."

"Okay, but I almost forgot why I called. I need to come and get a quarter for her going away party tomorrow."

"I'm at the crib," Slick invited. "Just come on through."

Sanya turned out to be a Godsend. She devised a scheme in which she and Slick could take joint ownership of the property using Slick's money and Sanya's credentials. The quitclaim deed that was executed allowed Stacey to be released from all assets and or liability associated with the property. Because of the large amount of equity she had it was a sweet deal for everyone.

It turned out that Slick wasn't the only crook in the neighborhood. Slick learned at Stacey's party that "going away" meant being sent to a federal prison for embezzlement. As an account manager for an oceanfront resort, she had swindled over a million dollars from the business in a four year span. When she planned to resign, the person that she was training spotted a small inaccuracy in numbers. A subsequent audit revealed the crime and it was traced to Stacey.

Even though she was sentenced to two years, she still had a large portion of the money spread out in different places. Her friend Sanya would help her hide and keep most of the money in similar transactions such as these.

Slick was able to move in the high end condo within a week. Stacey's things were already in storage and Slick had little to move so the transition was easy. After getting settled, Slick knew he had to upgrade. His furniture was out of place in the lavish three bed two bath condo. Over the next month, Slick purchased expensive furniture and accessories to decorate his new spot. With the furnishing complete, Slick was satisfied. He took in his surroundings and held the notion that he had finally made it.

When he'd been there about two months, Slick received a call from his cousin Rocko. Rocko lived in Goldsboro and had come to visit Slick on a few occasions. He'd expressed his fondness for the area and a desire to relocate. Slick never took him serious though. Many people from his hometown always said they wanted to get out, but took no initiative to do so. Slick sensed urgency in his cousin's voice, however as they spoke on the phone.

"Slick man I'm telling you. I got to get outta here before I kill this nigga man!"

"What you talking 'bout. What's goin' on down there in the 'Boro," Slick asked concerned.

"Some bama ass nigga down here tripping. I don't even know this whack dude, and he trying to beef over some dusty broad. Don't nobody want that chick! I knocked her off one time and was done! For real bro, this nigga riding by my momma house and everything. If I see him over here again on some funny shit, I'm a bust him. No questions!"

"Hold on homeboy. Easy! Just chill for a second. Ain't no need for all that." Slick tried to calm his friend.

"I'm trying to chill! Believe me! But I ain't no pussy! I done played the good guy too many times and I'm done walking away!"

"I ain't saying run or nothing. But you got to be smart about it. You got a daughter to raise, remember. If you get knocked with a body, who gon' take care of her."

After a few more words of wisdom, Rocko came to his senses. "You know what, cuz? You right. I don't know what's going on with me man. I guess I'm just frustrated. Things ain't going right. My baby mamma tripping. My money looking funny. Your boy just need a change."

Slick could relate. He had been in the same position amidst beef and despair three years earlier before moving to Virginia. The problems and lack of opportunities in the small town had him equally on the verge of drastic measures. Luckily, Wood had answered Slick's request and allowed him to come to Virginia before he self-destructed. Slick decided to offer the same lifeline to his friend. "Well, you know you could always come up here and chill for a minute if you need to."

Just like that it was done. About a week later, Rocko left Goldsboro. Slick welcomed him and began to show him around. Before long, Rocko had familiarized himself with the city and was making friends of his own. He had gotten a job, a few girlfriends and even began to sell weed. Slick was proud to have had a hand in his friend's newfound success.

The only drawback to the situation was that Rocko had a coke habit also. Slick knew this beforehand and didn't have a problem with it. He felt good having someone else to get high with. However, Slick's regular access to the drug and both men's high tolerance led to many long nights of indulgence and partying. Pretty soon, Slick was back to his old state of excess and perpetual downfall. Rocko had also lost his newfound ambition.

Slick started to frequent the dice games again. They were now being held at Fredo's who was making a killing with his new connect. He was now supplying most of the boys. Slick even patronized him sometimes. His prices were good but he was lackadaisical in his dealings.

Slick had once wanted to buy four ounces. When he arrived Fredo gave him nine. Slick considered telling him, but evidently, Fredo had so much that he didn't even recognize the loss. Being so lax, it was only a matter of time before the game flipped on him.

Every Sunday, Fredo and the boys would go to Virginia Beach's urban night club, Picasso's. It was the hottest spot for the younger crowd. All the hustlers, goons, and broads attended the club like it was the Oscars. Slick had even been pried from his white boy bars on a few nights. He liked the spot so much, that sometimes he would go by himself.

One night in the spring of 2005, all of the boys were at the club when Fredo received a call. His roommate, Jerry, a white boy from Kansas, had been robbed and beaten at their apartment. When they arrived, they found Jerry bloodied on the floor clinging to his life. The ambulance was called to take him to the hospital. Meanwhile, Fredo and the others piled into the bloody living room to plot revenge.

Slick was not at the club with the others, but out making runs. He received the call and since he was in the area, decided to stop by for a minute. He entered to find Spray, Flash, Grim, Banger and ten more of the boys. Blunts were lit, guns were brandished and murder was in the air. Slick, wanting no part of the action, stayed for a while but then decided it would be best to leave.

When he walked out the door, Slick spotted five police officers coming down the hall in his direction. Simultaneously, he remembered the twenty five grams of coke in his pocket. He thought of trying to walk past them, but retracted after considering what just happened. He figured he'd be searched. Rethinking, he doubled back inside and shut the door.

"Hey y'all, the police is coming down the hallway. It's about five of them and they look like they coming straight here." Slick warned the men, while stashing the coke in his boxers under his genitals.

Everyone scrambled, putting out blunts and stashing drugs and guns.

"Everybody be calm," said Fredo to no avail.

"Fuck you talkin' bout nigga," Flash replied. "I got all this work on me and the strap. Nah, G, they can't come in here!"

"If y'all niggas be quiet they might not fuck with us. You never know. They might just leave," Banger added.

"I know your stupid ass seen Slick just leave and come back in," Spray said. "They know somebody in this jank."

The conversation was interrupted by knocks that could be none other than police. Everyone stiffened with anticipation. Fredo manned the peephole, watching the officer's movements.

"Virginia Beach Police," a loud voice uttered. "Open up the door. We know you're in there. We're here to investigate an assault!" The silence inside continued. "If you don't come out we will come in by force!"

The men had no choice. The police were there to investigate the robbery. The beating was so severe they were called to the hospital. Spray and Flash ran into the back room and hid before Fredo reluctantly opened the door.

The law came in and searched all of the men. Slick was nervous when the officer grabbed his crotch. Upon contact, he thought the drugs would fall out. Fortunately, they didn't and the cop moved on.

While everyone else was being searched, Fredo was engaged in a conversation with the lead officer. They hadn't found any weapons but they had yet to search the whole house. When asked if they could search the back, Fredo informed them that there were two armed men in the back room. When Spray and Flash didn't respond to several calls, a standoff ensued.

Hours went by as Slick stood outside with the others. The police had detained and cuffed all of the men, while they tried to coax the outlaws out. After exhausting all options, the police released a canine unit into the room. Pleas of distress came from the young men as the dogs attacked. They were then quickly subdued and brought out.

At the end of the night Fredo was charged with multiple gun and drug charges. Everyone else was allowed to leave, except Spray, who had an outstanding warrant. Slick had missed several calls from business and personal contacts during the time period. The totality of what could have happened set in on his drive home. This wasn't the first time he'd been close to getting caught with drugs but his conscience was beginning to eat at him now. He once again made a conscience decision to change his life and associates.

An opportunity presented itself in the form of a letter from the Virginia Real Estate Board the next week. After two character hearings and many letters of recommendation the board had granted the hustler the privilege of practicing brokerage. He called everyone he knew and told them of the good news. He felt an extreme sense of accomplishment amidst all of his trouble. Ironically, he got a call from his friend Donnie that same night.

"Hey bro," Slick exclaimed. "You know they gave me my license today. 'Preciate the letter big dog!"

"Are you serious? That's great champ. I told you to just keep the faith and it will happen for you."

"Yeah, I admit I had a little doubt, but deep inside I knew I would get them."

"Look bro, we blessed. That's all it is. Just keep doing the right thing and watch everything fall into place. It ain't nothing God can't do. Look at me!"

"Yeah, I know he got something special for me. Sometimes the devil be trying to get me sidetracked but I know he can't win."

"Nah, he already lost. Just wait. Give it about six months and see what God can do. Just stay focused."

Slick took his mentor's advice. He transformed immediately into his role as a professional. He bought new suits, computer equipment, office materials, and other business supplies. He obtained a new phone strictly for real estate. He read many books on business and studied the lives of those who had succeeded. Mentally, he prepared to face the crooks and criminals in the so called legitimate business world.

Sanya along with many other of his associates noticed his fervor. She invited him to join her firm. Slick investigated the company along with many others and chose hers. He interviewed with the principal broker and signed the contract.

He was assigned duty and started working in the office. Although he was the only black man there, he was not intimidated by his counterparts. He carried himself with confidence knowing that he was also capable. He had no reason to feel inferior knowing that he generated just as much if not more income than his peers.

Still, he stayed humble. He showed respect and watched the techniques of successful agents. In his first month, Slick secured a listing to sell a $400,000 house. He was ecstatic as he thought about the possible $20,000 dollar commission. He realized the potential to make money and the fantasy of being legit became reality. Little did he know that market conditions, would not be the only factor that would hinder his success.

Slick still kept one foot in the streets however. The money was still calling but the coke had begun to get scarce. Slick was scrambling to obtain work from several different sources. He managed to keep a steady supply and money continued to flow.

Things were looking good on the outside, but on the inside the reverse was true. Slick and Rocko still were getting high nearly every night. Because of this, Rocko had lost all of his motivation. While Rocko would rather go hard in the game, Slick was trying to escape the trap. When it was clear that the two were on different pages, they chose to part ways and remain friends. It was best for both of them as their living condition had become horrid.

"I told you it was a bad idea from the start," Wood told Slick a few days later. "I knew y'all boys was gon' get up there, get on that stuff and it'll be over! I know how y'all do." Wood had warned him prior to the move that it was a catastrophe waiting to happen.

When Rocko left, things quieted a little. To combat the solitude Slick bought two pit bull puppies, one from Wood and one from Dooky. He brought them back from North Carolina when he visited his family. He called them Malice and Nightmare; Malice for her behavior, and Nightmare for his color. The two puppies became favorites of his lady friends. He walked the puppies more and realized that they were a girl magnet on the beach.

The puppies and girls were not enough for Slick. Against his better judgment, he began hosting dice games again. With all of the turmoil happening around them, no one had a stable place to shoot. Slick did try to limit the games to players who had real money. Normally it would be about four or five people shooting for a $100 a roll in c-lo.

One day that summer Slick received a call from K J to shoot dice.

"Bring it on nigga," Slick enticed. "I'll shoot your fat ass head up. Ain't nothing changed big boy."

"I'm on the way then."

Slick hung up the phone and grabbed a few hundred from his top drawer. K J arrived a few minutes later with Spoon. Slick knew Spoon from the other dice games. He shot dice but not for the amount K J did. Slick found it a little strange to see the two men together. He took no heed to this intuition and let the men in.

"Nigga, I don't even wanna talk," K J said walking straight pass Slick into the kitchen where the dice were. "Come on here nigga. I ain't got time to waste."

"What up my nigga," Spoon said extending his hand. Slick dapped him as he walked in.

"What up Spoon? You came to shoot too huh?"

"Nah, man, you know y'all boys got that big money. I was just riding with K J so I said I might as well come check my man Slick too."

"'Precitate that nigga. I got some liquor over there on the counter and some brew in the fridge. You good."

"Nigga come on," K J beckoned. "I ain't got that much time. Is you gon' shoot or bullshit all day?"

"Bitch, you ain't said nothing. Pee wee for the dice."

The two men started the game with the usual trash talk. Slick began to feel strange when his guests started acting suspicious. Spoon kept standing extremely close to K J when Slick would roll. Slick could not see what was happening because he was on K J's opposite side. Slick disregarded the movements while focusing on the money at stake. He went on a hot streak and ended up winning a quick grand from his opponent.

"I'm done!" K J said walking towards the door.

"Don't be like that homeboy," Slick joked. "I still ain't forgot that six g's I lost nigga. This right here ain't shit!"

"Fuck that," K J said seriously. "I'm in the car Spoon."

K J walked out and Spoon stood up. Slick's dogs began to bark ferociously as Spoon walked towards Slick. Slick tried to quiet them but they persisted. Before Spoon got fully out of the door he turned around.

"Yeah, Slick, matter of fact, let me get a cup of that liquor before I go."

Slick allowed him back in and pointed him toward the cabinet. "The cups are right there over the stove," Slick said still standing by the door.

Spoon walked to the sink and washed his hands. Something in his heart told Slick to be alert. His dogs were barking loudly, which they never did. He watched K J from the door while keeping a roving eye on Spoon at the sink. His senses stiffened when he noticed Spoon had not gotten a drink but merely washed his hands. Slick stood on guard while the man approached with his hand extended.

"Aight," Spoon said as he got to the door. "I'm a holla' at you later family."

When Slick stuck his hand out Spoon tried to pull K J's .45 automatic from his waist. Seeing the handle, slick grabbed the man's wrists with both hands. Spoon threw his body weight into Slick and both men tumbled out of the door onto the steps. After a scuffle, Slick was able to stand up and started to run down the steps.

"Don't run or I'm a shoot you in the back," Spoon warned from the top of the steps. Slick ignored the command and sprinted into the middle of the complex where people were outside. Spoon gave chase. Realizing he couldn't fire the gun with all of the witnesses, he went back to K J's car and the two left.

Slick was enraged. He knew that K J didn't have the balls to rob him. Spoon was just hungry and used as a pawn. Not knowing if they were coming back, Slick called Toby and asked to use one of his firearms. All of his weapons were taken in the last break in. Toby quickly came through and handed Slick a .9 millimeter pistol.

"You be careful with that thing though Slick," Toby warned. "It doesn't have a safety."

"That don't even matter. If them cats come back through here, it ain't gon' need no safety."

"I told you about having all of those thugs in your pad anyway," Toby chided in his country drawl. "You know better than that. You gotta watch yourself. You making a lot of money."

"I'll be okay," Slick said, in a hurry to get rid of him.

"Alright, buddy. Call me if you need me."

Slick gave Toby a couple of grams for his trouble. To quell his excitement, Slick took a large amount out of the bag and snorted it himself. When the drain hit, it did nothing but intensify the anxiety he felt over the robbery attempt. He grew angry, picked up the phone and called K J in a rage.

"You a fuckin' faggot. You a punk. If you wanted to rob me you should a been man enough to do it yourself bitch! Wait 'til I see your fat ass! You better have that pistol on you then!"

"I ain't have nothing to do with that," K J replied calmly. "I ain't no what that man was gon' do. But if you wanna bring it like that, it's whatever."

Slick made a few more threats and the conversation ended. Already, hype off the coke, he continued to get high into the early morning. Full of paranoia, he probed the house with the gun until he couldn't snort anymore. He finally laid down. With the gun still in his grasp, Slick drifted off to sleep. Slick would have no use for the weapon as K J's actions would return to him full circle in just a matter of days.

Fredo had fallen on hard times since the incident at his house. Because of the charges and the subsequent heat, his operation had crumbled. Feeling ill-will toward K J because of his success, he hatched a plot with three others to rob him. The scheme was poorly planned and the results were disastrous.

A few days after the attempt to rob Slick, Fredo, Gunman, Spray's brother Rome and Fredo's friend Knox went to K J's residence in broad daylight. Seeing his Lexus, they assumed he was there and kicked in the door. With guns drawn, they entered and found not K J, but his brother Larry. The gunmen interrogated him about the location of product and money but he wouldn't budge. A struggle ensued and Knox shot the man three times in the chest. Without the drugs or cash, the four men fled the home, leaving Larry dead at the scene.

Slick received the news via television. He was flipping channels the next day, when he saw the faces of the four men on the news. He watched the story and learned that homicide warrants had been issued for all four. He called around and got the inside story from Ski, who was too eager to reveal the details.

Slick was flabbergasted. If the men he associated with were heartless enough to kill a childhood friend, there was no doubt in his mind that he too was susceptible. Considering this last incident, he decided he would take no more chances. He would stay alert and armed.

When Toby came a week later to retrieve his pistol, Slick felt naked. The same day he went to a pawn shop and picked out a pistol. Even though he had a felony in North Carolina, Slick was under the false notion that it wouldn't apply in Virginia.

After paying the $350 for the .357 magnum, he was told that he'd have to wait twenty minutes for a background check. Having a run to make, he left his number with the clerk and said he'd be back. Thirty minutes later, Slick received the call.

"Mr. Richardson," the voice on the other end said. "This is John from Lynnhaven Pawn. Please come and pick up your money. Unfortunately, we cannot sell you the gun."

"Why not," Slick asked knowingly.

"I don't know. It just showed up in the computer as a denial. I have a number to the state police if you want it. Any questions you have can be directed to them."

Slick knew the felony was the reason for the rejection so he didn't even bother calling the 800 number. Undaunted, he called one of his loyal customers, Jeremy, who would do nearly anything for a gram or two. An hour later, Jeremy walked out of the same store and handed a box to Slick. Using his resources, he was able to possess the same .357 that he was refused earlier. It amazed him how much power he and cocaine wielded over the users he dealt with.

With his protection secure, Slick tried to remain productive. Though things in the streets were reeling, he still maintained his desire for success in real estate. He would stay at the office probing leads until five o'clock daily. After work, he'd go home, change clothes, and satisfy the many customers who'd called during the day. However, it had become increasingly hard to find dope as the drought worsened. He had even started resorting to his customers to find possible connections.

One such customer was Cody. He was a tall, lanky, dark-skinned twenty-one year old Slick had met through Boss. Cody had bought a few eight balls from Slick and the two had begun regular dealings.

As fall started the drought worsened. Slick hadn't had any work for three days and was getting antsy. Cody along with many others was calling several times a day. Slick had to keep denying them because he couldn't find anything. The situation was bad for everyone.

"You still ain't got nothing," Cody said on the fourth day.

"Nah man, it's dry as hell," Slick replied. "'Bout like the dessert out here right now. Shit, you don't know nobody else who might got something."

Cody was silent for a second. "Yeah, my peoples got that work but he don't sell nothing but deuces and up. That's why I be calling you."

"What it look like though? I mean, I can't fool with no garbage."

"Nah, bro, that joint fire. You know I mess around too, so I know. It's 'bout like what you be having."

"Alright, hit him up and see what kind of numbers he talking 'bout and get back at me."

Calls went back and forth and negotiations were made. Slick met Cody in the old neighborhood of Thalia Oaks. He arrived at the same time as Cody's connect. Cody grabbed the package from the truck and brought it to Slick, who immediately put it on a scale. The results disappointed him.

"Hold up man. This jank like twelve grams short," Slick alerted. "I can't take this."

"What," Cody said feigning surprise. "Let me take it back to this nigga, and see what he say." He went back to the truck and came back less than a minute later. "He said that's it. That's all he got left."

"Well I know he gon' come down on that number some then right?"

"Nah, he said it is what it is. You can take it or leave it. It ain't like it's a whole lot of work out here anyway."

"Man, get the fuck outta here with that," Slick said with an attitude. "That ain't what we talked about. What y'all niggas think this is? Matter of fact, don't even worry about it. I'm good."

Slick drove back to the oceanfront full of anger. He didn't like dealing with middlemen for just that reason. Something inside had told him not to mess with Cody from the start, but because of the drought he took the chance.

The next day, while at work Slick received a call from Cody. He apologized to Slick for the confusion. He offered a better condolence when he told Slick that he had the package with him and it was the correct weight.

"So you got the whole thing on you right now," Slick confirmed.

"Yeah, I'm in the same spot as last night so you can come get right now if you want."

"Nah, I can't come now. I am the office. But I can come get it at about five. That's cool?"

Cody agreed. It was one o'clock. Slick tried to focus on his work, while at the same time thinking about drugs. Something felt funny about the situation. His instincts told him not to meet the man, but he needed the dope badly. He felt even stranger when Cody continued to call him throughout the day, despite Slick telling him what time he'd be there.

By the time five o'clock came, Slick had decided not to go. He drove home, changed his clothes and began to relax. He walked his dogs with the intention of staying in for the night. But after repeated calls from Cody, Slick was persuaded against better judgment to meet him.

Slick returned from the walk and attempted to bring the dogs in. For some reason, Malice and Nightmare would not enter, but stood by the door barking loudly. When Slick finally got them in their cages, he grabbed the keys to a rental car and headed for the door.

The dogs barked more loudly when Slick closed the door behind him. This time he took it as an obvious sign not to go. But like he'd done so many times in his life, he ignored the inner voice that was crying to help him avoid danger.

Slick pulled into the parking lot and spotted Cody in front of the same building. Cody got into the car and gave Slick some dap. Slick pulled out the scale and set it on the console. He watched Cody dig into his right pocket expecting him to pull out the cocaine. The small black automatic pistol that he clinched instead made Slick's heart skip a beat.

"You know what it is," Cody said, coolly glaring at Slick. "Let me get all that up off you."

Slick looked in the man's eyes and then down at the gun. When he noticed that Cody had not pointed the weapon at him, he figured he could make an escape. Just as he grabbed the door handle, Cody snatched Slick's right shoulder and swung the pistol. The hard metal crashed against Slick's face causing blood to splatter from his nose.

Dazed and bleeding, Slick still tried to shake away from the man's grasp. He had one foot out of the car when Cody pulled him back in. He swung the gun again, this time catching Slick in the temple. Slick still did not stop struggling and Cody swung the gun again.

The loud bang shocked both men, causing the struggle to cease. Slick was the first to react and jumped out of the car. Cody sat looking confused in the passenger side. As Slick examined himself for wounds, his attacker drove off in the rental car. Slick gathered himself and neighbors came out of their doors to see what had happened.

When the police arrived, Slick told them that he was passing out fliers for his business when an unknown man attempted to steal his car. After a scuffle, the man succeeded in driving off. He gave them a description of the car and a list of items in it. They made a report and put out an APB for the vehicle. They also took Slick's information.

Two days passed before police found Cody, still driving the car. He also had the gun and was using Slick's phone as if it was his own. Slick couldn't believe how stupid the man was. He was called to the precinct to retrieve his things.

When he arrived however, Slick was treated like he was a suspect. The police asked him all sorts of questions that had nothing to do with him being a victim. It turned out that Cody had told detectives about his and Slick's previous dealings. With access to the phone records, they knew he was telling the truth. When Slick realized this, he refused to answer any more questions and left the station abruptly.

He felt the walls closing in. He figured that the police would definitely be watching him now. Plus, there was the ever constant threat of someone close setting him up. He would have to switch up everything or quit altogether. His already bad paranoia got worse and Slick began to sleep with his .357 magnum.

About three days after the Cody incident, Slick was in his living room watching television when he heard the sound of his gate slamming. He looked out the window to see Trap, one of the young boys from Pine Gardens, at the bottom of his stairs. Slick ran to the door immediately and addressed the eighteen year-old.

"A yo man, what the hell you doing out here in my patio. You need to take your ass on somewhere!"

"Slick, this is me," Trap said, starting to walk up the small flight of stairs. "You act like you don't know me or something."

"Yeah, I know you, but you don't got no business at my spot though. I don't know you like that nigga!"

"Come on man, just let me holla at you for a second. I need something," he said still approaching.

"Look man, I'm telling you to go 'head and get away from here. I ain't playing with you, yo!"

Trap continued to walk up the stairs. Slick closed the door and ran to the kitchen sink. He grabbed the .357 from under it and reopened the door. He pointed the gun at Trap as he reached the last step.

"Whoa man! Hold up Slick," he said with his hands up. "What's wrong with you homeboy?"

"Man I done told you to leave several times. I don't want to, but that's my word. I will pop your ass if you don't get 'way from here."

Slick watched the man back down the stairs, wondering how Trap knew where he stayed. He watched him walk around to the side of the building. When Slick checked the bedroom window, he saw three other guys meet Trap on the side of a bike trail. Slick concluded right then that he had to move. He also made the decision that he was through with the game. There was no way that he could live like that anymore.

About a week later, Slick received a call from his aunt Dorothy who stayed in the area. She had just quit her job and stated that she could use some help with the rent. Slick agreed in his haste to exit the life. He packed his things into a storage unit and within a week he was out of the condo.

His new residence was a gift from heaven. In Chesapeake, the apartment seemed worlds away from the problems he was having in the Beach. Even though his customers were still calling, he either ignored them or told them of his retirement. Some respected the decision and some tried to coax him back. Eventually, he disconnected both phones that he used for dealing, leaving only the one for real estate. He did keep his contact list however, but was proud of having taken somewhat of a stand.

Even though Slick still hadn't sold a house, he was working diligently as an agent. He met with loan officers, mortgage bankers, and other professionals in order to secure potential clients. He felt good that he was now able to devote more time to his profession. He still had thousands of dollars in drug money put away, so he thought he didn't need a thing. He had no way of knowing how fast ill-gotten gain could disappear, but he would soon find out.

In October of the same year, Slick was invited to a game by Donnie. He had chartered a bus and fifty family members and friends made the trip. Slick took the three hour drive from Virginia to Goldsboro to join the others. The trip was a much needed siesta considering all that Slick had encountered that summer.

When the bus arrived in Indianapolis, the guests were greeted by their host and treated to dinner and hotel rooms for the night. Slick and Wood, along with other immediate family would spend the night at Donnie's house. After the evening dinner, everyone settled in their hotel rooms and the rest went back to house.

Before everyone in the house could go to bed, Wood wanted to make a late night food run. Slick, who was normally all for late night escapades, initially declined. Something was occurring in him that he couldn't explain. But when no one else volunteered, Slick chose to ride with Wood. The two travelers pulled into the White Castle parking lot at 1:30 a.m.

Before entering the restaurant, Slick noticed two carloads of Latinos drinking loudly in the parking lot. He dismissed them quickly and he and Wood entered and ordered. Slick was excited, having never eaten a White Castle burger. While waiting for the food, they decided to go have a smoke.

While they conversed, two sheriff's cars screeched into the parking lot. They pulled directly in front of the two black men. Slick wasn't the least bit worried, knowing they had not done anything. He looked the two large white men in the face as they approached.

"How you gentlemen doing out here tonight," the fatter of the two said in a cowboy tone.

"We are alright," Slick said nonchalantly. "Just enjoying the cool night air."

"Yep," Wood added. "Can't wait to see them Colts in action tomorrow. That's all we came for."

"Well, all that's good fellows. But we had a complaint about somebody making noises and causing disturbances at this location. That wouldn't happen to be you guys would it."

Slick answered with the pride of not being the culprit for a change. "Oh no sir. That wasn't us. We just got here. There was a car full of people over there who left right before y'all got here. We just came from N.C. to watch the game and we outta here tomorrow."

"Yes sir," Wood said laughingly. "And we don't need no trouble. We just came out to get us a couple of burgers."

"Okay guys. Just let me see your I.D.'s just to be sure."

Slick eagerly gave the officer his card, knowing he was clean. His partner took Wood's and they retreated to their vehicle. They returned moments later and went straight for Wood.

"Put your hands behind your back Mr. Richardson. There is a nationwide warrant for your arrest."

Evidently, the cliché that all blacks look alike to whites was true. The deputies had identified Wood as Slick, and were leading him to the car despite protests. Slick stepped in instantly, knowing that it had to be a mistake.

"No sir. I'm Mr. Richardson. What seems to be the issue?"

The officers released Wood. They cuffed Slick while interrogating him at the same time.

"Have you ever lived in Virginia?"

"Yes, and I still do," Slick said still confused.

"Well, you have a warrant."

"For what?"

"Did you try to buy a gun a while back?"

"Yes, but they denied me. They didn't tell me that I did anything wrong."

"Well unfortunately, that is a crime in Virginia. We're gonna have to take you in. We'll alert them to your presence and they have fifteen days to come get you. If they don't, you'll be released."

Slick was dumbfounded. His first worry was what his friend Donnie would think. Even though he hadn't done anything wrong, it still looked bad. He didn't want to bring any negative attention to his friend's squeaky clean image. His second thought was of Wood, who would be left to explain to everyone else what happened. Lastly, he thought of the charges. If it was a crime, then why wasn't he arrested on the spot in Virginia? Eventually, he became irritated with the whole situation and took it out on the officers.

While being transported, he berated the officers about everything from their skin color to their sexual orientation. Slick even managed to take his penis out and urinate on the cruiser's floor. When he reached the station he became more confrontational. He was put in a solitary cell after arguing with a lieutenant. He continued to cause ruckus in the jail until physical force was threatened. He took the warning serious, knowing that the rednecks would love nothing more than to inflict serious pain on the mouthy nigger.

Slick finally calmed down and after being booked was released into regular population. Slick entered the large room of foreign faces without fear. He had been in numerous jail cells. Being in another state didn't make any difference to him.

He walked to the assigned cell and sat on the bunk. He took in the familiar setting of the jail. All were built the same with few variations. He by now had lost track of how many times he was in this situation. This time, a thousand miles from home, he wondered how it could have happened again.

He had moved to Virginia to avoid the pitfalls of jail and street living. After his short stint in the North Carolina Prison, he had declared that he would get his life together. Thinking of his time in the Portsmouth jail cell, Slick mused about the futility of plans one made while being locked up. It was easy to have positive goals without the pressure to complete them. He thought of all the good intentions that he'd had upon his release from Polk Correctional Center and how they crumbled. His mind drifted back to the period after his release from the North Carolina prison before he moved to Virginia.

10
The Great Escape

April 1999-2002
Goldsboro, NC

In the spring of 1999, Slick became an inmate of Neuse Correctional Center. The small prison camp on the outskirts of Wayne County housed misdemeanor prisoners and felony offenders who'd already completed the bulk of their sentence. The minimum custody facility provided a far more lax setting than Slick expected.

The location of the prison was also an advantage for the twenty one year old. It was not even two miles outside of the Goldsboro city limits. Consequently, Slick found that he knew many of the officers and inmates who were there. This gave Slick a renewed sense of comfort. While, walking on the yard his first day, he heard a familiar voice yell his name.

"Hey yo Slick! What the hell you doing in here boy?"

Slick turned towards the fence and spotted a man in his late twenties. He moved closer and recognized the face.

"Jeru," Slick yelled, excitedly walking to the fence. "What's the deal homeboy?"

"It ain't nothing, just finishing up this last four months on a dope charge. How much time they give you?"

"I got a year for my second DWI," Slick said sadly. "I just had to go through that booking process. Man, it's crazy."

"Yeah, you'll be alright," Jeru consoled. "You'll be over here when you finished processing. Me, Sty, Fatboy, Bootsy, Ant and 'bout ten other niggas from the 'Boro over here, so you'll be straight."

"Okay, tell them niggas I said what up," Slick said about to walk away. "Oh yeah let me get a cigarette from you?"

"I ain't got none, but here go a dollar," Jeru said, slipping the money through the fence. "You can get a pack of them cheap Mavericks with that. That's all I can do."

"'Preciate it," Slick called out walking away. "I'm a holla at you later on."

Slick went through the two week processing period getting used to life in prison. He adjusted to the everyday regimen. He was ecstatic, however, after learning from a counselor that he would not have to do the entire year. The DWI offense was under an older statute so the time would be cut in half. With good behavior, it was possible he could be released in four months.

After processing, Slick was reassigned dorms and given a job in the kitchen. In the workers dorm, Slick found the action. There were poker and tonk games daily, available marijuana and sports tournaments played for money. Slick quickly settled into a routine and was at peace with his surroundings. He suddenly understood how a man could return to prison after being freed. Once one accepted the conditions of confinement, it was possible to live content within the walls.

The next three months went by fast for Slick. Between working, lifting weights, smoking and gambling, the days passed like the wind. In July, however, Slick had to go to court for the hit and run case. His lawyer, Mr. Worley again, advised him to take a plea. He agreed and received a five month sentence to run concurrent with the time he was already serving.

With the felony conviction, he couldn't remain at the Neuse. A few days later he was transferred to Sandy Ridge. Thousands of inmates were housed daily at the holding center, while waiting on their transfer. The process took all day. Later that night, Slick finally arrived at the Polk Correctional Center to serve the remainder of his sentence.

Although it was a prison for younger offenders, Polk was built for maximum security. The large walls inside the high barbed wire fences intimidated Slick. It reminded him of Attica or one of the prisons he'd seen on television.

The conditions were worse on the inside. The large pods that the inmates were housed in did not have air condition. Slick was suffocated by the humidity when he entered his assigned block. He barely had a chance to take in his surroundings before he heard someone shout his name.

"Slick! Oh my god, nigga! What in the world you doing in this joint man?"

Slick knew that voice anywhere. It was King. He turned around to see the friend he'd known since junior high. The two had spent many days in the projects getting drunk and high. In fact, it was at King's house where Slick had his first shot of whiskey. Slick was glad to see a familiar face and walked up the stairs where King was.

"What's up with you my nigga? How long you been in here?"

"Man I been in this joint for twelve months. You remember I kept catching all them yak and gun charges. I still got 'bout two and half left. And I still got some shit pending. Them crackers got me buy the balls," King said laughing. "But you know they can't hold me down. What kind of time you get?"

"I ain't get nothing but five months. Y'all niggas better chill though. I done did three months at the Neuse and I can't see how y'all stand it. I like my freedom too much to be coming in and outta here."

"Nigga quit being soft! You gon' be alright. Everybody in here. Big Yat got the canteen on lock. C-Rock working in the kitchen. G-man doing the laundry. Man, we lunching in here."

"Oh yeah," Slick replied. "All them niggas on the yard."

"I'm talking 'bout a lotta niggas; Bobo, Ray, Johnboy, Don, Booty, Corey and a bunch of other niggas I don't even know. We got shit on smash. Eating good, smoking good…whatever you want."

Slick was relieved to hear the names of so many people he knew. He was comfortable with the fact that he was not alone. He even ended up on the bunk next to King. The two stayed up all night joking and trading war stories. King kept Slick laughing with his recollection of events.

"Nigga, I ain't forgot you and Cisco snuck up behind me that day and put them guns in my face too," he said laughing. "I like to had a stroke."

"Nah, nigga, you peeled your pockets like we was going rob you," Slick said laughing also. "Thought you was 'gon get us a charge didn't you?"

"No, what I was doing was trying to throw Cisco off. He already had caught one body and I ain't know what that nigga was thinking."

"Yeah, but we won't even after you. We were looking for C-Rock. But since y'all was so close, we knew you was gon' give him the message."

As they talked, it baffled Slick how the two of them could sit and joke about trying to kill one another on the street. Now, they were forced to be allies. The stupidity of it all became evident to both as they discussed all of the foolish events that had occurred in the streets.

Slick made the adjustment to the new setting well. The yard was bigger and held more people. Since everyone went to rec at the same time, Slick was able to see many of his associates from the streets. After continuing his workout plan, the hundred and seventy five pound man was soon bench pressing more than three hundred pounds.

Because of the conditions and the youth of the men however, Polk was more violent. Slick had watched several beatings and altercations on the yard. Most of the offenders were already hardened criminals who had been locked up since juvenile. Slick was astounded at the amount of twenty-one year old murderers he met. Sentences of eighty and ninety years were not unheard of amongst the inmates. With this many violent offenders in one place, it was nearly impossible to avoid a confrontation.

One day after coming in from the yard, Slick discovered that his locker had been broken into. Feeling violated, he challenged the thief by calling him out in front of the whole block. When no one responded, he continued to shout insults, looking to spark anger in whoever did it.

"Whoever did it, they momma is a trick," he provoked. "Nigga probably broke as hell and can't buy his own hygiene. Probably is a faggot on the low too!"

With still no response, Slick stopped. Unfortunately, the rouse worked. Slick was lying on his bunk later that night with his headphones on and his eyes closed. His state of rest was broken when a stinging substance was thrown in face.

"What the fuck," Slick said rising up and grabbing his eyes.

Before he was fully erect, Slick was struck in the face with a glancing blow. He rolled off the other side of the top bunk to avoid more punches. He wiped his eyes, gaining his balance at the same time that his attacker came around the bed. The two engaged in a sixty-second slug fest until deputies arrived. Both were then taken to the hole, but Slick was returned to population the next day after an investigation.

When Slick returned to the block, he was greeted by threats from the man's homeboys, Brad and Khalid. They were upset that their friend had gotten in trouble and Slick had not. Though they were in different blocks, Slick knew that they would eventually meet on the rec yard. The next day Slick awoke and prepared for the inevitable.

Slick knew he could hold his own against anyone. But both of the men who'd made the threats had been down for longer and had longer sentences. They were also bigger and had less to lose. When the time came, Slick surprisingly felt fear when he saw Khalid standing by the entrance to the yard.

Slick exited the door and ignored the man as he passed. Khalid wasted no time making good on his threats and punched Slick in the back of the head. Slick turned around to find Khalid with his hands down. He quickly started to punch him in the face. Khalid backed into a brick wall under the assault and Slick pinned him in.

Out of the corner of his eye, Slick saw a figure running towards him. The body type resembled that of Brad's. As soon as the person got within range, Slick turned and caught him with a left cross. He then engaged with Brad, while Khalid watched. The officers came and broke up the affray. Slick was once again spared time in the hole but the others got a month for a two on one fight.

Slick was surprised how good he had handled himself. He didn't consider himself a fighter, but he wasn't a punk either. When he returned to the population, this time he had no further problems. Many people who saw what happened confirmed that Slick had proven himself against the two.

The only other incident he had was a misunderstanding between him and a female guard. While exiting the cafeteria one day, he brushed up against Jefferson. She took offense and pushed him back. When he voiced his displeasure she got irritated and pulled him aside. He was charged with two offenses and received twenty one days in the hole.

The solitude was not an issue. Slick loved to be alone. He preferred his thoughts instead of the rhetoric of those in population. The worst part of the bid was when his mother came for a visit. Slick had asked her not to come. He knew that she was having a hard time and he didn't want to see her hurting. Slick decided to use this as motivation to do better upon his release.

Because of the incident, Slick had to complete the full five months. At the end of November, a month before the Y2K scare, Slick was released from the prison. The guards drove him to a bus station in downtown Raleigh. He was given a ticket to Goldsboro, dressed in a white kitchen uniform and state issued sneakers. Slick arrived home two hours later and called his mother to pick him up. There was no fanfare or welcome home party. Slick returned back to the same situation as before, but this time he was a felon.

His first day out was full of anxiety. He couldn't wait to hit the streets. He called a few close friends. His homeboy Ronnie came through with a couple of outfits. Wood came from Raleigh to check him. That night, Stubbs came through with the weed and liquor and Slick got drunk until he could stand no more. He called an old girlfriend to come get him and they went to a room. Slick released eight months of frustration all over the girl throughout the night. Drunk and drained, Slick fell asleep on his first night out with a big smile on his face.

The next couple of weeks were more of the same. Slick smoked, drank, and even did a little coke. Along with the partying, he caught up with old friends and made new ones. He made up for lost time by screwing as many girls for as long as he could. He found it fascinating how the girls gravitated towards men who just got out of prison. He didn't care why at the time as he was too busy enjoying himself.

One night while at home, Slick received a call from Ronnie.

"What's good Slick? What you up to tonight?"

"I ain't doing nothing too much. I ain't got no paper. Why, what up with you?"

"You want a job nigga?"

"Man it's almost twelve o'clock and you call me talking about a job. What you smoking on?"

"Nah, I'm for real," Ronnie said seriously. "I'm out here at work and this Mexican just walked off and quit. They need somebody right now to take his place. They asked me if I knew anybody and I told 'em I did, you."

"Okay, I might as well," Slick responded. "I ain't doing nothing else. Just call me tomorrow and I'll be ready."

"No Slick, they want you to come out here right now; like within the next fifteen minutes."

Slick managed to make it to the site and started working. Even though the hours were long, the work was fairly easy. Working seven days a week with forty hours overtime, the job provided a nice weekly sum. Besides that, Slick enjoyed having something to do. The job also kept him out of trouble.

Slick took another step towards rehabilitation by enrolling in school. He decided he would complete the business degree he had started nearly four years earlier. He worked the job until the year ended and prepared for the task of school.

The Y2K date came and the world did not end. In the beginning, Slick held his focus in school. But as the year progressed, Slick fell prone to the usual distractions. Soon the girls and socializing became more important. Before long, Slick was right back to hanging with his old crowd, doing the same things that got him time.

One day in the middle of the semester, Slick and his cousin Quay were about to leave the campus when they were approached by campus security.

"Are you Mr. Richardson," the large black man asked Slick. "Do you have a red Daytona in the parking lot?"

"Yes sir that's me," Slick answered. "And yeah, I do have a red car out there. What's the problem?"

"It seems that someone has broken into your car. The window was smashed in and glass is everywhere. I've called the police and they're outside waiting to question you."

Slick had bought the car a month earlier. Always the schemer, he had used the tags from the Buick that he'd stolen back from the impoundment for the new car. He suddenly remembered that and raced to the parking lot.

Upon reaching the outside he saw no police. He hurried to the car and removed the fictitious plates. He inspected the glass and wondered who would have done this for a few school books. That became the least of his worries as he spotted the police car coming down the aisle.

"Mr. Richardson," the cop addressed, struggling to get out. "Is this your vehicle?"

"Yes sir. Apparently someone broke in. I don't know what for though."

"Well, how long have you had this car?"

"About a month or so," Slick asked becoming frustrated. "Are y'all gonna dust for prints or anything?"

"Well, the problem is this. The plate number that was reported to us does not match a red Daytona. They actually belong to a Buick that also happens to be registered to you. This same Buick was impounded a while back and subsequently stolen from the lot. Now tell me. You wouldn't happen to know anything about that would you?"

Slick answered carefully. "No sir, I don't."

The officer walked to the back of the car. "Where are the tags at now then?"

"I have no idea. When I came out here they were gone," Slick said, hoping they wouldn't search his bag. "I don't know what to tell you officer."

"Honestly, something seems strange. I'm gonna keep this report. And I certainly will be keeping in touch with you. I have all of your information so don't worry about a thing."

"You act like I'm the criminal or something," Slick said with a scowl. "You need to be finding out who broke into my car. Sorry ass clown!"

After a few more choice words, Slick dismissed the police and went back into the building. He waited until nightfall and then drove the car to his parent's house. The next morning, he took it to a local shop to have it repaired. Slick used the incident as an excuse to quit school and never returned to the college.

With no school or ambition, Slick again started to wander around aimlessly. He went from set to set, girl to girl and card game to card game. He would pick up an occasional job, only to hold it for no more than a few paychecks. Instead of work, he preferred hanging in the familiar setting of the streets.

By the end of the year, Slick was in the same position as he was before he went to prison. He started to get high and drunk more often. He did have some good fortune however. Danny didn't come to court so the robbery was dropped. The felony gun charge was also dropped to a misdemeanor. Therefore, in January 2001 when he went to court for the third DWI he didn't know what to expect. Slick readily accepted the thirty day plea agreement, which was good considering the year he had gotten for the second.

The thirty days evaporated like mist. Once again, Slick was released, clean, sober and with good intentions. He got a job again but didn't like it and quit after three weeks. It seemed to many around him that he had committed himself to becoming a hardened criminal.

So busy getting into petty trouble, Slick was unaware of the change in the streets around him. A lot of the major players in the small town were getting knocked. The rest were scared and moved away, fearing all of the federal informants that were turning state. The town was so small that nearly everyone was affiliated so therefore everyone was hot. No one knew who to trust.

It was at this time that Brain retuned from South Carolina. Brake also had returned from Raleigh. He and Big Sal had moved to the state capitol to escape the round up and Crazy Stan was on the run. The heat and a few sour deals had caused their operation to go south, so Brake was now scrambling to get back on his feet. Slick was happy to have his old peoples back in town and began to chill with them like before.

Due to the changes within the game a new drug emerged on the scene. Ecstasy became a favorite among many of the party goers in the town. Pretty soon it spread like wildfire. Slick had heard of and seen people rolling, but he preferred to sniff coke and smoke. He was leery after watching a couple of his homeboys overdo it and get turned out on the colorful pills.

His opposition wouldn't last for long. One night, while Slick was at Brain's house, Brake came through with Big Sal and Snake. Snake was a longtime associate of all the men. Slick knew him as good basketball player. The others knew him for the cold-hearted hustler that he was. The five men sat around drinking and smoking for a while until Brain wanted to go further.

"I know you got some of them poppers Brake," Brain slurred slowly. "Go 'head and come up off some. Your boy trying to get right!"

"How many you need," Brake said, pulling out a large Ziploc bag full of multi-colored pills."

"Give me two," Brain said pulling out a twenty.

"Shit, let me get two then," Snake said smiling. "Matter of fact, you might as well put one on the table for everybody."

"Hell yeah," added Sal, grabbing the bag. "This knuckle head got a thousand pills in his pocket and actin' like that. He gon make me go upside that round head of his."

"Y'all humpty-dumpty ass niggas act like this shit grow on trees," Brake said smiling. "You better dig them paws in them pockets and pull out some bread. Y'all niggas trippin'"

Brake was only joking. He opened the bag and laid out five triple stacks for the crew. Slick loved to see how his people looked out for each other. Everybody had been through tough times together and was just glad to be able to sit back and talk about it.

"Slick, you got to pop with us tonight," Brake added. "I know you ain't never did it before, but fuck it. You with us tonight, so don't trip."

Slick took the pill with everyone else. They popped and chased it with liquor. It took almost twenty minutes for the drug to take effect. When it did, the euphoric stimulation was like nothing he'd ever felt. His whole body filled with warmth and a sense of pleasure. Twenty minutes later, the drug was at full blast. Slick was extremely horny and needed relief. He left the men right there and went to one of his freak's house.

The pain and pleasure that he gave to the girl had her asking him what was wrong with him. Slick pounded the girl for hours. The drug kept him extremely aroused, but would not allow him to climax. After mentally forcing himself to come, Slick got up and left the girl writhing on the bed. He walked out of the house coldly. He was still aroused however and he went to yet another girl's house to finish his mission.

Slick continued to frolic around for most of 2001. One morning, he was sitting with Tasha, a girl he had known since high school. The two had been up all night getting high and were still going at about 9:00 a.m. Slick was in the bathroom freshening up when he heard a scream.

"Aaaaaahhhhh! Oh lord! Slick! Come here and look. Quick!"

Slick ran into the room to find out the commotion. He entered and found Tasha staring stupidly at the television. "Look at that," she said pointing. "They saying that we being attacked."

"What in the world," Slick said, watching the planes slam into the towers over and over.

"They said that some Muslims or somebody did it form Iraq or Saudi Arabia somewhere over there. Slick this is crazy man. I'd probably be scared if I didn't have this coke."

The chaos on television didn't curtail their usage. Actually, the excitement induced them to get more. Slick and Tasha sat and watched the coverage all day, while getting high and drunk on her couch. The president addressed the nation, and vowed that the attackers would pay dearly. However, during the upcoming year, Slick would see no difference in the violence overseas and the battlefield that his environment had become.

■■

By the beginning of 2002, things had returned to normal. People returned to their everyday lives and hustlers returned to the streets. Because of the new 9/11 safety standards, there was difficulty getting a hold of drugs in many states. Somehow, the small city of Goldsboro managed to keep a steady supply of everything.

Along with the drug activity, Goldsboro had many liquor houses. These were spots that one could go to at any time of morning or night to buy alcohol. Many, also doubled as number houses and gambling joints. Inevitably, when money, liquor and drugs were involved, there would always be volatile circumstances.

A month after New Year's, Slick started to frequent one such area. Devereux Street was a residential area that held five such houses in a two block stretch. The houses had been there for years. Even though the occupants came and went, the illegal activity remained. The location was a haven for crime, despite the elementary school across the street.

A corner house was owned by two sisters. One of them, Nika, he had known from school. The other, Meesha, he had seen around town, but she was younger and he didn't know her that well. The girls had started selling liquor and Slick went to their spot more because of the smaller crowd. It was also a convenient place to sell his products. It was in the heart of the town and near the old projects where he spent most of his time.

The more he went it seemed the more people came. Word spread quickly and the girls began enjoying regular business. One night Slick was there playing cards, when he realized that no one else was there but him, his opponent, a few drunks and Meesha. She had been flirting with him all night as he sent her for drinks. Slick had ignored the light-skinned cutie with the petite frame for most of the night. But now with the alcohol and lateness of the evening, he began to pick up on her hints.

"This is gonna have to be the last hand," she said. "It's already three in the morning and I'm 'bout to close up shop."

"Okay baby," Slick said without argument. He had already won enough and was about done anyway. Also, he knew he had a chance with Meesha and was eager to dig her out. "This is gonna be the last hand and we out."

"Well Slick, I was gonna ask you if you could help me clean this mess up and take these bottles out for me."

"I got you lil' mama. Don't worry about nothing," said Slick smiling. He looked at Meesha and she licked her teeth with her tongue sticking out. Slick knew he was in from then on.

The hand ended and Slick's opponent left. Slick got up and started to clean up the kitchen while Meesha was in the living room. She then called him back up front and pointed to a drunk, still sleep on the couch.

"I keep trying to tell him to leave but he won't get up," she complained. "I'm tired of his ass. He always do that."

Slick walked over to the man that he had known since childhood and shook him. "Ty! Ty! Get up man! Shorty trying to close up, nigga. You got to get up. You don't got to go home, but you got to get the hell outta here!"

Slick continued to prod the pan until he finally left. He locked the door and began to help her clean. After everything was done, Slick grabbed Meesha by the waist and led her to the living room. She offered no resistance so he took off her clothes. He put it down on her in the living room that night and many thereafter.

From then on, he centered his operation at the liquor house. He and Meesha became close even though they each had other friends. It was more of a business relationship. The sex was just extra. He was there so much, however, that people started to think he ran the house.

Occasionally during the summer, the house would get pack. One night, Slick walked in to see three other girls he was involved with. He played it tight by ignoring all of them. He figured the best way to avoid a riff was not to acknowledge any of them.

At the end of the night when everyone was leaving, Slick walked onto the front porch. He saw Snake standing in the street arguing with three men. He listened to the quarrel from the porch.

"I ain't gon keep telling y'all to back up from around me," Snake warned with his hand in his pocket. "I ain't playing with y'all. I already feel threatened."

"What you gon' do then. If you feel like that you'd a been did something. That's the problem though. You ain't gon' do shit." Terror, a local drunk who always started trouble, inched closer to the Snake.

"I'm done telling y'all to back up. Y'all think it ain't real then, huh?"

They got within a few feet from Snake. Without warning, he pulled a small pistol and fired into the group. People scattered as two of the men hit the ground. Slick got low and watched Snake run down the street. Even though Slick was cool with everyone, he got in his car after Snake to make sure he was okay. He found him a few blocks away and took him safely of the west side.

A couple of weeks later, Slick found himself with Brake and Snake one Saturday evening. They were out riding and ended up on the north end of town. There, they met up with Fo-Five and Seymour at a liquor house. The five smoked and drank until the club was about to close.

When they were high enough, they decided to go to Lynn's, another liquor house that got packed after the club. They arrived before the crowd and had the bar to themselves. Snake, however, had stayed outside with some of his young shooters because of the beef.

When the club closed the liquor house began to fill up. Just as it got crowded, Khalid, a hustler with ties to Terror, the guy Snake shot, entered. His appearance was magnified by the machine gun slung over his shoulder. His words pierced the air as he spoke.

"All hoes please leave!"

The attention was now on the gunman. Both men and women scattered for the exits. Slick was not worried because he was also cool with Khalid. He took no hurry in getting out while the gunman patrolled the house. Slick finally made it to the front door with the gunman close behind.

Soon as Slick reached the bottom of the steps, gunfire rang out. Slick ducked off to the side of the steps and saw Khalid go down. Rounds continue to fly above his head while he ducked for cover. After the shooting stopped, Slick ran to the car, where Snake and Brake were already there waiting.

"Hurry up nigga," Brake yelled. "What the hell you doing? We got to get away from here!"

Slick hopped in and listened to Snake rave about the shooting. "See, I knew that nigga was gon' come round here with some trouble. I just felt it. Y'all see I didn't even go in."

"But who started busting first though," Brake asked. "Only thing I heard was shots out the blue."

"My young niggas let off soon as he got out the door good. I got off a few rounds but he was already hit by then."

"That nigga crazy as hell to come in your hood with that bullshit," Brake said. "Niggas just ain't got nothing better to do 'round here than act stupid.

When the dust settled, Khalid had been shot multiple times, all below the waist. He was hospitalized for a few days then released. The streets kept silent about the shooting and no one was ever arrested.

Life continued to spiral for Slick. The pills, coke, and weed had him running around for days at a time. He had several houses he could go to and lay up with various women. Normally, he stayed mostly around Devereux Street and the projects, where he felt most comfortable.

Late in the summer, Slick was at Boots, a liquor house in the back of the projects. While there, he ran into his cousin Tray, who had not long come home from a murder charge. Slick was glad to see him. He sat outside in the car with him doing coke while they caught up on old times.

"So what you gon' do now that you home," Slick asked. "What kind of plans you got going on."

"Nothing much," Tray responded in his quiet demeanor. "I'm just out here trying to get this money. That's all I know how to do."

"Ain't nothing wrong with that," Slick said switching subjects. "But who in the liquor house though?"

"Nobody for real. Just a few whack broads and some clown ass niggas. Speaking of that, I'm a rob this dude right here in the truck when he come out." Tray revealed a black sawed off shotgun from within his army jacket sleeve.

Slick brushed the comment aside and kept getting high. He knew his cousin was a livewire, but was too engrossed in his own world to care. He didn't really know if he would try to stop him if he did.

"Forget that crazy shit," Slick said finally responding. "Let's go in here and get some drinks and see what these stragglers talking about."

The two men entered the small house and mingled with the few people there. Slick however, kept a close eye on his cousin. While Slick bought the drinks, Tray stayed quietly detached from everyone in the corner. Slick knew that he was hungry and plotting heavily.

When the house was clearing, Slick walked back to his car, while Tray lagged behind waiting for his victim. When the man emerged with the three women, Tray approached them and started talking in a friendly manner. Slick knew the girls and also talked with them. Tray was focused on one and Slick thought he had abandoned his plan.

Things were going good until the man attempted to enter his vehicle. Tray held the door and prevented him from getting all of the way in.

"Hey, my man," the guy said. "What's wrong with you? Let me get in my car!"

"Nah, you can't leave," Tray answered coldly. "You don't got no business around here anyway. This my hood."

"Man if you don't get your hands off my door and let me go. What the hell you talking about, this your hood? Man you're crazy!" The women began to get antsy and each one opened their door.

"Nah nigga, you ain't finna go nowhere." Tray removed the shotgun and trained it at the man's face. "I need everything you got right now or I'm a blow your face off."

The man pleaded for his life. Slick watched stunned from the driver's seat. The screaming from the women roused Slick out of his stupor. He tried to diffuse the situation by calling his cousin.

"Tray! Tray! Come on man. Let's go. That nigga ain't got nothing!"

Tray kept the gun trained on the man. "I don't care. Whatever he got, I need it." He turned slightly to Slick. "Go 'head and pull of if you ain't with it."

The brief distraction allowed the victim to push the gun away and shut the door. Tray struggled to get the door back open but the man sped off. Dejected, he got in the car with Slick. "Damn, man. I coulda' had that nigga."

Slick rode off and called Brake, who was on the west side. Slick drove his cousin with him to pick up some pills. When they arrived, Slick got out and went into the house. Brake and a few others came out with Slick and walked him back to the car. When Mark, who lived at the spot, notice who Slick's passenger was, he gave him some advice.

"You better get that boy outta here as fast as you can. You must ain't know he don't supposed to be on this side. He got a bounty on his head from niggas around here. The only reason I'm doing this is 'cause I know his mama. But you got to take him somewhere."

Slick knew about the beef between Webb Town and the North, but he didn't realize his cousin was involved. Tray was either fearless or crazy because he said nothing when Slick arrived in the area. He still accepted the warning and took Tray back to the projects. Slick would continue to hang with Tray, despite the issues. Once again he would make a bad decision regarding the company he kept.

Life got more turbulent for Slick. Selling weed, crack and pills kept him moving in every direction. In addition, using coke and popping pills kept his mind in a constant state of disillusion. Adding the women, he barely had a chance to assess his lifestyle. One day, Boot, the liquor house owner, took him aside.

"Boy, I don't know what's wrong with you. You got a serious problem. I'm only telling you this cause I like you. I don't know what it is. But if you keep going like you going, somebody gonna stop you. I'm telling you now, so you better get it straight."

The stern look and hard tone let Slick know the older man was serious. Slick considered the words if only for a day. He knew Boot had been in the game a while and knew what he was talking about. Slick had no intention of slowing down however, because the excitement and fun was too much to leave.

Time progressed and Devereux Street was live as ever. One night, Slick entered Nika's, and found it as packed as it had ever been. When Slick came up, people started to ask him for drinks. It was so crowded they had no chance of getting to the bar. They figured Slick, with his relationship to the owner, could get drinks faster.

As Slick squeezed through the mass of bodies, the scene was disturbing. The sea of people was crammed into the small space, making it nearly impossible to move. He finally made it to the bar and secured himself a drink. After surveying atmosphere, he decided to leave until the crowd decreased. Nothing good could ever come out of this many people in such a small place.

His suspicions were right. Before he made it to the back door, he encountered a scuffle. Terror, always drunk and armed, was in a dispute with an unknown man a few feet away. The quarrel became physical when Terror shoved the man hard. The man stumbled backwards. In the confusion, Terror's gun dropped and smashed to the floor.

When people saw the gun, everyone tried to rush out of the back door. Slick knowing the layout, moved towards the front door. Before he reached the door, gunfire erupted inside and out.

Shots rang from every side. Rounds flew inside bouncing off walls and furniture. From the sounds, Slick thought everyone in the house was shooting. He made it onto the front porch and was greeted by more fire. He ducked for cover, hearing the whiz of bullets zip past his ears and hitting the house.

The firefight continued for what seemed an eternity. Slick was praying out loud as the bullets landed close to his proximity. When the firing ceased, Slick scrambled around to the back of the house. He was let in and sat and talked with the two sisters about what had happened. It was evident to all three that by the morning the house would not be open for a while.

The next morning, Slick went home to find his parents leaving for church. The irony of their life compared to his was disconcerting. Slick longed for the simpler days that his parents enjoyed. The drugs and violence around him was eating at his core. He removed the smokescreen and examined his life for what it really was; a straight line road to death or the penal system. Slick preferred to see neither one.

After they left, Slick stepped outside to smoke a cigarette. Half way through, he saw a white van stop in front of his house. Something drew him towards the vehicle as if he were in a trance. When he reached the van, he saw that it was his cousin Latisha.

Slick had been tight with his older cousin since high school. She considered him like a little brother and was always there for him. This time it was no different. Latisha sensed a problem when Slick just stood there not speaking.

"What's wrong baby," she asked in a sympathetic voice

Slick became full of emotion. The drugs and the events around him had come to a boiling point. Tears streamed down his eyes as he thought of all the loved ones he'd disappointed and the mistakes he'd made. Seeing his pain, Latisha got out the car to console him.

"Don't worry about whatever it is. You know God got it all under control boo. And I love you too, nigga. If you ever need anything, you got my number. Make sure you call me. I love you, boy."

After a few more hugs and kisses Latisha left. Slick felt better after talking to her. He also knew that the same temptations were waiting for him as soon as he came back out. He was not quite ready to give himself to God, but he needed a change. Slick walked into the house and fell into a deep sleep.

That night, Slick was awaked by his mother. She extended the phone to him and left the room.

"Who is it," he yelled out.

"It's Wood," his mother called back.

Slick started not to take the call. Wood was also one of his friends that could tell when something was wrong. There was no way he felt like talking to Wood about what he was going through. Having no one else to turn to, he spoke into the receiver.

"What's up Wood?"

"Antonio! My man, what's going on? I been down here the whole weekend and I ain't seen you yet. What's good?"

"I'm chillin'. I been right 'round here," Slick said in a monotone voice.

"Man, get out that bed boy. I know you probably done been out for 'bout three days, wilding out. I done called the crib I don't know how many times."

"Oh yeah, I didn't know that."

"I bet you didn't. You ain't never home."

"What you doing down here anyway," Slick said diverting the pressure. "You probably down here running around with some of them stragglers."

"Nah, not really, but what's going on for real, Slick?" Wood could detect the distress in his friend's voice and got serious. "Come on man. I've known you too long and heard this voice too many times. Go 'head and talk to your boy."

Slick didn't know where to begin. He felt like a failure. His life was a whirlwind futility and he was going nowhere fast. "I don't know man. It feels like I'm trapped or suffocating around here. I don't got nothing to do. I feel like I'm about to go insane or something."

"Well, what you want me to do. You know anything you need, I got you. What you want?"

"Nothing for real. I just feel like it's time for a change. It's like if I stay down here, either I'm a end up hurting somebody, or somebody gonna end up hurting me. That's just the way it is."

"So what, you wanna come back to VA with me. You know you good."

"When you leaving," Slick asked skeptically.

"I'm a hit the road in a couple of hours. You think you'll be ready by then?"

"Man...I don't know about just leaving like that. You talking about tonight."

"Yeah, man, that's what it is. Matter of fact, gon' and have your stuff ready. You coming, like it or not. I done heard this shit too many times and I ain't gon' let you sit 'round here and keep doing it. I'll be there at about eleven, so be ready."

Wood hung up the phone, leaving Slick with mixed feelings. Leaving Goldsboro was something that he never even considered in life. What would he do? How would he survive? The questions were endless. However, Virginia did offer an exciting new place and a fresh start where nobody knew him. Slick decided to take his friend's offer and became enthused about it.

Slick packed up quickly and waited for Wood. Slick surprised his parents with his suitcase. He announced to them that he was moving to Virginia as he walked to the door.

"Well, hold up," his mother said. "Who you gon' live with.

"Wood!"

"Well you sure it's alright with him."

"Yes ma. We already talked about it."

"Well how you gon' survive? You got a job already? Have you thought about this good?"

"Yes ma'am," Slick said exasperated. His mother's questions were evidence of her concern, but Slick thought her worries were small. The main objective was that he was getting out of Goldsboro. Slick expected her to be happy and proud of him for making the decision.

"Okay son," said his father. "You be careful up there. You know I used to be stationed up that way myself."

"Yeah, but I'm a be in the Virginia Beach. You was in Norfolk."

"It's pretty much the same thing," his father said standing to his feet. "Anyway, we love you son and we wish you the best of success in anything that you do."

When Wood came and tooted the horn, Slick walked to the door. Before leaving, he was interrupted by his father.

"Oh, I almost forgot. Let us pray with you real quick before you go."

Slick joined hands with his mother and father. Since he was little, they had the habit of praying before departure. Slick welcomed the blessings and bowed his head, listening to the words of the prayer.

"Heavenly Father, we come to you in Jesus name. We're asking you to watch over our son as he moves to Virginia. Lord we ask you to protect him, lead him and guide him in everything he does. Let your Spirit be upon him, and your face shine upon him and give him peace. Bless his life in a mighty way and keep him from all temptation. Lord we plead the blood of Jesus over him now and commit his life into your hands. We ask all these things in Jesus name, counting them already done, Amen."

Slick gave his parents hugs and left with Wood. He stayed mostly silent during the three hour drive. He assessed his life up to this point, all of the chances he'd blown. He also considered the new opportunity presented to him.

He knew that Wood was responsible, and would take no foolishness. He would not allow Slick to self-destruct, or live the way he'd been living. He would hold him accountable. Slick knew that only under conditions such as these could he make a change. He silently made a vow to make the most of his friend's sacrifice.

What he didn't consider was the same temptations, vices and evils were waiting for him in Virginia with open arms. He would come to learn the hard way that's it's not a different environment that changes a man, but the difference in his inner self that brings about a transformation.

11
Calm before the Storm

October 2005
Virginia Beach, VA

Slick was a prisoner in the Indianapolis jail for ten days. He passed the time by watching television and playing cards during the day. The natives took a liking to Slick and gave him the nickname Juvi, saying that he favored the Cash Money rapper. Slick joked with the men like they were lifelong friends. At night, however, he found himself praying to God for help. He knew he didn't want to resort back to the life upon his release. The only power he knew that could help him was the God he talked to every night.

On the eleventh day, two Virginia Beach detectives arrived to extradite Slick back to Virginia. The black and white officers represented the system that Slick detested. Slick proceeded to voice his opinion of them from the backseat on the way to the airport. The words he used were harsh and vulgar. He continued until the white cop, Miller, had enough.

"Listen, son," the gruff man said looking back. "Our only job is to bring your body back to Virginia. It doesn't matter how we do it. It can be in an ambulance, a bag, or a hearse. It doesn't matter to me. So I suggest you just sit back there and cool it."

The threat was clear enough and Slick gave it a rest. When they arrived at the airport, Slick felt the stairs of other passengers as he walked through the airport. He was between both officers, with a towel covering the handcuffs. He kept removing the towel. It was obvious that he was a captive so why try to hide it he thought. He imagined the thoughts of the people. Even though he hadn't done anything, the way they had him bound made him look dangerous.

The plane ride was short. Slick chatted with the black cop while the other slept. They arrived in Virginia Beach and took Slick to the precinct. Not to his surprise, he was again denied bail. He went through the normal procedures and finally received another $10,000 bond after two more weeks. He was released and went back to his aunt's house to try and resume a normal life.

When he returned to the real estate office, he learned that he had lost his listing. Sanya had tried to cover for him while he was away, but the owner got skeptical and pulled the house from the market. Slick still remained encouraged by the support he was receiving. Sanya brought up a different option.

"So what you gonna do for money now. You haven't sold a house yet and you're not dealing any more right," Sonya asked as they sat in her car. "How are you gonna make it?"

"Well, I got some change saved up, so I'll be straight for a minute. And let's not forget. I'm a be pushing houses like they was coke in a while. Everything gon' come together soon."

"If you say so, Slick. I'm gonna tell you right now. This business is kind of shaky. Especially since the market has slowed here recently. I haven't sold a house in three months myself. That should let you know how hard it is."

"See," Slick exclaimed sarcastically. "You ain't made no money in a while and you don't look like you missed any meals. Trust me, I'll be fine."

"Yeah, but I got Jim. He has his own business so I have something to fall back on. You, on the other hand, are out here by yourself. Don't you have bills? Are you sure going to make it?"

"I got to make it. I'm a survivor. I just got to do it the right way."

Slick tried hard to stay true to his word. He kept his hands clean for the most part. He still had contact with many customers so he would play middleman on some occasions to a make a dollar. This led, however, to his continuous use as he would take some for himself each time. This made his situation worse, because he then began spending his own money, something that was dwindling quickly away.

When Christmas came around, Slick visited family and friends in North Carolina. He had fun socializing with people he hadn't seen in years. He passed out real estate cards and many people congratulated him on his success. He felt like a legitimate businessman. The façade would quickly start to unravel when Slick returned after the New Year of 2006.

Although Slick's income had changed, his living expenses didn't. He continued to spend money like he was dealing. His lavish tastes for food, clothes and women still enticed him. His cocaine use continued although at a lower level. The thousands of dollars he had to pay the lawyer for the gun charges also put a dent in Slick's pocket. Slick was happier not in the game but was definitely feeling the effects financially.

In addition, his living arrangements began to sour. One morning, his sleep was broken by muffled arguing. The voices of his aunt and her boyfriend became louder. The words the man spoke to Dorothy made Slick fume. He held his peace and tried to ignore the incident. He didn't even mention it to his aunt at the time.

A few days later, Slick was awakened to the same noise, this time louder.

"Go 'head and leave Bobby," he heard his aunt say. "This is my house. If you can't act no better than that, you know what to do."

"Fuck you and this place. I don't need you. I never did!"

"Get out of my face now, Bobby. You need to leave before you get yourself in trouble."

"I ain't going nowhere until I feel like it," Slick heard the man say. "It ain't nothing nobody can do about it!"

Slick tried to ignore the fuss but couldn't. He left his room and saw his aunt and her boyfriend standing in the doorway. Slick looked at the man with disdain. He also looked at his Dorothy with disapproval. Slick spoke with her when the man finally left.

"I can't do this. This ain't the first time I done heard y'all early in the morning. I didn't say nothing out of respect. But I can't just sit here and listen to that."

"I know Slick," she responded. "I'm so sorry you had to hear that. It's crazy. He only act like that when he been drinking a lot."

"Well, if you don't want me to interfere with your relationship, then I think it's best for me to leave. I just can't sit here and do nothing. If you're okay with it, that's fine, but I can't handle it."

"I can understand how you feel. I should have told you about him earlier."

"It ain't no problem. I'm just giving you two weeks-notice."

Slick once again had to resort to his client base in order to find somewhere to live. He called around and found that Slack the bail bondsman was selling his house. Because of the slow market, he had his brother Brock and Gino staying there until it sold. After learning of Slick's predicament, all three men agreed that Slick could share the three bedroom house for a portion of the rent.

Slick knew that staying in the house with two hard core coke users was going to be a challenge. Brock and Gino partied nearly every night. Slick would indulge with him, but still wouldn't sell it. Before long, Slick saw no reason to let the money get buy him. He started to serve his roommates, along with a few other select customers. But this time, his conscience convicted him like never before. Slick felt inside that if he went full-fledged something drastic would happen. He kept this in mind and treaded lightly.

In an attempt to stay straight, Slick got a job with a collection agency. He was still a licensed broker, but the market had caved and nobody was selling anything. He got the job for the extra cash and the numerous women. Slick loved the environment and actually did well, until his drug use caused him to be late constantly. He was dismissed only two weeks after the three week training period.

Within a few months, his living arrangement grew sour also. Slick found out that Gino wasn't paying Brock and Brock wasn't paying the rent to his brother. Slick found himself caught in the middle of a dispute between the three. He felt that it was his fault for bringing the coke into the house. Even though he wasn't deep in the game, the constant access was enough. By the start of the summer, Slick was once again facing homelessness.

Through a real estate connect, Slick found another broker who was renting out her house. Slick made contact and agreed to rent the extra room. He was able to escape the chaos of the party house but the damage had been done. His habit had been reborn and his tolerance surpassed previous levels.

Amidst all the discord, Slick did manage to secure four legitimate clients during the summer, simultaneously. His ground work was beginning to pay off as contacts called and literally gave him customers. He was able to help the clients with their needs and all of a sudden had four deals going.

The gun charges were also disposed of at this time. His lawyer had negotiated a plea where he would receive only probation for the felonies. It seemed like the black cloud was being lifted from his head and he used these things as an incentive stay clear of the law.

Unfortunately, Slick descended again into a pattern that characterized his life. Just when everything seemed fine and success was on the horizon, Slick found a way to sabotage his own progress. He digressed into a self-destructive state.

Slick began receiving the commissions from his deals in July. By October, all of the money was gone. He had spent the interim in the bedroom of the large house getting high off cocaine. All of the summer holidays had passed and Slick had celebrated neither. He had forfeited all of his ambition to the substance. In the confusion, he didn't even realize he missed his high school's ten year class reunion.

As Fall 2006 arrived, Slick was broke and struggling with his rent. He hadn't been to the office in months. He continued to stow away in the small room. He had no control over the habit as it consumed him day by day. He religiously ignored calls from close family members who were worried. His landlord also expressed her concern one day when she knocked on the door.

"Taylor," she said softly, peeking through the door. "Is everything alright?"

"Yes ma'am," Slick said opening the door. He looked disheveled from staying up all night. "Why you asking me that?"

"Just because. You've been spending a lot of time in here lately. You said you sell real estate, but every time I leave or come back, you're still here."

"I took some time off," Slick lied. "It's been kind of slow but I'm going back to work soon."

"It's not just that. You're running in and out all times of the might. You smoke all the time, when you told me that you barely smoke at all. I just didn't expect this."

"I'm sorry. I'm just going through something right now. I'm gonna get it together in a few."

"Well, it's almost the fifth and you haven't even said anything about the rent. Do you even have the money?"

"I have most of it. I'm about two hundred dollars short, but I can have it by next week."

"No sir, I can't do that. I told you at the beginning I needed the money on the first. This is the second month in a row you've not paid on time. I can't do business like this because I have things I have to do. I'm sorry Taylor, but you have to go."

Slick was too high and drunk to argue. He gathered all of his things and piled them into his car. After a few trips to his storage, he was out of the house the same day. For the first time in his life he had nowhere to go. He thought about calling his parents but his pride wouldn't let him. He drove around aimlessly before pulling into the back of his old Thalia Oaks apartment, where it had all begun. He cut the car off, climbed in the back seat and went to sleep.

He woke up the next morning with new resolve. After bathing in a convenient store sink, he went to a temp service to find a job. Immediate warehouse positions were open and he got the job starting that same night. He worked the job, sleeping in his car for about a week and a half. Somehow, he managed to keep his nose dirty by still supplying some of his clients through other connects.

On the second weekend, Slick was in his car getting high when he received a call. It was Spray's momma inviting him to play cards. Slick took the thirty minute drive to Portsmouth to see if he could improve his luck.

He got to the game and started off winning. After drinking too much liquor, he lost focus along with all of his money. Without a dollar to his name, Slick took the drive back to Virginia Beach with the intentions of sleeping in his car.

On the interstate he drove erratically under the influence of brandy, gin and cocaine. He took toots as he swerved between lanes of the road. He sped needlessly, having no destination.

Halfway there, he attempted to change lanes without looking. The horn from the other car was the only thing that stopped Slick from running the driver off the road. The sirens that sounded next were probably the best thing that could have happened. Slick stuffed the cocaine down in his drawers before pulling over on the shoulder.

The young white trooper looked worried as he approached the car. He lowered his head to the window slowly.

"Can I see your license and registration sir."

"I don't have neither one," Slick said, already belligerent. "And I'm drunk as hell. So if you gonna take me to jail, I don't care. Just hurry up and do your job."

"Yes sir, I can definitely smell the liquor on your breath. How much have you had already tonight?"

"Do it look like I know," Slick said smartly. "You look like the wiz kid. How about you tell me."

"Well you're so drunk that you almost ran that car off the road back there. That's why I stopped you."

"Okay man, so what you gon' do. I aint got no license and I'm drunk. If you gon' take me to jail, come on. I ain't got no time for this. This is like my fifth DWI anyway. What they gonna do to me?"

"Okay, step out of the car and put your hands behind your back then." Slick obeyed and the officer frisked him. "Do you have anything else on you or in the car?"

"No faggot," Slick said becoming impatient. "Let's go. It's cold out here and I want to get some rest. I ain't been to sleep in three days anyway! What you know about that, punk boy?"

Slick antagonized the officer throughout the sobriety tests. On the way to the station, Slick continued to be unruly towards the younger man. The trooper was relieved when they pulled into the precinct. He took Slick before the magistrate and explained the charges and his behavior.

The magistrate, a young black guy with dreads ignored the trooper's statements. The trooper had tried to give Slick more charges because of his actions. Sympathetically, the magistrate gave him a $5000 bond and he was assigned to the fifth floor of the Norfolk City Jail.

When he reached the floor, Slick pulled out the cocaine that he managed to sneak passed the search. He got high right there on his bunk. Nobody noticed and he sniffed all night and the next day until it was gone.

Without money and a place to stay, Slick resolved to sit in jail until his court date. He felt like he had come to the end of his rope. He got familiar with the jail and began to converse with a few cats he knew on the streets.

After a few days, he was told about pre-trial release, a system that allowed an offender to be released on probationary terms before the court date. Slick applied for the program that day and awaited the results.

Three days later, a large black woman came to his cell and asked Slick questions about his circumstances. Slick gave answers he knew would satisfy the woman. After the interview, Slick was told that he would know the outcome in a day or two. A letter came from booking the next day stating that he would be released later that night. Slick was happy until he remembered he still had nowhere to go.

When they let him out at twelve a.m., Slick wondered around the downtown Norfolk area aimlessly until about two. He came upon the bus station, entered and sat down. He called a few people but was unable to reach anyone that time of the morning. He sat on the hard bench and tried to formulate a plan. He could not go to sleep for the anxiety and remained awake until daylight.

The next morning, he called his aunt and told her what had occurred. She came to get him and first took him to get his car from the impound. He was told that it would be over a thousand dollars to get out. Slick didn't have the money and after a protest, decided to leave. She then took him to pick up his last check from the job. After running a few more errands, she took Slick to her house to get settled.

"Okay Slick," she said. "You can stay here for a few days until you can find something else. I don't mean no harm, but I think we both know that you and me can't stay together for long. I'm just used to my own space."

Slick agreed that he would find a place soon. The next day, he looked in the paper and found a room in the Park

Place area of Norfolk. For a $100 a week it wasn't the best spot, but it would have to do. In the same paper, he also came across an ad for a sales position. He called and set up an interview with the manager. Within a week of his release, Slick had already found a job and an apartment.

Slick moved into the house on 34th street that was shared by two others. Without a car, he had to catch the bus to work. The hour ride there and back allowed Slick to think and get his mind in order. He welcomed the time that he had to connect with his inner self.

Life Assist was a small office of about twenty-five phones and computers. Employees called prospective customer under the guise of working for the blind. The customer was then offered everyday household products at astronomical prices. The pitch played on sympathy for the handicapped and Slick was surprised at how many people were duped. Using his charm and persuasive ability, Slick nevertheless excelled and was promoted quickly.

New Year's 2007 came and Slick was settled into a routine. He would work all day and get back to the lonely room around eleven. Then he would read or talk on the phone until he fell asleep. The next day he would do it over again. The strict discipline lasted for the first few months and kept Slick out of trouble. Even though he was by himself, Slick enjoyed the peace that came with solitude.

When spring approached, Slick was making nearly a thousand dollars a week. He had learned a technique from Charles, a top seller, and tailored it to himself. The more hours he worked, the more money he made. The more money he made, the more he began to socialize with his co-workers.

The office manager's name was Robbie. Like Slick he was young, black and had been to prison. He was a strict boss who was known for angry outbursts and embarrassment of his employees. He exploded sometimes without warning. This was strange to Slick considering the large amounts of weed Robbie smoked.

Melanie was his assistant. She was a petite, caramel complexioned beauty who had taken a liking to Slick. Through conversation they found they had a lot in common. Both of their parents were Christians. She also shared Slick's passion for reading. It would only be a short while, before discovering they had more sinister vices in common.

Charles was the fifty-year old who had trained Slick. He was the top seller and very good on the phone. His attitude, however, turned many of his peers off. His arrogant and egotistical nature caused those around to detest him. Slick would not know how spiteful the man was until later.

Kia was an eighteen year old hot girl. Fresh out of high school, she was green to the ways of the world and excited to have new freedoms. She was very open-minded and many of the horny individuals in the office would take advantage of her naivety. Slick had even refused her advances, when she offered to perform random oral sex on him.

Two more good friends were Ray and Pam. Pam was a churchgoing, mother like figure. She always encouraged Slick to follow his roots after learning his background. She was a stabilizing force in the otherwise worldly office. Ray was a chubby, lively black guy. He loved to talk about sports or women. Either topic could set off a debate lasting the whole day. The two were comical, because they always found some issue to disagree on.

Numerous others came and went. Michelle was a white girl who was pretty much black. She only liked blacks and had three kids by the age of twenty. Her hard life shown in the way she drank excessively. Slick liked her because of her gangster ways and they became close. Slick had no attraction to her, contrary to what others at the office thought. He was content making money and staying out of dangerous situations.

When the summer came, the office grew lively. Everyone was selling and the office resembled a lounge or nightclub. Michelle and others brought bottles to work.

Robbie smoked blunts like his mind was bad. Fresh new young girls showed up weekly to try their hand at selling. Many only succeeded in getting caught up with one or more of the womanizing men in the office.

One day during the reverie, Slick was on the phone when he heard a voice through his headset. "Slick," Melanie's voice said. "After you finish that call, come into the office real quick. I got something for you."

Slick closed the call, turned off the phone and walked into the small room. "What's up Ms. Sexy?"

Melanie blushed as she reached into her purse. "Like I said, I got a little something for you," she said handing him a folded bill. "I remembered you said you mess with that white girl from time to time. My peoples came through earlier with some fire and I thought about you."

Slick took the bill and unfolded it. He inspected the white powder and then started to refuse. It had been months since he had gotten high. He had smoked and drank, but ever since the last DWI he had remained clean.

"I didn't know you got dirty though," Slick said still debating. "I would've never known just looking at you."

"I didn't wanna let you know cause you said you was trying to chill. But I know it's the summer and niggas be getting loose. So I said I'm a turn by boy on."

Slick fell victim to the pressure and ingested the drug. He was accosted by the feeling he had craved so much before. The high overcame him and he no longer wanted to work. He convinced Melanie to allow him to leave and get more. She agreed and when the office closed, she and he sat and got high until leaving.

This first act had reopened Pandora's box and Slick couldn't close it. Now, every night after work he would by a gram or more of cocaine. He'd usually sit up all night buy himself in the little room and sniff.

Before he knew it, he was in the same state as the previous year. Summer again disappeared without him realizing it. The only difference is that he continued to work.

Soon, the money that he was making was barely enough to cover his habit. He had nothing to show for the thousands he was making.

When fall began, the office calmed a bit. Complaints from Charles had reached the corporate office. Robbie began to tone things down along with everyone else. Michelle reduced the alcohol consumption and there were no more wild antics.

One day, a dark-skinned petite chick entered the office looking for a job. Slick paid no attention at first, being more concerned with sales. Leah was given the job however, and Slick spoke to her on a few occasions. He was friendly with everyone at the job and Leah was no different.

A week or two had passed and Slick began to talk with her more frequently. He enjoyed intelligent conversation and was always happy when he could find a woman on his level. He found that she also had a religious background. The two started to talk on the phone and engage in deep chatter for hours. Leah, however, threw a wrench in the game one night while they talked after work.

"Slick," she said tentatively. "I really don't know how to say this. I feel so awkward asking you this."

"It ain't never stopped your nosy ass before. Ain't no cats out here. Say what's on your mind," Slick responded harshly.

"Well," she said laughing. "I feel sort of bad, Slick." She hesitated once more. "I was just thinking. Oh my god, I can't believe myself. Okay. I was just gonna ask you if you wanted to get up one day."

"I see you every day at work," Slick joked. "Don't you think that's enough?"

"No crazy," Leah said and punched him in the arm. "I'm talking about me and you silly. Just us."

"Hold up. I thought you had a man already. I know he ain't gon' like that too much."

"No, I don't think so. But he don't have to know. It's just something I want to do. I haven't cheated on him before, but it's just something about you I have to experience."

"Listen shorty," Slick said seriously. "I don't know about that right there. I mean, we're really good friends and I don't want to complicate things. I think you might better chill with that."

"It's only one time. I promise. I just wanna see what it's like. I got to have it."

"For real, if you get this it's gonna be more than one time. Trust me on that. And frankly, I don't think I want those problems."

Slick knew that if he hit it, she'd be calling. Also he didn't want to cause any problems at the office. Slick could already see that her wants could put both of them in a bad position. He held her off for a while until her persistence caught him in a bad position.

One Saturday, Slick was closed in his room with a bottle of liquor and a bag of coke. He was content by himself until he received a phone call from Leah.

"Slick," a soft voice said when he answered. "What you doing tonight?"

"Nothing much." Slick, numbed by the coke, kept his answers short.

"Look nigga, I'm a be straight forward. My boyfriend just went down to Florida to see his family. I'm at the crib by myself. I want you to come tonight so we can go 'head and get this over with. I already told you I got to have it."

Her bluntness caused a sudden arousal in Slick. He had never been pursued in that manner before. Thinking with his sexual organ, he agreed. He showered anxiously and called a cab to her apartment.

When he arrived there was little talk. She was already clad in skimpy pajamas. Slick lay on the bed next to her. She instantly began to massage his already erect manhood. Then she performed oral sex before straddling atop of him. Slick allowed the girl to fulfill all of her fantasies as he laid still.

Throughout the night however, Slick would take control. Turning, twisting, and flipping the small bodied girl, Slick released his pinned up frustrations in an onslaught of punishment. Moans and groans accompanied deep breaths as the two climaxed several times. In the morning, Slick caught the bus back to Norfolk feeling used and drained.

The next week at work was awkward for Slick. He tried to play it cool while Leah clung to him whenever she could. Against her word, she continued to invite Slick to her place in spite of her live in boyfriend. Slick caved in to her demands and kept seeing her at her house with no respect for the danger. He felt even worse seeing her man pick her up from work every night.

Soon, word got around and Slick noticed a change. Melanie and Kia were practically begging Slick to get at them. It was obvious Leah had told his business and the two were eager to try some too. Also, Leah started getting jealous when Slick talked to them or any other female. It would soon be revealed that Slick and Leah wasn't the only ones involved in an office romance.

Slick also got a much needed change from his single room. His aunt had bought a new house and once again offered him a place to stay. Against his better judgment he moved to the ocean view area house.

When football season started, office personnel started projecting their favorite team's success.

"I think the Steelers can win it this year Charles," Ray boasted. "We got almost the same team as last year. Mike Tomlin gon' have that defense ready this year too."

"No, no, no," Charles responded. "There ain't no way on this earth that's gonna happen. Not with the way Romo was looking in camp. You wait! The Cowboys gonna surprise a lotta people this year."

"All I'm saying is keep your eyes on Vince and them Titans," Slick interjected. Donnie had been traded the year before and Slick adopted Tennessee as his official team.

"You see what they did his rookie year. And they got that boy Johnson from ECU. Have y'all seen how fast he is?"

"Young is a head case," Robbie added laughing. "He out there 'bout to kill himself. Y'all better get him a counselor or something. What you need to be scared of is them Skins right now."

"What," Pam screamed. "Ain't nobody I know worried about them dead skins. Everybody know that the championship got to come through New York. Eli and my Giants ain't playin' no games with nobody."

The debates continued all throughout preseason. As the regular season began, Slick slated the games that he would attend. He informed Robbie of the days he needed off. The supervisor had no problem and even expressed his desire to attend a game or two. A few in the office were envious and began to hate. When he started to take off Saturdays to attend the games, objections were voiced. Robbie ignored them and allowed his friend to go.

In October, Slick made plans to go to a game in Denver. While on the bus to the airport, Slick spotted a girl he had seen many times before. She worked in the same area and got off a few stops ahead of him. Slick made it a point to watch her each time she exited. Her hips and rear mesmerized him more and more each time she got off the bus.

This day, he struck a conversation with her. With a little small talk, he ended up with her number and said he would call. Feeling himself, he arrived at the airport and checked in. He called his father who was scheduled to meet him in Denver when he arrived. It was his first time going and he was excited.

They both arrived at the same time and caught the shuttle to their hotel. Slick and his dad were greeted by Donnie and the rest of the team in the lobby. After socializing for a while with family, the players went to their rooms.

Slick and his father went out to eat later that night. They enjoyed father and son time as they discussed various issues that were facing them both. Slick realized that he was fortunate to have someone that he could voice his cares to. A wise man that gave sound advice was exactly what Slick needed at this point.

After eating, Slick and his father went back to the room where he fell asleep. Slick took that time to call Shea, the girl he met on the bus. The two talked about many things late into the night. Slick learned a lot about her that night including the fact that she had three children and was from Indiana. Slick was attracted to her straight forwardness as she spoke in the phone.

"I ain't ashamed to say that I got three kids by three men and I take care of them all by myself, you know what I'm sayin'. I don't get no help from nobody, for real. And they good kids and don't get in no trouble.

"How old are they," Slick asked.

"Fifteen, thirteen, and four. They straight. My girl, Misty, she kinda prissy. She like to do hair. My oldest son, Marshawn, is into all kinds of sports and the baby Jaquan is just into everything. I got my hands full but we straight."

Slick instantly felt a spot for the kids even though he hadn't met them. His recent sitting with his father made him realize how blessed he was. He learned more as the conversation continued.

"Look. I don't have no time for games. What you trying to do? You just trying to hit this or is you looking for something else. Just let me know so I know how to do me."

Slick was stunned by her bluntness. "I usually just let things flow. I ain't gon' make no plans or sell you no dream or nothing. We'll just play it light and see where it goes from there."

"Well it don't matter to me either way. But the most important thing when you dealing with somebody is trust and communication. Without that, ain't nothing good gon' happen for nobody.'

"I can't argue with that," Slick added. "Honesty is always a plus too. If you gonna be with somebody, you should be able to tell that person anything."

They talked until Slick fell asleep on the phone. He woke up the next morning and he and his father caught the shuttle to the game. As usual, Slick had a wonderful time and his father enjoyed himself as well. After the game, the two went back to the hotel, gathered their bags and went to the airport. They shared a hug and a prayer before departing on separate flights.

When he returned, Slick resumed talks with Shea. He talked to her on and off throughout the day while both were at work. He also continued to creep with Leah. This arrangement was growing sour, however. Slick found himself more attracted to other women such as Kia, whom he learned was involved with Robbie. Slick would find out soon enough that everyone was fair game.

The next Saturday after the game, Slick returned home to find his aunt in an uproar. She had blamed him for a problem in the bathroom. Slick had notice the issue with the toilet before, but had said nothing. He didn't argue with his aunt about it. He had begun to see a change in her attitude and behavior towards him. Slick got the strange feeling that he was soon going to be looking for another place once again.

The last straw came a few days later. Slick was asleep in the middle of the night when he was awakened by a loud scream.

"Slick, Slick," his aunt yelled. "Come here quick! I need your help!"

He heard a loud banging noise downstairs. He got out of the bed and walked to the top of the stairs. He saw Bobby, who was staggering drunk, standing by the broken screen door. His aunt stood scared nearby.

"Slick make him leave. I done told him I don't know how many times to leave but he won't," his aunt cried.

Slick groggily looked at both adults. Slick knew that even if he intervened, they'd be right back together the next day. He resigned that there was no reason to put his self in the way of harm. "Y'all two need to just stop it," Slick said sleepily and walked back to the bed. He fell asleep and heard no further noise that night.

Even though she apologized the next day, Slick knew he had to leave. His aunt had put him in a dangerous position in which he was trying to avoid. He talked about it with Shea on the phone. In blunt manner, she offered him advice.

"Yeah, you sho' got to get out of there. It's gon' be the same thing all over again," Shea said. "You said that ain't the first time, right?"

"Yeah,' Slick responded. "it ain't the first time. But I should be able to save up enough money in about two weeks to get a spot unless you gon' let me crash with you until then."

Shea was silent for a minute and then spoke. "Okay, Slick. Two weeks and that's it. And, I'm gonna need a hundred dollars a week for rent, partner."

Slick agreed and moved in that same night. They drank and talked as Slick got familiar with her family and friends. When everyone left, Slick and Shea continued to drink. Before morning, the two ended up in her bed naked. Under the influence of the liquor and beer, the two consummated their relationship many times that night.

Before they realized, two weeks had come and gone. Slick had become spoiled by Shea's actions. She kept his clothes washed and folded. Every night when he got off of work, a hot meal was waiting. The best part was that after he showered, he was always greeted by a nude body in the bed. Food, shelter and sex were the only things needed at this time to keep Slick satisfied.

It soon became apparent that Slick wasn't going anywhere. Without having to move, Slick used the money he saved to buy an old school Chevy Caprice from a friend. The new vehicle allowed him to abandon the bus and get more accomplished.

While things were improving at home, at the office problems were emerging. One day, Slick walked into the office to find Melanie in a heated discussion with Robbie. After the argument, Slick noticed Melanie packing up all of her things. When Robbie emerged from the room, Slick asked him what had happened.

"She's done," he said still reeling. "She's outta here. Fuck her. I'll find somebody else!"

This came as a surprise to Slick as the two were close friends. Leah let Slick in on what had happened. Melanie had had a bi-sexual episode with Kia, who was involved with Robbie. Robbie had a wife, but was more infatuated with the younger Kia. Melanie also had a live in girlfriend. Somehow, all parties involved found out and the chaos ensued. Robbie felt betrayed by Melanie, whose own girlfriend found out and left. The end result was Melanie suffering the most with the loss of her job.

In December, Slick made plans to attend another game. This time he went to Tennessee and was a guest at Donnie's new house. He enjoyed an awesome time with family and friends. The Titans won the game and his trip was again rejuvenating.

He got back to Virginia and returned to Shea's. When he entered the bedroom, she was laying on the bed with a concerned look. Beside her lay a pregnancy test. Slick grew excited as he thought of the possibilities of a child.

"So is this your way of telling me you're pregnant," Slick asked as she lay silent. She shook her head yes. Slick smiled inwardly, not wanting to show too much emotion. He turned around to unpack his bags, smiling all the while.

"So what, this means you gonna leave me now," she said. "Or do you want an abortion?"

"What," Slick frowned. "Are you serious? I told you how much I always wanted children. I ain't going nowhere. You can bet that."

"That's what they all say," Shea said tearfully. "You say that now. But when the baby get here, you just gon' leave like all the rest."

Slick took the time to sit down and express his feelings. Through her tears, he could see all the pain and the hurt that she had told him about. The abuse, abandonment, and other relationship problems were all she could think about in the face of this pregnancy. Her experiences told her that she would probably have to raise the child alone.

Slick assured her that he was different. He vowed to be there for her, and her children as well as the newborn. He explained that he took the responsibility of fatherhood very seriously. After an hour of talking, Shea was finally calm and comfortable. The two lay down and Slick held her securely in his arms.

The excitement was formidable and he couldn't sleep. He realized that the time had come for him to become a man and accept responsibility. With his good income and support system, he knew he was in a good position to provide for the child. Little did he know, after the New Year he would no longer have a job. Additionally, the loss of employment caused Slick to make ill-fated decisions that would put both he and his newborn child's life in danger.

12
A New Life

January, 2008
Virginia Beach, VA

The New Year arrived and things were finally calm in
Slick's life. His skills at Life Assist were netting him no less
than $1200 a week. His long hours and new residence had
made it impossible to use the coke any longer. Ever since he
found out about the pregnancy in December, he had no desire
anyway. He still smoked a few blunts with Robbie at work
and had a drink or two, but as far as the hard drugs he
refrained.

Part of this was because of Shea. Being totally honest,
he had told her of the problem before. She expressed the fact
that she wasn't going to deal with that behavior. Her firm
stance kept him in line. He wanted to do everything in his
power to accommodate her, since she was pregnant with his
child.

He even interacted with her children regularly. He
took the youngest to school each morning before work and
spent time with him on the weekends. Because of this, Slick
could see a change in the four year old. The once rowdy, dice
shooting, gun toting tyke, was now being more respectful and
asking questions about God.

Marshawn, the oldest boy was more reserved. He and
Slick would watch and talk sports together. Initially, he was
skeptical of Slick at first because of the other men his mother
had dealt with. After seeing Slick had no ulterior motives, he
loosened up and began to talk more freely. Slick attended his
games and practices while he played football for his junior
high school.

Misty, the only girl was the princess. With a keen eye for fashion and an ability to do hair, she kept herself looking like a diva. Slick loved to tease her and hear her sassy, quick-witted comebacks. He developed a bond with the girl and would take her to and from work whenever he could. She even opened up and started to ask Slick questions about life situations she was dealing with.

During the holidays, Slick went home and told his parents the news. Surprisingly they were excited about the pregnancy. They expressed their desire to meet Shea and sent him back with gifts. His sisters, however, would take longer to accept the girl they knew nothing about.

After the New Year, Slick returned to Virginia with fervor. Examining his pay stubs, he realized that he had made $55,000 dollars the previous year. He knew he had only put forth half the effort with all of the drugs and drinking. He concluded that he could reach the six figure mark with hard work and dedication. His new desire for success was driven by his goal to provide support for his daughter.

The first few weeks after the New Year, Slick sold a company record of 2500 units in a week. The commission netted him the same amount of dollars. Everyone at the office congratulated him and was happy about his success. Charles, always seeking attention and recognition, was the only dissenter.

"The only reason he made that many units because he's here all day," he complained. "If I stayed here that long, I'd do that every week. Plus, Robbie is giving him the best leads anyway. This is ridiculous."

"Shut up Charles," Michelle said. "You just mad 'cause somebody beat you for a change. Didn't you make sixteen hundred dollars this week too. And you still mad? Stop being a bitch."

"Yeah Charles, don't act like that," Leah added. "You make the most money all year 'round. What's one week?" Even though they still talked, Slick had slowly terminated their sexual relationship. He noticed a negative change in her attitude towards him after that.

"It's alright," Slick said. "Just let him keep hating, while I'm on the fifty yard line at the playoffs next Saturday." Slick took further opportunity to flaunt his success to Bill. "Then, he can have all the sales he wants. I'm a be having a ball."

Slick didn't really care who sold the most. All he wanted was his $1000 a week minimum. Charles on the other hand, had to have the title of lead salesman. On days when Slick sold the most, he would complain to headquarters about favoritism and other acts around the office. It was a preposterous assumption, but Charles' frustration and envy caused him to act childish. Soon, his behavior would undermine the entire company.

In February, Slick took Shea to see comedian Nephew Tommy for her birthday. They went out to eat before making the thirty minute drive to the Hampton Coliseum. At the show, the two laughed at the jokes, while enjoying their time together. Slick was happy to put a smile on her face because of all that she had done for him.

When Slick returned to work after the weekend, he received word that Charles had called the corporate office again. He had complained about the drinking, smoking and unprofessional atmosphere of the office. He had also voiced his opposition to Slick's many Saturday's off to attend games. Slick was called into the office that Wednesday.

"You know you my nigga right," Robbie told him. "And I'll do anything I can for you. But I might can't let you go to the game this time."

"Nigga what," Slick said unbelievingly. "What the hell you been smoking this morning? You tripping on acid or something?"

"Nah, it's that nigga Charles. He called corporate again," Robbie explained. "Told 'em we be smoking, drinking, freaking and all types of shit my nigga. He trying to especially get me and you fired. He a bitch, talking about I be letting you go to the games all the time."

"Man, fuck that faggot," Slick said angrily. "I'll go out there and punch 'em in his face right now. He ain't nothing but a fifty year old telemarketer with nothing else better to do. I'm going to the game and I don't care who like it. As much money I make for this company, I don't even got to talk about it."

"I feel you bro'. That nigga is soft as hell. I'm a see what I can do, but I might need you."

"Homeboy, this is the playoffs. This shit don't happen every day. Come this weekend, I'm a get off work, back my bags, and hop on that plane to California. Now, if I still have a job when I come back, that's cool. If not, I'll cross that bridge then."

Slick developed a loathing for Charles that instant. He thought how could a black man not celebrate the success of another? Slick then vowed to out sale Charles every week and make him miserable in the process. His first priority was the game and after that to antagonize his enemy.

Slick flew out that same Friday to San Diego. He met Wood this time and the two fans enjoyed their usual time out. They went out to a few clubs and ended the night with another drunken episode. The next day, Slick drove to Tijuana by himself and got lost in Mexico. He was driving in the downtown area when he made a few wrong turns. A store owner saw him circling around and pointed him back towards the border. Slick made it back across in time for the night game. Unfortunately, the Chargers beat the Titans in overtime, and their Super Bowl hopes were doused.

Slick returned to Virginia and had not forgotten Charles' acts. For the next two weeks, Slick did everything possible to disturb him. He talked extra loud, turned the radio high, opened the outside doors, rotated the fan; anything to make Charles uncomfortable. He even smoked blunts in his car with the window sealed so that when he entered the building, he would reek of marijuana. His plot worked.

Charles continually complained and tensions rose between the men.

At the end of February, Slick was at work when he received a call from Shea. She told him that her stomach hurt and she wanted to go to the hospital. With an hour left on the clock, Slick said he would be there when he finished.

Before it was time to leave, Slick received another call. Michelle had just gotten out of jail for a ten day driving sentence and needed a ride home. Slick agreed to help his friend. He left work early so that he could pick Michelle up and be there in time to take Shea.

When he arrived home, Shea was cold towards him. The extra time he took had made her mad. He offered to take her still but she ignored him. Actually, she stayed silent the whole night until the next morning. Slick drove her to work and Shea said not a word. Slick did not yet understand the hormones of a pregnant woman and grew furious because of her attitude.

While at work that afternoon, Slick received a call from Shea. Still irked, he reluctantly answered the phone.

"Come get me," Shea said stoically.

"What," Slick raged.

"Come get me from work. I'm ready to go."

"You must be crazy," Slick yelled. "You ain't talk to me all night and day and now you want me to do something for you. What you think this is? That ain't how it works shorty!"

"Look, are you gonna come get me or not, Slick?"

"Hell no! Get home however you can. You don't run this over here. I do!"

Slick slammed the phone shut, nearly breaking it. He didn't understand how she could treat him like that and expect him not to be sour. His anger boiled to the point of needing a drink. He drove to the liquor store, got a bottle of brandy, and returned. He sat in the car and guzzled half of the liquid before going back to work.

Back in the office, his anger turned to Charles. Emotions, mixed with the liquor in his coat pocket, had him ready to settle the feud with the older man directly. He found a method to start an argument. He placed the industrial sized fan on high, and turned it to blow on both he and Charles who was only a desk away. Even though it was cold outside, Slick opened the back door so the draft could be felt even more. When Charles felt the air he addressed Slick.

"Come on Slick. What are you doing? There's no need for the fan. It's cold outside and I can't hear my customers."

"I'm hot nigga. You ain't the only person in this office. If I wanna be comfortable, I'm a keep this fan on," Slick said.

"If you're so hot, then take your coat off. That don't make no sense!"

"Nah, man, I need the coat on. I'm anemic." Slick gave the man a look, inviting him to react.

"This is crazy," Charles said. He got up from his desk and turned the fan off.

Slick turned the fan back on without saying anything and went back to work. This time instead of turning it off, Charles unplugged the fan and turned it around. Slick took this as a challenge and removed his headset.

"Well, what you wanna do then? I'm tired of you anyway, always crying like a bitch! Do something faggot!"

"You ain't said nothing Slick. I'm not gon' get into it with you, but don't think for a second I'm afraid of you."

"Well do something then! I been waiting for this anyway. I know you the one doing all that hating!" Slick's voice got louder with each word and others in the office noticed the riff.

Voniqua, the night manager who replaced Melanie, came out of the office to investigate the commotion. Since Charles was older and had seniority, and she was new, Voniqua sided with Charles and asked Slick to leave. Slick walked out still fuming. Mad that he couldn't get to Charles, he took the frustration out on the man's truck. Slick took his size eleven Timberlands and kicked the rear end of the Navigator, causing extensive damage. Knowing that he had went too far Slick went to a local bar to drink some more.

The reality of what he had done did not set in until the next morning when Slick was sober. He got dressed and prepared for work, barely speaking to Shea. When he got to work, he was called into the office by Robbie.

"Look man, I heard you and Charles got into it last night. What happened?"

"Nothing for real. I just got fed up and snapped. I was about to dig into that old nigga's ass," Slick answered.

"Slick, don't let that nigga fuck up your jet set lifestyle. You getting money, you flying out to games. Don't let that hater sidetrack you. You know he already called Jeff in them this morning."

"I figured that much. But it's straight. I ain't 'gon do nothing to him now. I just had to get something off my chest."

"Alright then my nigga. Don't worry about it. Just go get that money."

Slick worked for about an hour before Charles came into the office. Upon seeing Slick, he turned around and walked out. A few minutes later, Robbie called Slick back into the office.

"I just got a call from Jeff at corporate. They said that somebody damaged Charles' truck and they think it's you. I don't care if you did it or not. Fuck 'em. But they think you did. So they told me to send you home for the day. I'll call you later on and tell you what's going on."

Slick ended up sitting home for a week. He had spoken back and forth to Robbie, who was trying to save his job. He was vouching for Slick's ability and overall character while Charles was portraying him as a thug. The elder's pull was too strong and Robbie soon found his own job in jeopardy for trying to help Slick.

Robbie had went over Jeff's head to Marty, Jeff's superior. Marty saw no reason to lose a top seller so he told Robbie to call him back to work. The day he returned, Charles made another call, this time to the corporate head. After twenty minutes, Slick was called again to the office by Robbie. He was handed the phone and listened to the white man on the other end.

"Mr. Richardson, you are to leave right now. You are no longer an employee of Life Assist and if you do not leave promptly, you'll be arrested for trespassing. The police are on their way and additional charges may be brought for injury to property. You are officially done!"

Slick started to plead his case but stopped short when he saw the police pull up through the window. He hung up the phone and slid out the back door. Familiar with the area, he ran to a nearby apartment complex and hid for a while. After an hour he returned to the business to retrieve his car.

When Slick got home, he explained the situation to Shea. The solemn look on her face displayed her displeasure.

"So you mean to tell me that you done lost your job. You got a baby coming in four months. How you plan on supporting her now."

"Well, they still talking and trying to work something out. I might be able to go back. I make too much for the company for them to let me go."

Shea shook her head. "I am not crazy. You can't fool me. I already know what you 'gon do."

"What you talking about," Slick said confused. "What you think I'm a do?"

"I already know. You 'gon go out there in them streets and do the same thing you been doing all your life. I ain't stupid."

Slick started to disagree but couldn't. He let the legitimacy of her words set in. He knew that he couldn't transition from $1500 a week to nothing without problems. He hadn't really saved any money as of yet, because of his expensive lifestyle. There was only one way he knew how to make that much money with as little effort.

A couple of weeks went by and all options were exhausted. Charles had succeeded in his plans to bring both men down. For his role in trying to keep Slick employed, Robbie was also fired by the company. Slick was told by the headquarters that he could never work for them again. The termination was final.

The first couple of weeks were tough. Slick filed for unemployment and was told that it could take up to two months. Realizing his plight Slick started to get depressed. He would sit around all day and drink liquor. He didn't even bother to look for another job. He just stayed home in a drunken stupor for days. Shea finally had enough and snapped him out of it.

"I don't wanna hear no excuses and I'm not gonna feel sorry for you. You know what you did. You made your bed now you have to lay in it. I ain't gonna sit around and have no pity party with you!"

"This ain't no pity party," Slick responded. "What you talking about?"

"I'm talking about you sitting around drinking and sleeping all day like the world done came to an end. You better get up and do something with yourself. You ain't helping' nobody like this."

"Don't worry about a thing. I'm finna step the game up right here in a minute."

"But I ain't talking about selling drugs neither. 'Cause that shit ain't about nothing, and you know it."

"I don't want to, but sometimes you just gotta do what you gotta do."

Slick felt the pressure increasing. He already knew deep in his heart what he would do. But a voice within, a voice of caution, told him that his decision would lead him to perdition. He felt that the moment his hands touched a package of dope would signal his demise.

The events of his last stint in the game had him leery. He was certain that if he got deeply involved again he would die. It was a clear picture in his head. But with only five hundred dollars and a baby on the way, he decided he had no choice. He called Spray to see if he knew who had any coke. Spray said he could find the desired amount. When Slick met Spray later that day he bought the drugs. With the purchase of a half-ounce of cocaine, Slick's appointment with death had just been set.

It wasn't even a week before Slick was hustling full scale again. He had called most of his old clients back. They were happy to hear from him and started patronizing him exclusively. They also introduced him to more of their friends, whom Slick hadn't known. Everyone complained about the product they had been getting. Slick made it a point to keep the best and they loved him for it.

He had pretty much hidden the fact from Shea. One day, however, while riding with her, he received a call from a customer. Pressed for time, he decided not to drop her off before making the sale. When he pulled up to the bar, she still had said nothing. He pulled out the bag of powder and Shea finally spoke.

"What I tell you? I knew you was gon' do it. I'm telling you right now. If you get locked up, don't call me. I ain't doing no more bids with nobody."

"You ain't gotta worry about that. I got this over here," he replied. "You just take care of that baby in your stomach."

It was a quiet ride home. She never again spoke about his dealings. The money started to come and he became comfortable. Inevitably, his hours grew later and he was away more. The strain on their relationship increased from the onset.

Along with the money came the usage and other temptations. Slick couldn't resist getting high once he was around the product full time. He stayed out later and later as the abuse worsened. Sometimes he would sit outside in the car all night in order to keep sniffing.

His actions and absence caused arguments between him and Shea. The constant drinking also made him more confrontational. She was five months into the pregnancy and was feeling ill-will towards Slick. The disputes were daily even though they made up shortly after. When she started to reject him sexually, however, Slick felt slighted and caused more friction with his reaction

He soon turned his attention to other women. Now that he was in a position of money and power, he once again had his choice of girls. He began to carouse with several of his old friends and a few new ones. He had even started to pluck Kia when he found out that she was sniffing too.

One night during that April, Slick had gotten Kia to pick him up. Shea had his car and he had needed to make some runs. After handling business, Slick and Kia started to get high. And of course when they got high they screwed. After the episode, Kia drove him home at about one in the morning. Unable to stop, he and Kia continued to get high, parked on the side of the apartment.

About an hour later, Shea came out of the house to give Misty's boyfriend a jump for his car battery. He and Kia were parked right beside the car. Slick slouched in the seat hoping Shea didn't notice him. After she finished, Shea walked directly over to where Slick was in the passenger side putting away the coke.

"Get out of the car, Slick," she yelled grabbing the handle. "What the fuck is going on out here. Get out nigga, what you waiting on?"

Slick got out of the car and tried to calm her. "It ain't nothing going on. Why you out here trippin' like that? This is just my home girl from work. We won't doing nothing but talking."

"Oh yeah," she responded. "Then why your pants unzipped then?"

Slick looked down at his pants and thought fast. "I just took a piss, girl. Damn!"

"Oh hell nah, y'all think I'm stupid. Look shorty," she said addressing Kia. "You got to go right now or we gon' have a problem." She stepped within inches of Slick's face. "You better tell that bitch to carry her ass!"

"It ain't nothing. I told you she just gave me a ride. That's it!"

Shea grew more animated the more she talked. Kia didn't make it any better by acting like she didn't know how to get home.

"Which way do I go to get to the interstate," She yelled from the window. Slick looked at her like she was foolish.

"Shorty, you better go 'head before I catch a case out here," Shea warned. "I know what to do. Kayla! Kayla! Kayla, get out here! Hurry up!"

Shea called her younger sister from inside. Kayla, who was always ready to rumble, came running out. "What's the matter Shea? What's all this noise for?"

"Nah, this nigga Slick got this girl out here and he think I'm stupid!" With her sister present, Shea walked right up to Slick and punched him in the face. "See nigga. Now what you wanna do? We get do this right now!"

"Keep your hands off me now," Slick warned. "You better get your sister Kayla."

"It ain't worth it Shea," Kayla chimed in. "I told you that nigga won't no good in the first place. Don't get upset. You know you pregnant.

"When I get to the end of the street, do I take a left or a right?" Kia continued to make the situation worse by acting dumb.

"Shorty, I'm a fuck you up if you don't get outta here," Shea raged. She started walking towards Kia's side when the girl smartly drove off. Shea then threw the keys at Slick and walked in the house. Slick stood outside for about thirty minutes trying to figure out what to say.

When he finally got the nerve to go in, Slick found all of his clothes in a pile by the door. He stood in silence not knowing what to do. Even though they always made up in the past, it was apparent that Shea was fed up. Slick remained downstairs that night, but he knew he would have to start looking for a place fast.

The next day, Slick searched Craigslist for an apartment and found a house with a private owner. With no credit check required, Slick showed up with the deposit and first month's rent in hand. He was given the keys after a brief conversation with the young white man who owned the place. He moved in the next week.

Located on Chesapeake Boulevard, the house was only a few blocks from the Norfolk Ocean View Beach. It was a quiet area and provided solace for Slick. He enjoyed the first few days of solitude in peace. He was glad to have money stashed away and to be living in his own place again.

Within a few weeks Slick resorted back to his old ways. With the freedom to sniff at his leisure, he started to spend days in the apartment getting high as before. This time however it seemed that when he started he couldn't stop. It got so bad that sometimes he wouldn't even answer the phone for clients. Four or five days would pass with Slick cooped up in the room with a bag and a random chick.

Slick saw no problems with himself as long as the money was coming. However, in June a considerable drought hit the area. It once again became a scramble for Slick to maintain a supply. He grasped at straws while dealing with new and old connects. He managed to keep a decent product and kept his business flowing.

By the end of June things had gotten worse. There was no cocaine anywhere. People were selling pure garbage and getting away with it. Slick found whatever he could whenever he could. He began to deal with people he hadn't seen in years.

One day he ran into Mike, a Puerto Rican, who used to sell him work. Mike told him that he had a connection.

Slick checked it out the same day and it was fine compared to what was available. Slick allowed Mike to play middle man and started to contact him regularly.

About two weeks passed and Slick needed to re up. After talking to Mike, Slick agreed to meet him later that night. Slick picked him up and they rode to meet the connect as usual. Everything seemed normal as Slick pulled into the parking lot and stopped.

"Alright listen," Mike said. "I'm a go in grab it real quick and come right back out. That's straight?"

"Alright, go 'head and do your thing," Slick said. He waited for the man to get out. When he didn't Slick asked what the problem was.

"I need the money so I don't have to run in and out."

"Nah, homeboy, I can't do no business like that. I got to at least see it first 'fore I hand somebody my money."

"Slick, you know it's straight. It's the same people we been getting it from. It ain't never been no problem before has it?"

Due to the dire situation for good dope, Slick senses were clouded. He knew better than to give the man the money beforehand. But Mike had been trustworthy before, so he handed the man the brown bag of money.

"You know you responsible for my cake yo," Slick informed. "No matter what you do, I'm a need my money or my dope."

"I got you my nigga," Mike said getting out of the car. "Just give me a couple of minutes and I'll be right out."

Slick felt a bad omen watching the man walk away. The uneasiness worsened when he watched Mike disappear into the maze of buildings. One side of his mind wanted to get out and chase him. The other part told him not to waste his time. His money was already gone.

Slick waited for ten minutes, not believing what he'd just done. He finally called and there was no answer. He dialed the number repeatedly, only to keep getting the voicemail. Finally, he left the parking lot, screaming useless threats and promises into the phone. He got home and stayed up for the rest of the night, snorting the little bit of coke he had left.

The next afternoon, Slick got a call from Boot Lee, an old associate from Thalia Oaks. He told Slick that he had been trying to get in contact with him. Boot Lee said that he had some good product at a fair price.

"Man, I wish I you would've called me last night," Slick said. "Then I wouldn't have to kill this nigga when I see 'em again."

"What you talking about now, Slick," Boot Lee asked.

"I don't even wanna talk right now. I'll tell you when I see you. But you already know what I need."

"Alright, but you better hurry up. You know it ain't nothing out here and these things going like hot cakes."

"I'm there now," Slick said and hung up the phone.

Slick travelled to his old neighborhood and met Boot Lee at his crib. He explained what happened and had to endure the ridicule from his friend. After chatting for a while, Slick purchased what he could. Boot Lee also gave him some extra on consignment to help him make up for his lost.

Slick then returned to business. He was burning inside over not being able to find Mike. This, along with the drug use, frustration, and the pressure of a coming child made Slick volatile. He became hostile towards customers, family and friends alike. If things didn't go as he wanted he would explode. His attitude towards women, particularly Shea, grew cold and demeaning.

The way Shea treated him was Slick's own fault. She just did not want the headache that came along with him. Because he felt so bad about himself, he countered it by criticizing and downing her. This led to constant disagreement between the two. Slick started to spend less and less time with Shea and she developed a barrier.

At the same time he was still running into trouble on the streets. The drought had got worse and nobody was moving. After several attempts, his old contact Fardo finally answered the phone. Fardo said he did have something and was out and about. Since he was so credible, Slick asked no questions and placed the biggest order he could.

When he met Fardo, Slick took the product and examined it. It looked like the same garbage he'd had to turn down before. Out of need, he took it. When he got home and tried it, he was disgusted. It was pro-cane. Slick called Fardo to get his money back, but of course there was no answer.

Left with no choice, he had to sell the counterfeit cocaine to his customers. He endured the complaints from his clients, who were just as upset. He told them that he had bought it just as they had so it was nothing he could do. It was so dry however, some that complained, called him back to buy more. He kept selling it while trying to find a solid source. Calls to Fardo still were ignored, but Slick definitely knew that he would see him again.

The next week, Slick had to take Shea to court. Ironically, the first person he saw was Fardo standing in the child support line. Slick raised his hands in a matter that said "where is my money or better dope." Fardo immediately exited the line and came over.

"I already know man. Everybody been calling me. I had to give Fat Boy nine ounces back the other day. I bought three kilos of it myself. You still got some of it left, right?"

Slick listened to the false explanation with contempt. The fast talk was nothing new to him. He chose to play it cool and answer the question. "Hell yeah, I got almost all of it," Slick lied. "What the fuck you think I'm a do with that. It ain't nothing."

"Alright, call me later on after you leave here. I'm a have something for you and see if I can't get you straight."

Slick knew when Fardo walked away that he wouldn't be reimbursed. He had already counted it as a loss. It wasn't exactly a loss since he had already made the money back he'd spent. Slick was still disappointed at his friend's business dealings.

Later that day, Slick took Shea to doctor's appointment. While they drove, Shea expressed her intention of getting her tubes tied after the birth. Slick voiced his displeasure because she knew he wanted more children.

"You know I ain't gonna have no more babies by you. After all this you putting me through now."

"Come on yo," Slick pleaded. "Stop playing. You know I want me a son. How you gon' do that if you gon' be with me."

"Who said I wanted to be with you. You better go have one with somebody else if you want to."

The conversation lasted until they arrived. Shea went in while Slick stayed in the car drinking a bottle of Hennessy. When he walked in, the appointment was over. The doctor told Slick that they didn't have long, two weeks at the most. Slick was excited as they left the office.

While walking to the car, Slick remembered a statement the doctor made before they left. "What other appointment was he talking about when I came in," he asked Shea.

"I just told you I was getting my tubes tied. He said I couldn't do it until two weeks after I have the baby."

Slick felt disrespected. The liquor took effect as anger rose up in him. How could she blatantly go against his wishes? He grabbed her by the arm firmly.

"Quit playing Shea. We just talked about this. You can't do that to me."

"Get off me, Slick," Shea said, pushing his arm away.

Slick refused to let her go and she continued to resist. In a fit of rage, Slick head butted her. He didn't realize the effect until a large, plum-sized knot appeared on her forehead. He instantly tried to hold her but she wrestled away.

Shea then ran towards the hospital. Slick gave chase until he saw the parking lot attendant coming to her aid. The lady screamed at Slick that she had seen what happened and had already called the police.

He knew that he could not drive off and risk another DWI. The attendant knew his car. He decided that he would stay and face the law. When they arrived, Slick concocted a story that the affray was mutual. He said Shea had struck him in the head with a bottle. Both of them were admitted to the emergency room for treatment.

While Shea was being talked to by police, Slick was getting his vitals checked by the nurse. When she finished, Slick went to the bathroom. While passing the admissions desk, he overheard the officer tell the nurse not to let him go. Slick walked right pass the bathroom to the emergency exit on the side of the building. He snuck through the door and hopped on the first bus he saw.

When he arrived back to the apartment he called Fardo again, desperately needing a good high. He still got no response. After calling around, he found a white girl, Crystal, who said she could get him a half-ounce.

When nightfall came, Slick got Melanie to take him to get his car. He then met Crystal's people and scored. To help relieve his stress, he invited Melanie and Kia to come get high. Having already had Kia, he knew he could have them both. The three ended up getting high and before the night was over, Slick had the pleasure of having both girls at the same time.

In the morning, Slick still had not been to sleep. When the girls left, he continued to get high and think about his problems. His binge was interrupted at about 9:00 a.m. by a knock on the door. He peeped out the blinds and saw two police in his driveway. He wondered how they got his address, as he hid the coke. He watched the police from the upstairs window for fifteen minutes until they left.

He immediately called Shea and began to curse her for sending the police. She said that she had not sent them but they came on their own. Abnormally, she listened until Slick got out all of his words. She remained calm until Slick could argue with her no more. He hung up the phone still fuming about everything in his life as a whole.

A few days went by and Slick calmed down. He had finally gotten some much needed sleep. Shea called him and acted like nothing happened. She invited him to come to the baby shower that weekend. Slick agreed.

Instead of attending, however, he took Jaquan to a water park at the beach. After entering and seeing her head, he couldn't look at her like that. Also, he didn't want to be embarrassed around her family and friends. Even though no one said anything to him about it, he knew they didn't approve.

When he came back with Jaquan that night, Shea treated him so nice that he stayed. They ate, talked, and planned as if they were the perfect couple. She even allowed Slick to sleep in the bed with her that night.

The next morning, Shea woke up and cooked breakfast. After eating, Slick was in the bathroom washing up when he heard screams.

"Slick! Slick! Come here real quick," a voice said from down the stairs.

Slick went downstairs and saw Shea standing in the kitchen looking down. "What's wrong with you woman? What you doing all that yelling for?"

"Come over here and look at this," she said pointing to the ground. "I think my water just broke."

"I thought it was supposed to be more than that, though."

"That's what I'm saying. I just don't think it came all the way yet."

"Well, we better go 'head and get to the hospital," Slick instructed. "You had an appointment today anyway, right?"

"Yeah, it wasn't 'til eleven though. But we might as well get up there now just in case."

Shea packed a small bag and Slick took her to the doctor. When the doctor examined her, he observed that she was already dilating. He immediately had her admitted to the pregnancy ward. Slick accompanied her to the room. Other family members also came. When the doctor told Slick it would be a while, he left instructing Misty to call him when it was time.

Slick wanted to stay, but the cocaine in the console of his car was calling him. He also wanted to get to the bottle of liquor that was under the seat. The excitement of the moment had triggered Slick's need for a rush. He started to hit the cocaine even before he pulled out of the parking garage.

Hours later, Slick still had not made it back to the hospital. He had rode around sniffing, and drinking, while making drops. Though he kept checking on Shea, he still made his rounds informing every one of the good news. He was still getting high when he got the call that Shea was about to go into full labor.

Even though he still had the warrant, Slick walked into the building with both the coke and the liquor bottle in his pocket. When he got to the room, Shea's pleasant demeanor gave no indication to her being near birth. He chatted for a while with everyone before leaving the room again. He searched for the nearest bathroom in order to hit the coke and take a drink. Afterward, he went outside to smoke a few cigarettes.

When he returned, the doctors had Shea's legs already in the stirrups. She had dilated the full centimeters in his absence. Slick stood by as the contractions worsened. Shea began to cry out in expressions of pain. Slick walked over and held her hand. He also helped her with the breathing as he was instructed by the nurse.

Surprisingly, after only a few strong pushes the baby's head popped out. Slick was amazed to see the black haired head dangling out of Shea. His astonishment was broken by pleas from the doctor.

"Push! Push, girl! You gonna choke the baby if you don't keep pushing!"

"Yeah," Slick agreed. Heightened paranoia caused Slick to panic. "Push Shea! Push! Please Lord, don't let my baby die! Lord I'm asking in Jesus name, to help her come out!"

With a few more pushes, the baby's full body squirted into the doctor's hands. The feeling that Slick had was unexplainable. His little daughter had made it into the world and was healthy. He watched as the doctor cleaned her and cut the cord. They laid her in the incubator and Slick walked over.

"Look at little Italy," he said to the doctor. He and Shea had agreed on the name months before. "Don't she look just like me doc? Look at those lips. Yeah, that's mine for sure."

"Yeah, and she even has your hairline too," the doctor added smiling. He tried to get the baby's attention but her eyes were locked on Slick.

"Look doc! Everywhere I move she's looking at me. She must know my voice already. And look at her eyes. They so big and round. She's adorable."

Slick and the others gloated over the baby until the doctor's took her away. The attention then turned back to Shea. Everyone consoled and comforted her. Slick joked about how easy it was for her. Seeing everyone was there, he figured that Shea would be alright. He had few runs to make and told Shea that he'd be back later.

After going to get high and drunk for two more hours, Slick returned to the hospital. He found Shea and the baby in the room by themselves. When she looked in his eyes, Shea could tell he was high. She gave a sigh of despair as he tried to avoid eye contact.

"So you left your newborn daughter to go out there and drink. That just don't make no sense. What's the matter with you? Are you gonna keep doing that forever? Just look at her for a second."

Slick tried to ignore the stinging comments. He walked to the sink and washed his hands before taking his child from the mother's arms

"Italy, Ktana, Taylor," Slick said, kissing the baby's cheek. He held little Italy in the air, admiring her.

"Don't forget Tyann," Shea added.

"I already told you I don't like that name, but you insist on adding it in there, don't you?"

"I sho' do," Shea responded. "So you might as well get used to it. And watch how you holding her before she fall!"

Slick sat on the bed beside Shea. He was still in awe of how the child kept her eyes on him. Shea's words really began to cut deep as he thought of his future. There was no way he would live long enough to be a good father, if he continued at the present rate. He knew he would have to change.

"Honestly Shea, I'm gonna get myself together. You are so right with everything you said," he confessed giving her a hug. "And I'm sorry for all that I did and the way I've been acting. I'm a make things better for all of us."

"All I'm saying is that you got a daughter now. I don't care about all of that other stuff you out there doing as long as you're here for her. I know what it's like, so I don't want her growing up without a father"

"You don't have to worry about that. I'm a be here for mine. I just want to show her the right way."

Slick stayed and chatted with Shea for about an hour until his phone started to ring. At one o'clock in the morning it was only one of two things: a coke sale or a woman. Slick answered the call and told the customer he'd be there in twenty minutes. Shea frowned as he closed the phone.

"See, I knew you was just talking," she said. "You talk all that mess about changing and look what happens when your phone ring."

"What you talking about," Slick said defensively. "What your face frowned all up for?"

"'Cause, you on the phone talking about you going somewhere. You can't even sit still for a good hour before you gotta run off. That's what I'm talking about, Slick!"

Slick was torn between going to make the money and staying with Shea and Italy. What influenced the decision was his desire for more cocaine. He knew he wouldn't be able to stop when he had started earlier and he could hold out no longer. He chose the drug over his daughter.

"Look Shea, don't trip. I'll be back," he lied. "I just got to go get this paper real fast. You know we need the dough, with all the baby stuff we gotta get." He stood up and prepared to leave.

"Slick," Shea said. She struggled to get out of the bed. Finally standing, she held the baby out to him. "Don't go nowhere, just look at her. Think about her."

Slick was touched by the tears flowing from Shea's eyes. He walked over and gave her a hug and a kiss on the cheek. He then kissed the baby's forehead. Even though he wanted to stay, the urge to do the coke was too strong.

"I'll be right back baby," he said with another kiss. "Just let me do this real quick. It ain't gonna take that long."

Tears started streaming down her face as Shea sat back on the bed. Slick stood by the door speechless. He was powerless . It hurt him to see the woman who had birthed his first child in that manner. With a sickening, empty feeling in his stomach, Slick turned the knob and walked out of the door.

Slick got to his car and immediately opened the bag of cocaine. Feeling energized, Slick drove to meet his customer at the bar. After having a beer, he left the club with the intention of going back to the hospital. When he was halfway there, his phone rang again. It was Kia.

"Oh hey, Slick. What you doing?"

"I'm my way back to the hospital. Shorty had the baby earlier tonight. I just had to take care of something. But the question is what are you still doing up?"

"I don't know. I just can't sleep. And then I figured you was probably up so I called."

"Yeah, you know I'm up. My baby came so I had to celebrate. You know me."

"Ah man. I knew it. I wanna play some too. Don't you wanna come get me?"

"Yeah. I could do that. I need some company anyway. I'll be there in fifteen minutes so be ready."

Slick back tracked and picked up Kia. He took her to his apartment and she started getting high with him. Instead of using her in the normal way, Slick spent most of the night ranting to Kia about his relationship with Shea and his desire to get clean and be a good father. His instability at a time when he was supposed to be a foundation was troubling for him. Kia listened and gave advice but it was to no avail. He was too far gone. It would take a miracle for Slick to wriggle free from the clutches of his lifestyle. Less than four months later, however, Slick would have his eyes opened to the power of God and to just how vulnerable to death he was.

13
Death in the Flesh

Italy hadn't been home a week before the problems started for Slick. His landlord informed him that he had to move out. The house was sold and he had to prepare it for the buyers. Slick knew that the house was for sell, but he didn't think it would go that quick. He asked Shea could he stay with her until he found somewhere else. As usual, she agreed with minimal fuss.

Slick was not ready to stop using. He still stayed out all night and partied hard, often not sleeping for days. Before long, the arguments and discord started again. Tensions mounted as Slick continued to try to force his will on her.

He was especially upset about Shea's plans to visit her family in August. She had already planned the trip to Evansville, Indiana and was scheduled to leave at the beginning of the month. He was angry about not seeing his daughter for the two week period. He also didn't feel like the baby should travel such a long distance at a young age. He called his mother and vented a few days before Shea left.

"Ma, ain't no way that she should be taking that baby way up there. She only two weeks old. What kinda sense do that make?"

"Taylor," his mom responded. "That girl got four kids. She knows what she's doing. That's Italy's family out there too. She should go see them. You can't keep trying to tell her what to do. What you need to worry about is getting yourself together. You running around drinking and all that stuff. You might be the one who doesn't need to be around."

The words pierced Slick's heart. His mother made it clear that he couldn't stop Shea and he accepted the fact. On the day Shea and the kids were leaving, Slick took them to the bus station. After seeing them off, Slick headed back to

Shea's house. She was nice enough to let Slick stay while she was gone, despite his behavior.

When he got there, the first thing he did was get high. With everyone gone, he sat comfortably in the house, staying up for two and three days with the drug. His only exits were to the liquor store or outside to meet a client. He had become so lazy and sloppy that he was even allowing people to come to her house. His discontent and bitterness grew with each sleepless night.

A week into the binge, Slick received a call at 3:00 a.m. He answered and found the voice of an old friend on the line.

"Hey Slick, this is Rizzio. What up man?"

"What's good Rizzio," Slick said with a headache and a nose full of coke.

"Nothing man. I'm just cooling out her in Chesapeake at my boy's house. We having a party. I thought about you and my man told me to invite you over."

Slick knew that Rizzio wanted some dope. However, the young Italian was prone to have short money and always complained. Slick was too high to deal with any conflict and was satisfied getting high alone.

"Man, it's late. What y'all trying to do," Slick said, getting to the point. "I ain't trying to come out there for no bullshit. What you need?"

"Nah, it aint no BS this time," Rizzio said in his hyper erratic tone. He spoke with someone in the background and came back to the line. "We gonna need like a quarter or two. I'm not sure. But it's a house full of people and all of them want something. We got beer, liquor and girls. I told you to come hang with us."

"Okay," Slick succumbed. "I'll be out there. Give me a minute to get myself together."

Slick hung up the phone. He didn't want to go. He was already too high. His paranoia level was on one thousand. The twenty minute drive to the Hickory section of Chesapeake seemed continents away. After several persistent calls from Rizzio, Slick got dressed and drove cautiously out to the country area.

When he got to the house, he was greeted by ten men and six women; all of them white. Even though it was a weekday, they were partying like rock stars. Lines were laid out, music blasting, and beer cans covered nearly every surface in the house. Slick was introduced by Rizzio to the people in the front rooms of the house. The owner of the house was a short, muscular dude with long hair. He spoke like he'd known Slick forever when they met.

"My name is Brad. This my shit. These are my friends. You can come on in, make yourself at home. You're welcome to anything in here. Don't worry about any of these clowns, especially Rizzio," he said with a serious smile.

Slick grabbed the man's hand and felt the energy. "Okay my man. I appreciate the hospitality. It's good to meet you."

"Yeah, like I said, you're good. This is mine. Rizzio, he ain't shit. I'm the one who need that. I usually have my own but my peoples been having some bullshit. So I said I'll try you. I been hearing a lot about you from this clown."

"Brad, come on," Rizzio interrupted. "Why you talking 'bout me like that. You act like I just ain't call the man for us. Give me some credit."

"Fuck you," Brad snapped. "You can carry your ass for all I care. I don't even know why you're here." He then turned to Slick. "Let me see what you got 'fore I smack this faggot. It ain't no garbage is it? I know good dope. I been doing this for a long time. I told you I usually keep it."

"Nah, it ain't no trash over here," Slick answered. "I don't fool with nothing but that primo. I do it too, so I know what's what." Slick pulled out the bag and allowed the host to taste it. He normally wouldn't do it, but something about the guy Slick liked.

"Oh yeah," Brad said rubbing his gums. "This is definitely some good shit. Let me get a quarter of that. And if you got another eight ball, let me get that too."

Slick gave the man what he wanted and ended up staying. He mingled among the crowd all morning. The host also took a liking to Slick. He told the dealer all about his landscaping business, family, and band. Slick sat on the couch and listened to Brad as the two continued to sniff.

It was hours after dawn when Slick prepared to leave. He was walking to the front door when he noticed an empty room by in the hallway. He inquired about the extra space to Brad who explained.

"Yeah man, I had to kick my sorry ass roommate out just last week. He didn't wanna pay the rent on time so now it's just me and my son James."

Slick seized the opportunity. "Well shit man, I need a place to stay. Me and my baby momma alright, but I don't wanna be ass out if she starts trippin'. I need my own just in case."

"I'm a tell you up front, I want three hundred a month and I can't play no games. Can you handle that?"

Slick reached in his pocket and pulled out three hundred dollar bills. "The first is already past but I'll still give you the full rent for this month. I can move my stuff in a couple of days if that's alright with you?"

"That's cool brother," Brad said shaking Slick's hand. "I think you're okay. We might just be able to make a few bucks together as well."

Slick and Brad agreed to the terms. Afterwards he went to Shea's house to get some much needed rest. When he woke up later that evening, his phone was filled with missed calls. Many of them were from Brad, who had never gotten to sleep.

When Slick returned the calls, Brad told him that he needed more coke. A few of the friends were still there and a few more had shown up wanting to party. Slick made the journey again when night fell. Things continued as before when Slick stayed again for the night.

The next few days were the same when Slick moved in. Brad had introduced him to so many new customers, that he barely had time for the older ones. The money began to pour in rapidly. He was surprised at the amount of drugs Brad and his friends consumed. He found that he would get little sleep in his room as Brad would have rowdy company every night.

Slick began to bond with Brad, however, through their nights of getting high. He found out that his roommate's mother was a preacher also. The two spent hours doing drugs and admitting the futility of their lifestyles. Both knew right from wrong and were suffering the consequences of their actions. It was at this point that a conviction set in and Slick grew deeper into despair.

When Shea and the children returned, Slick tried hard to be normal. He told her of his new place and his plans for the future. Shea continued to be nice to him, further confounding his disturbed mind state.

In early September, Slick again flew out to Tennessee for the Titan's season opener. He met Brake, Rocko, Wood and other friends that weekend. As usual, the boys went out on the town the night before the game and partied. Slick had even snuck some cocaine on the plane for the occasion. He, Brake, and Rocko sniffed discreetly in the company of their peers. It had become apparent to Slick that he needed the drug and he would go nowhere without it.

When he returned to Virginia, Slick mostly stayed away from Shea and his daughter. He preferred to stay in the environment of drugs and junkies where he lived. It also had gotten to the point where Slick would rather sit and use the drugs than to sell them. To counter this, Slick began giving a certain amount to Brad so that he could sell them and bring Slick the money. This act did nothing but provide Slick with another incentive to get high.

About mid-September, Slick received a letter from the courts stating that he was a month behind in child support. Slick was furious to find that the papers had been initiated by Shea. He was spending hundreds of dollars of week on things for the baby, so he couldn't understand why she would do that. Also he was angry because she hadn't told him. He went to her house the next day to address the situation.

"What is this right here," he said throwing the envelope on the table. "After all the money I done spent on my child you gon' go and take out child support on me!"

"I don't know what you're talking about," Shea said.

"This letter right here, it says Shea Forbes vs. Taylor Richardson. How you don't know what I'm talking about and your name right here in black and white?"

Shea started to stutter as she sensed Slick's anger boiling. "They must've done it when I went down there to fill out the paperwork for the TANF check. I don't know?"

"You do know," Slick yelled. "You got four kids so you knew what they was gonna do that if you applied for assistance. What you need a check for anyway? Don't I take care of mines? Don't I help you out? Look at all this stuff I bought around here! That don't mean nothing to you?"

Shea tried to keep the argument down. "I told you I didn't know it was gonna happen like that. I'm sorry."

"Whatever, Shea, you knew what you was doing. You can sit there and act stupid if you want, but you ain't dumb. And for what, three hundred a month? That's all they giving you." Slick reached into his pocket and pulled out a wad of money. He counted out three hundred dollars and slammed it on the table. "There you go. If that's all you wanted, you could have just asked me!"

Slick left the money on the table and stormed out of the house. Anger built up as he thought of having to pay a third party for his child's care. He didn't need anyone to monitor if he provided for his own or not. He drove back to Brad's and started getting high. Anger was quickly becoming a catalyst for his use. Constant ranting also became a by-product of the usage as he called and vented to anyone that would listen.

"And this silly ass broad gon' go down there and take out papers on me," he said to his cousin, Sumiyah, over the phone. "After all I do for her over there. That make me just want to kill somebody."

"Slick, you have to understand," Sumiyah spoke calmly. "She has to look out for herself. She has three other kids to look after. She's not used to somebody that's trying to stick around and who is going to be there. She's just doing what she knows to do. Look at things from her perspective."

Slick exploded with responses justifying his point of view. Sumiyah tried to calm him down with gentle words. It was she who was there for him in times past and he could always confide in her. This time, however, he was in his own zone and nothing she said could soothe him.

His soul was aching. The fact that he could not see his daughter on his own terms disturbed him. The cocaine continually clouded his mind from making good decisions. The pain was indicated by his many emotional outbursts to family members who were worried. Several already knew about the struggle that he was having with alcohol and drugs.

Later that night, Slick received a call from Ava. She was a twenty-one year old Slick had met a few weeks earlier. He was captivated by her body when he saw her in the Seven-Eleven. He approached her and got the number. A few nights later, he picked her up and took her to a hotel. They talked, smoked, and Slick ended up conquering her body the same night. Later, he found out that she had a live-in girlfriend. She also told Slick that she was a set up girl who liked to stage robberies. These facts further attracted Slick to her as is preference was a fly chick with gangster ways.

This night Slick agreed to pick her up after the call. When he arrived she got in the car and asked him to do her a favor.

"Can you take me to the Hampton Inn on Military Highway," she asked. "My girl got this nigga out there that's slipping. He got a forty cal. in his truck and she stole the keys. She put them outside and he in the room knocked out. I'm trying to go get that joint."

"Alright," Slick agreed without thinking. "I can do that."

"Hell yeah, let's go then. I got to have that. The nigga soft as shit anyway. I should get somebody to rob his ass."

Slick laughed lightly. This wasn't the first time Ava had mentioned her M.O. She had even asked him to accompany her on a lick. He told her that he wasn't that hungry. She left it at that and never asked him about it again.

When Slick pulled in the parking lot, Ava got out. He watched her disappear inside the hotel. In her absence, Slick opened a bag of cocaine and started to sniff. When paranoia started to set in, he decided that he didn't trust the girl. He took out the four grand in his pocket and tried to stuff it into the cusp of his seat.

Before he could get the cash out of sight, Ava appeared at the window and hopped in the car. She noticed the amount of cash as Slick pulled it from the seat and squeezed it back into his pockets. The language of her eyes spoke volumes before she opened her mouth.

"That's a whole lot of money you got on you nigga," she said smiling. "You might should a left that at home."

Slick gave her a sideways glance. "Nah, shorty, I'm straight. I ain't worried about a nigga taken nothing from me. Anyway, what's up with that thang? Did you get it?"

"Yeah, I got it. Now come on let's ride out before he come out here looking for us."

"Hold on," Slick said with precaution. "Let me see that joint before we pull off."

Ava reached under her jacket and handed Slick the lightweight plastic gun. "Hell yeah, she is cute," he said, sliding the gun under his seat. "I'm a hold on to it until we get where we going. I don't want nothing to happen if we get stopped or something like that."

Slick made it to the room and left the gun in the car. This time he couldn't help himself and pulled out the bag in front of her. She admitted that she used and they both got high together.

After a while, Slick started to rave about the problems he was having with Italy's mother. The more he talked, the more emotional he got. He continued until he realized that Ava was tired of the subject. After a weak attempt at sex, Slick decided to take the girl home. He dropped her off, only returning the gun after she was out of the car.

The rest of September was a blur for Slick. At the beginning of October, he prepared to attend another game. He had arranged for Marshawn to accompany him on the four hour ride to Baltimore. Slick watched the excitement in the young man as the date approached. The two would ride with Wood's friend Seaberry, who stayed in Virginia Beach.

The night before they were to leave, Slick picked up Marshawn and went to Seaberry's house. When they arrived, Seaberry showed them their rooms and went to bed. After Marshawn was sleep, Slick started sniffing. As usual, he couldn't stop and stayed up all night. When it was time to leave in the morning, Seaberry found Slick still drinking in the living room.

"What up man? Is everything alright," Seaberry asked. "You been up all night?'

"Yeah," Slick responded. "I guess I'm excited. I couldn't sleep for nothing."

"Well, it's that time. You and your boy 'bout ready?"

"Hell yeah, let's do it!"

Slick roused Marshawn and they went to the car. Slick allowed Marshawn to ride in the front so that he would be alone in the back. During the four hour ride, Slick continued to secretly sniff. By the time they arrived, Slick was wired. They met up with everyone else at the stadium and went in.

Slick's sister, Sharon, along with Wood and many other friends were there. However Slick couldn't enjoy the game because he kept going to the bathroom to get high. He also had snuck a small bottle of liquor in to help balance the cocaine.

Upon returning from the bathroom once, he saw a commotion in the area his sister was sitting. Slick rushed up the stairs to find out what happened.

"Everything straight now," Wood said. "It was a problem but it's over now."

"Well, why Sharon over there looking like that? What happened?"

"One of them dudes behind her spilled some beer on her and acted like he didn't want to apologize. But it's all good now. We got him straight."

Rage mixed with the cocaine in Slick's system and caused him to snap. "Which one did it," he said moving towards the crowd.

"Chill out Slick, man," Wood said. "It's over!"

The drugs and the liquor were louder than Wood's voice. Slick approached the group of white men behind his sister. "Which one of y'all up here acting like he want a problem."

Several of Slick's friends grabbed him when they noticed his anger. The two men behind his sister stood up and began to curse Slick. He was blocked from reaching them by other fans. When he realized that he couldn't get to the men, he gathered two mouthfuls of spit and hurled it the men. A scuffle ensued as they tried to retaliate. When Slick saw the security personnel approaching, he slipped through the confusion, went down the stairs and ducked into a bathroom. After taking more toots, he watched the rest of the game from the television in the hallway from the smoking section.

After the game Slick rejoined the other guests as they waited for the players to come out. It was obvious to everyone that something was wrong with him. He stood off to the side with a scowl while the others chatted happily. Wood looked at his friend with contempt. Donnie had already been informed of the incident, but didn't show any displeasure when he came out. He greeted everyone as usual and then got on the bus.

On the way back to Virginia, Slick continued to sniff in the back seat. Slick was not aware or didn't care that there were others in the car. He hardly said a word the whole trip. He was already feeling embarrassed by his actions at the game. He felt that his life was out of control and there was nothing he could do to stop the spiral.

When they arrived back at Seaberry's that evening, Slick and Marshawn got in the car and left without going in. Halfway through the twenty minute drive to Norfolk, Slick couldn't resist taking a few snorts. He was totally consumed. He opened the bag, not caring if the fifteen year-old in his passenger seat noticed or not.

"You know that stuff is bad for you," Marshawn said a few minutes later. He looked at Slick like a concerned parent.

"I know." Slick hung his head in embarrassment and then took a long swallow of the liquor between his legs.

"You might as well pull over and let me drive if you gonna be doing all that," Marshawn advised.

Slick pulled over on the interstate and Marshawn drove the rest of the way. When they got to the house, Shea was up washing dishes. Slick walked in and stood behind her in the kitchen with his head down. Shea detected that something was wrong.

"Oh lord, what happened, Marshawn," she asked.

"Nothing ma," he said going up the stairs.

"Whatever," Shea said turning to Slick. "I know something done happened just by the way you looking."

Slick just shook his head. He looked up at Shea with solemn eyes and finally spoke. "I messed up this time."

"What," Shea said with a frown. "What you talking about now?" Slick didn't answer, but continued to shake his head. "Look, I'm tired of this. I don't even wanna know about it. Just get out Slick! I'm not going through this with you tonight!"

Her tone triggered anger in Slick and he started to flip out. He thought about his daughter and decided better. "Well, just let me see Italy real quick before I go."

"No Slick, it's too late for all that. Just go 'head and leave now."

"Look, I just took your son to Baltimore for a game and you trying to act like I can't see my own daughter. You crazy!" Slick started to go up the stairs while Shea called to her sister.

"Kayla, Kayla. Call the police! This nigga down here acting stupid!"

Slick stopped in his tracks. "What? You gone call the police on me and I only wanna see my daughter. You got to be the dumbest broad I ever seen in my life. Don't worry about. You can have this sorry ass place!"

Slick stormed out of the house and went to his car. When he got home, he couldn't sleep. The thought of his actions earlier caused him to be mad at himself. Shea's denial of his right to see his daughter fueled his animosity towards her. He got high the whole night with intentions of returning to see his daughter in the morning.

At around eight o'clock the next day, Slick drove back to Shea's. When he got there, he found Shea and Misty getting into her sister's car. He didn't see the baby, however. He stopped beside the car and she pulled off without acknowledging him. He followed her over the bridge leading to downtown Norfolk. When she parked at the courthouse, Slick parked nearby and got out of the car.

"Hey yo," he yelled when she got out of the car. "Where's my baby at? I wanna see her."

Shea continued to walk towards the building, ignoring Slick. This made him angrier. He followed her inside the courthouse until she came to the clerk's window. He listened a few feet away as she talked to the clerk.

"I wanna take out a restraining order on someone. I also want to file for custody of my daughter and take out a warrant."

Slick was so furious he could've struck Shea on the spot. He thought about where he was at and used caution. "You are a silly broad, you know that," he said to Shea calmly. "After all I do for you and my child you gonna try to put me in jail. For what? I didn't even do nothing. You just don't got no sense at all."

Slick left the courthouse in a fury. He drove around for a while not knowing what to do. He called Shea's mom thirty minutes later to vent to her.

"Do you know what your daughter did? She went down there and took a warrant out on me. I didn't even do nothing to her. And she taking out a restraining order, so I can't see my daughter."

"I know baby. I got Italy right here," her mother replied. "Where you at?"

"I'm way out here by Ocean View, but I wanna see my daughter though."

"Okay baby. You can come and see her for a minute before Shea get back."

Slick drove back over to Shea's. He parked on the side of the house and went to the back door. When he knocked, he saw two police cars pull up behind his car. He watched them get out and walk towards the front. He knew they were there for him.

Slick ran through the parking lot into another cluster of apartments. He saw a girl standing in her doorway and ran up to her.

"I'll give you $50 dollars if you let me use your phone to call a cab from here."

The girl looked at her boyfriend who agreed to let him in. He gave them the bill and called a taxi. When he made it home, he remembered he had no cocaine to sniff. Unable to get high, he walked around the house calling anyone he thought would listen to his problems.

"Man, who that chick think she is," he yelled to Wood. "That's my child. She can't keep me away from her!"

"Yeah, that's true but you gotta understand," Wood replied. "That's the momma. They gon' always side with her in that situation."

"Well, I'll just go out there and kill everybody then. If I can't see her, nobody will. I don't even care about nothing no more!"

"Hold on homeboy. You tripping yourself. Don't do nothing crazy. And I know you still messing with that stuff. You just need to calm down some."

"Fuck that," Slick said, growing more emotional. "I done told you I don't care! Everybody can die if I can't see mine. That's the way I feel, point blank, bottom line!"

"Who you yelling at," Wood said. "You need to take a step back and slow down. Just like at the game. Do you realize how crazy you was looking? Everybody was asking me what's wrong with you. Seaberry even said you was pulling that shit out in his car. You really losing your mind. You the one who might need to check yourself. You might need to stay away from your baby the way you acting."

Slick continued to go back and forth with Wood in the heated conversation. His excitement led him outside on the front porch. He stood talking for a while until three Chesapeake police cruisers passed his house. Upon seeing him, they slowed and turned around. Slick walked immediately back into the house. When he peeked out the window, the police officers were parked in the yard. He hung up the phone and called to Brad's son, James, in the next room.

"Look, James," he informed. "The police are outside three deep. Whatever you do, don't open the door."

"What happened," the sixteen year-old asked. "What did you do?"

"I didn't do nothing. I told you about my crazy baby momma. She took out a bogus charge on me."

"So what are you gonna do," he said walking to the window. He looked through the curtains and surveyed the scene. "Oh shit Slick. There's about ten cars out there and more of them across the street. Hell nah man, this is serious."

Slick looked through the blinds in his room and saw the officers setting up across the street and on the side of the house. Shotguns and pistols were being positioned as the officers canvased the yard.

"There he is at the window," a voice said from the outside. He looked to the right and saw an officer with a shotgun pointed his way. He closed the curtain and paced the floor.

The police began to knock. Slick looked at the twelve gage shotgun that Brad kept by the door. Slick envisioned ending it all by running out of the house with the shotgun raised. His life was in shambles anyway so why not ended right now, he thought. He continued to contemplate his fate amidst the officer's banging.

When the two men refused to answer a SWAT team was called. A standoff ensued as Slick continued to appear and disappear from the window, taunting the lawmen with his actions. Slick kept up the antics until his phone rang.

"Hey brother, what's going on out there," Brad said. "I just got a call that it was about twenty police officers on my property and around my house. What the hell's going on Slick?"

"My daughter's mother called the police on me. I didn't do nothing but somehow they found out where I lived. They saw me standing on the porch and they came. It's some bullshit for real."

"Well, you gotta come outta there. I run my tree business from the house and it don't look good. I already got a call from my landlady. And you know I do my own thing on the side too. I can't have this going on like that. I mean, do what you gotta do, but don't put me in jeopardy."

Slick understood Brad's point. He decided that he would end the standoff. He instructed James to exit first and tell the police that he was coming out unarmed. When James opened the door and walked out, Slick waited to see what would happen. After a few minutes, Slick carefully eased out of the door with his hands up. The officers cuffed him and led him to the car. They informed him that he was being charged with assault and trespassing. Slick didn't protest. He said not a word on the ride to the Norfolk jail, after being handed over by the Chesapeake authorities.

Norfolk was more considerate than Virginia Beach and gave Slick a $3500 dollar bond. He posted the bond with the money in his pocket and went to get his car. He then called his connect to score some coke and drove home.

When he got there, the house was empty. He walked in his room and found all of his clothes in a pile on the floor. He took this as an eviction notice and packed all of his things into the car.

■■■

"Mad live, could learn to bounce out on a bad vibe…or either keep a gun in your cab ride…Have I thought about my life as a bad guy…made a little money selling rocks that was capsized…robbed a lot a people like I never was baptized…"

The dark lyrics of Styles P's "Alone in the Streets" guided Slick towards the Virginia Beach oceanfront. The strip of hotels was as destitute as Slick's soul. The summer had ended and the tourists had left. Slick spotted a Red Roof Inn and pulled in. Emotionally, mentally and physically exhausted, Slick purchased a room for a week and went to sleep.

When he awoke the next day, Slick went directly to work. Determined to find a place to stay, he searched the familiar strip. He found a two bedroom apartment on 25th Street for rent by a private owner. He made a call and arranged to meet the owner, Mr. Bribble. He filled out the application using false information and the elderly man told him that he would contact him with the results.

Slick then went to a local real estate agency. His license was still valid and he decided it was time to get back into the business. He interviewed with the manager of Executive Realty and signed the contract. He left the company feeling encouraged as he tried to regain control of his life.

After not talking to Shea for a couple of days, he called and she answered. As usual, she talked as if nothing had happened. She even asked her to bring her a Pepsi if he was coming to see the baby. When he did, she allowed him to keep the baby for the night. He took Italy to his room that night and brought her back the next day. He was happy for the time he was able to spend with the child and glad that he and Shea were on good terms.

He still had his share of playmates however. A few days later on the weekend, he received a call from an old friend named Geneva. She was at a beachfront club blocks away from his hotel and wanted him to come. Too high to be in public, he told her to call him after the club and they'd meet then.

When she called, Slick drove to pick her up. He took her with him on a few runs before returning to the hotel. After having sex with her for a while, Slick wanted to keep getting high. He got dressed preparing to take the girl home. Before they left, he checked his pockets and counted the money in them. Feeling that his money was short, he blamed the girl.

"I didn't take nothing from you Slick. You've known me for five years and I would never do that," Geneva explained. "You might better check one of them customers. They probably didn't give you all your money. You didn't even count it when they gave it to you."

Slick considered her statement but was already too far gone and frustrated. He kicked the girl out of the room without letting her get all of her property. Seeing her phone on the table, Slick took it and put it in his vehicle. When she called from a payphone nearby, Slick denied having anything, cursed her and hung up the phone.

Geneva came back a short while later with the police. Slick let the police in the room and insisted that he didn't have the phone. After a brief search the police left not convinced that Slick was telling the truth. Slick stayed for the rest of the night but decided to move the next day because of the heat he'd just created.

The next morning he moved across the street to the Cascade Motel. Unbeknown to Slick, the three story building was already known as a haven for drug activity. Nevertheless, he rented the room for a week, while waiting for the call from Mr. Bribble.

He still kept up his excessive use at the new room. His first few days were spent mostly in the room drinking and getting high. Despite his condition he still wanted to see daughter. Shea had softened her shell once again and allowed Slick to see her whenever he wanted.

On a Thursday night at the end of October, Slick sat in his room in a state of loneliness. He neglected several calls from family and friends alike. He was tired. In the depths of his heart he wanted to quit. He was sick of losing the constant battle against cocaine. He examined his life and figured that he'd be better dead. He picked up the phone and called Shea.

"Hey," she said sleepily. "What's up?"

"Nothing, for real. I was just sitting here thinking and I'm tired of doing the same thing over and over again. I just wanna live a regular life and be around my daughter. I know I said this before but now I'm serious."

"I know what you mean," she responded. "I'm fed up with all that fussing and stuff too. It ain't no good for the kids. You don't want them to go through all that."

"That's right. And I just miss being there with my little princess so much. I know it's kinda late, but do you mind if I come get her."

"As long as you ain't been drinking or nothing it's fine with me."

"Nah Shea, I ain't been doing nothing. I'll be by there in a little while to get her."

It was about 12:00 a.m. when Slick returned to the room with Italy. He got the baby comfortable, feeding and changing her before she went back to sleep. He admired her as she lay on the bed peacefully. The tranquility in the room was too much for Slick and the urge arose to get high. Unable to resist, he opened the bag and started snorting. An hour later his phone rang.

"What you doing baby? Where you at right now," Ava asked excitedly.

"I ain't doing nothing now," Slick said, really not wanting to be bothered. "Why, what's good with you?"

"Nothing, I'm trying to come out that way and see you. I wanna chill with you for tonight if you don't care."

Slick heard the anxiety in her voice. Now that he was high, nothing appealed more to him than having Ava do whatever he wanted. However, he had been feeling leery about her lately. All her talk of robbing people began to sink in and he ignored most of her calls. He could sense that she was dangerous. On the other hand, she did fulfill his every wish and wasn't hard to please. Slick stalled for time as he battled his instincts.

"Tonight I got my daughter here with me, so I don't know. Give me about an hour to get her straight and I'll let you know what's poppin'."

Slick closed the phone and commenced to getting high. An hour came and went. Slick had ignored several of Ava's calls in order to keep getting high. The calls became so frequent that he couldn't enjoy his high so he finally answered.

"I'm in the cab on my way down there. What hotel you gonna be at?"

Slick shook his head at the girl's persistence. It was almost three o'clock in the morning and she still insisted on seeing him. He went against his first instinct and decided to let her come.

"I'm at the Cascade on 28th and Pacific. Call me when you get outside."

Ava called about twenty minutes later. He gave her the money for the cab. After going back down stairs to pay, she came back in. Even though he was high and drunk, his first concern was the gun.

"You got that gun on you," he asked before Ava sat down.

"You know I do daddy. I got the keep the strap on me these days."

"Aight then, let me see it. You see I got my daughter in here tonight. I'm a put it up for you."

Ava pulled the silver handgun from her waistband. She ejected the clip along with the round that was in the chamber.

"I'll just put it under the couch right here so we'll both know where it is," she said walking towards the couch.

"Aight, but just be careful with it ," Slick said watching her hide the weapon.

"I feel you nigga. You already know I got four kids so I ain't gon' put your baby in danger," she said, walking towards Italy. "Especially not your pretty little self." She picked up the girl who was now awake. "See, look at her smiling. That's right little mama. Uh oh Slick, I think she wet herself. Where her bag at?"

Slick gave her the bag and watched as Ava tended to his baby. His paranoia about the girl subsided as she changed and fed his daughter like Italy was her own. With his comfort reassured, he pulled out the bag of cocaine and started sniffing again.

"Boy, you got to be crazy," Ava said when she noticed. "You sittin' in here getting' high with your baby in this room. You don't even give a fuck do you? If you don't then me neither. Let me get some."

Slick handed her the bag and she took a few toots. When the drug took effect, Ava began to rub her breasts and thighs in a sexual manner. Slick grew aroused seeing her wallow on the bed. He grew more anxious when she spoke.

"Damn! That's why I hate doing coke. That shit make me so horny. Come on, I ready to fuck."

She began to take her clothes off. She then got down on all fours and crawled over to Slick who still had the bag in his hands. Without saying a word, she unzipped his pants and inserted him into her mouth. Slick's nervousness disappeared as he became a victim of her seduction. He sat the bag down and engaged himself into the escapade.

His performance was mediocre. Slick was preoccupied with the location of the gun. He had also been up for a few days so his energy was low. Ava expressed her dissatisfaction when he finally was able to ejaculate.

After the episode, the two smoked a couple of blunts. Slick however was on edge. Still getting high, he sat in the chair by the door, while Ava lay on the bed by the baby. He began to rant about his lifestyle and his child's mother to Ava who once again grew weary of the conversation.

When the sun came up, Slick was still paranoid. Ava had been talking about her need for money the whole night. She even attempted to sell Slick the gun. Her constant talk about robbing caused Slick to keep a close eye on her even though she was being pleasant.

When the time for cleanup came the maids knocked on the door. Slick opened the door and greeted the maid.

"Do y'all want service this morning," the elderly lady said.

"Yes ma'am, hold up a minute," Slick said. He walked back in and addressed Ava. "Make sure there ain't nothing laying around in here. They finna come in here in clean."

"Hell no," Ava said in a hush tone. "I got this gun in here and you got that coke and the baby. They don't need to come in right now. Just get some clean towels and we'll be good."

Slick walked back to the door where the maid was standing. "No, we don't need nothing but some towels and rags right now. I'll get y'all to clean the next day."

The older lady looked at the disheveled occupant. "Is everything alright young man?"

Slick's despair showed in his eyes. He dropped his head and shook it. "No, not really."

"Well baby, I don't know what's wrong, but whatever it is just plead the blood of Jesus about it. I had a brother that was out there in the streets and everybody was saved except for him. And we kept praying for him but it didn't make no difference. But we kept praying and pleading the blood of Jesus and now he's off drugs, and married and got a family and all that. So I'm just telling you, whatever it is just trust God baby. And plead the blood of Jesus. That always works."

When the lady finished talking, Slick thanked her and closed the door. He began to feel a gloomy sensation in the air. When he sat the towels on the bed his phone rang.

"Mr. Richardson," the voice said when Slick answered. "This is Mr. Bribble. I decided to go ahead and rent you the apartment. You seem like a nice fellow and I'm comfortable with your information. Can you meet me there in an hour to sign the lease?"

"Yeah, I can do that," Slick said excitedly. "Thanks Mr. Bribble. I'll see you in a little while."

Slick was elated. He hung up the phone and told Ava that they had to leave. He told her about the apartment as he was getting Italy together. She stood up and began to get her things in order also.

Within minutes, his phone rang again. This time it was a customer. Shane, a funeral home director, wanted a quarter. Slick had been wasting a lot of dope and needed the money for the apartment. He told the man he'd be there and began to move faster when he hung up the phone. When he had everything in the bag, his phone rang once more. This time it was Shea and she sounded upset.

"What's up Slick," she said softly. "What you doing right now?"

"Finna go handle some business real quick," he said coldly. He felt good about his new place and wanted to show her he could make it without her. "What's up? What you want?"

"I just miss my baby Slick. I just feel like I need to see her. Could you bring her to me now," she said with a weary voice.

"Well, what you crying for," he said even more distant. "What's wrong now?"

"I don't know. I just need my baby now. Can't you bring her now Slick," she said between tears.

"Look, Shea. I ain't got no time for this right now. I got to go handle some business. I'll call you when I'm on my way there. I got a couple of stops to make first though, but then I'll be through there." He hung up the phone before she could respond.

Slick then picked up the car seat and sat it on the bed. When he picked up Italy, Ava asked him to use his phone because her battery was dead. Slick walked over and handed her the phone still holding the infant.

When he got back to the bed, he put Italy in the car seat. Slick's phone rang and when he turned around he saw Ava answer the phone with the gun in her hand. Slick figured that she was putting it in her waist and kept strapping the child in. When he noticed that she still held the weapon, Slick unstrapped the baby and walked to the door. He opened the door and looked down the hallway to make sure the maids were still close by. Leaving the door opened, Slick entered the room to grab the car seat and leave.

As soon as he stepped in his conscience told him it was a mistake. Ava was still on the phone but the gun was now out of sight. Slick bent down to grab the baby bag before putting Italy back in the seat. When he stood upright he heard the door slam. He turned around to see Ava blocking the door with the gun pointed at his face.

"Alright, you know what it is nigga. I need that dough in your pocket right now. My kids is hungry yo!"

Slick turned his back partially to the girl to shield the baby from the line of fire. "Come on shorty," Slick calmly responded. "What the fuck are you doing? You know I ain't got nothing but this little bit of money in my pocket. You ain't got to carry it like this. You see I got my daughter in my hands. Just chill out. I got you."

Slick turned around half facing her. Her nervousness was evident by the way the gun shook in her hands. Her words were even more erratic as she grew more anxious.

"Come on yo, I done told you I need that," she insisted. "I ain't got no time for games now. Oh…you think I'm playing or something nigga!"

Ava cocked the gun back while holding the trigger at the same time. The loud boom surprised both as Ava jumped back towards the door. Slick felt the stinging burn of the bullet as it pierced his hip. As he looked at Ava coming closer with the gun, he felt death enter the room. It was at that moment that he knew it was his time to die.

In an attempt to save himself, he started to knock on the wall where the maids were in the next room. "Help me! Help me somebody, please! Help!"

Ava ran up to Slick and put the gun to his head. "If you yell one more time I'm a blast you right in your head!"

Slick felt the steel at his temple and ceased all movement. He clutched his daughter closely, ready to embrace his final moments. The room grew colder. Italy was eerily silent, unaware of the danger they were in. Slick knew he had to act but didn't want to grab the gun because of his daughter. He once again appealed to Ava.

"Come on shorty. Please don't do this right here. I told you I ain't got nothing. You can have this little bit of shit, just let me go."

"Shut up nigga," she said as she searched him cautiously with her free hand. "If you keep talking, I'm a shoot you in your dick and tell them you was trying to rape me."

Slick knew that the girl was serious. He also felt that she had no qualms about killing him. With his baby in his right arm, Slick attempted a desperation grab for the gun with his left hand. The weight that shifted to his right leg caused increased pain from the gunshot wound and Slick fell to one knee.

When he slipped, Ava pounced on him, swinging the gun at his head. Slick deflected the blows with his free arm while still holding the now screaming child. With Slick wounded and off balance, the girl pushed him all the way to the floor. He fell on top of the child expecting a bullet to the back of the head. When no shot came, Slick tried to get up on his knees despite the pain in his hip. The girl easily pushed him back down. Slick then felt Ava shove the gun against his rectum and pull the trigger.

In Slick's mind, the shot signaled the destruction of all of his sexual organs. He writhed in pain on the floor, while still covering his daughter. His will to live began to flee. The amount of blood filling his pants when he rolled over was shocking. The sight of Italy covered in blood further dampened his spirits. He looked up at the girl with the gun, closed his eyes and waited to die.

When Slick felt the girl going through his pockets, he sensed new life. He opened his eyes and saw her stooped with the gun at her side. Slick lifted his left leg and tried to kick the girl away from him. She avoided the kick and started swinging the gun at Slick again. In the midst of the scuffle, Slick grabbed the girl by the face, trying to distort her vision. Undaunted, Ava placed the weapon in the center of Slick's pelvis and fired a third time.

This round signaled the end. There was no fight left in the man. He looked down at his blood soaked groin area with sorrow. He was sure that his manhood was destroyed and he would never again live a normal life. With that in mind, he decided to lie down and bleed to death. He put up no more resistance as the girl searched his pockets. After she pulled out the blood stained wad of money, she walked calmly out the door.

Everything was now in slow motion. Slick lay there thinking of all the things he'd done in his life: good and bad. He envisioned the reactions on the faces of his loved ones at his funeral. He'd been waiting for this moment. He knew it was coming all along. He had actually started to beg for death. Slick relaxed his body as he began to pray the sinner's prayer for salvation.

His words were overshadowed by the cries of his daughter lying next to him. The words that were previously spoken by the maid resurfaced in his mind. Slick instantly began to plead the blood of Jesus over his life right then and there. With all the strength and passion in his body, he prayed and asked the Lord to save him and help him survive.

With a new will to live, Slick tried to stand up but fell back down. After falling three more times, Slick mustered up all of his energy and dragged himself to the door with his arms. He was able to open the door and crawl halfway out before his body gave way.

"Help me, please! Somebody please help me! I've been shot! Oh Lord Jesus, please help me!"

Suddenly doors began to open. The maids came out of the next room. A young white lady came running from down the hall and two lesbians came from down stairs. They hovered over him as Slick continued to pray. His prayers stopped when he remembered Italy.

"My baby, my baby," he yelled. "My daughter in the room too. Please somebody help her. Oh lord, my baby. What have I done?"

The white lady ran in the room and came out with the baby, who was dripping in blood. Slick barked out Shea's number to the lady as he lay bleeding. With his daughter secure, Slick resumed his prayers.

"Lord, forgive me Jesus for my sins. I know I have done wrong, but I accept Jesus into my life and I plead the blood of Jesus over me right now."

"That's right baby," the maid said. "Keep praying, keep praying. The blood of Jesus! The blood of Jesus!"

Slick and the lady prayed until the ambulance arrived. Everybody gave the paramedics room and they attended to him. When they cut his pants off to see the damage, the bag of cocaine fell out of his drawers.

"We have dope," a paramedic yelled out. The lady held the blood filled bag in the air. A police officer confiscated the drugs and put them in an evidence bag.

Slick could've cared less. He was fighting for his life. All he could think about was the condition of his genitals as they placed him in the ambulance. He continued to pray en route to the hospital. When the morphine took effect, his entire thought process went blank. His voice trailed off in the distance along with his prayers. Slick then slipped into a morphine induced trance not knowing whether he would live or perish.

Epilogue

November, 2008
Virginia Beach

Slick stayed in the hospital until the next evening before sneaking out. He went directly back to the hotel in which he was nearly killed. He stayed there for the night and was arrested by police the next morning.

The Commonwealth had charged him with cocaine distribution for the bag of dope they found. He was denied bond and admitted to the medical ward of the jail. He remained there a week until a bond hearing was arranged. After being given a $10,000 bond, he called Joe once again and posted the bail.

Instead of going back to the ill-fated room again, Joe dropped him off at a Fairfield Inn in the downtown area. Though he could barely walk and still needed treatment for his wounds, all Slick wanted was coke. He called Boot Lee and was able to get a couple of grams. Slick stayed up all night thinking about the money and drugs he'd left at the room.

When it was checkout time, Slick called a cab to take him to the oceanfront. When the cab arrived, Slick made a detour to the liquor store before going to the beach. He sipped the venomous liquid on the ride there in an attempt to drown his sorrows.

When he arrived back at the Cascade, management told him that the room had been cleaned. His property was put in a storage area on the premises. A few guests and the manager helped the injured man with packing the bags into the rental car. Slick then signed a release paper and got into the car.

Slick could tell that some of his things were missing by the number of bags. Nevertheless, he searched them and found the old leather coat in the back seat. To his surprise, both the money and the cocaine were still in place.

With the security of a package and money, Slick went right back to work. He made a few calls and orders followed. He rode around with a packed car, using and selling as much as he could. He had no plans on what he would do next. The recent close call did little to alter Slick's course of self-destruction. His rate of consumption had grown to the verge of overdose.

When nightfall arrived, Slick was super high with no place to go. He had not seen Italy or Shea since his release. He drove to Shea's house. All the lights were out when he got there. After sitting in the car for a few minutes, Slick reluctantly got out and knocked on the door.

Shea came to the door with Italy in her arms. It was the first time Slick had seen her since she was covered in blood on the hotel floor. Shea allowed Slick to come in and gave him the child. Slick held the baby tight as emotions overflowed within.

"I love you," he whispered to the infant. "I love you, I love you. I'm so sorry. I'm sorry baby. I love you. Thank you, thank you Jesus for watching over her. Thank you. I love you."

He continued to hold the child and thank God for their survival. The danger that he'd put them in became vivid as he looked into her eyes. Slick was scared thinking of the alternative outcomes to the shooting.

Not wanting to face Shea, Slick handed Italy back to her. Without saying a word, Slick walked out and got into the car. As he sat, tears welled in his eyes when he realized that he had nowhere to go. He was even more saddened by the current state of his life. He was nothing. A small time drug dealer who had almost gotten his daughter killed.

All of his hopes, dreams and ambitions, where were they now? What happened to the innocent choirboy who loved school and basketball? Who was this hardened, lonely criminal that he'd become? What had occurred to bring him to this destitute state?

Emotions began to rise. Slick fought the tears with the machismo that he was taught as a child. Men don't suppose to cry. He couldn't cry. He couldn't stop now. This was nothing. People get shot every day. I'm alive. It's just life. I can keep it moving.

Slick tried to convince himself, but knew he was wrong. Death had come for him. He had stared the reaper in the mouth. He wasn't supposed to live. He had already been warned. God told him what would happen beforehand. And yet, death was turned away when he prayed. He was granted mercy in the midst of the gunfire. Even the doctors couldn't explain how he hadn't bled to death with a bullet hitting his femoral artery. No, this wasn't minor. Slick knew that he'd experienced a miracle and had been given a second chance.

He thought of his parents, who were worried. They expressed their concern after the shooting. They even asked him to come home. He denied the request initially. Sitting in the car now, it didn't seem like a bad idea. He needed a change. He could go down to Goldsboro and think while he recuperated. Family and friends equaled love to Slick and that's what he needed.

Slick decided right then to leave. He cranked the Buick Lacrosse up and headed for the interstate. His spirits rose when he thought of the changes that he needed to make. He knew it would be a challenge, but something deep inside told him it was possible. He had to remind himself that he'd done it before.

Slick rode the dark highways of Interstate 264 until it turned into highway 58. An hour later, 58 brought Slick to I-95 as he flipped the dial on the radio station. He felt dark, lonely and pain from his wounds. His mood darkened when he stopped at the words of a song he'd never heard before.

"You can think about the woman…or the girl you knew the night before…when you're riding sixteen hours…and there's nothing much to do…and you don't feel much like riding…you just wish the trip was through…"

The song was about a lonesome rock star who was tired of the road, the useless women and the demands of the life. He was always under constant pressure, always on the stage. When he performed, everything was fine. People loved him. But off the stage, when the show was over, he was nothing but a poor, miserable lost soul.

Slick could relate. Out of everyone he'd dealt with over the years, he was all alone now. Out of all the parties, women and fun, he had nobody he could call. He empathized with the singer as he dissected the lyrics.

"Here I am…on the road again…There I am…up on the stage…Her I go…Playing start again…There I go…turn the page"

Like the man in the Bob Seger's "Turn the Page," Slick wanted out. He was just as worn and torn as the singer. The life, however, had Slick entrapped. The perks, the women, alcohol, drugs, money, power were all vices that appealed to his physical lusts. When he participated in these activities, he would have pleasure but his spirit was being destroyed. His inner man was empty even though he possessed a lot on the outside.

Slick addressed the emptiness while still listening to the words. He made the same decision as the character in the song. He would get off the stage. He resigned to quit once in for all the life he was living. The writing on the wall was clear. Only God could foresee, however, how hard it would be for Slick to turn the page.

The song was barely over before the urge for cocaine surfaced inside him. He reached in the bag unable to resist and took two large toots. When the drug reached his brain, all of his previous thoughts disappeared. The righteousness he declared he wanted to pursue seemed far in the distance through his cocaine clouded lenses. Without thinking, he searched the rap stations for music.

He turned up the volume on the dial like nothing was happening within him. The beat instantly had him bobbing his head and mouthing the lyrics of the chorus. He lit up a cigarette and rolled the window down. The words that he spoke were a contradiction to the mindset he'd had minutes earlier. Like the foolish, double-minded person he was, Slick leaned out the window and screamed the lyrics as if he was talking to God himself.

"Every day I'm hustling! Everyday I'm hustling! Everyday I'm, Everyday I'm Everyday I'm Hustling!"......

To be continued....

Works Cited

A Plus f/ Prodigy. "Gusto." *Summertime Shootout Pt. 1.* Desert Storm. 1995. CD.

En Vogue. "Hold On." *Born to Sing.* Atlantic. 1990 CD.

Fifty Cent. "Life on the Line." *Get Rich or Die Trying.* Interscope. 2003. CD.

Fifty Cent. "Many Men." *Get Rich or Die Trying.* Interscope. 2003. CD.

Jaheim. "Put That Woman First." *Still Ghetto.* Warner Bros. 2002. CD.

Jay-Z. "Can't Knock the Hustle." *Reasonable Doubt.* Priority. 1996. CD.

Jay-Z. "D'evils." *Reasonable Doubt.* Priority. 1996. CD.

John P. Kee. "Jesus is Real." *Wash Me.* Tyscott. 1991. CD.

Authorized King James Version. Oxford, New York: Oxford University Press, 1997.

Nas. "Black Girl Lost." *It was Written.* Columbia. 1996. CD.

Notorious B.I.G. "Warning." *Ready to Die.* Bad Boy. 1994. CD.

Tupac. "Ambitionz Az A Ridah", "Blasphemy." *Makaveli: Don Killuminati.* Death Row. 1996 CD.